Global Villages

Global Villages

Rural and Urban Transformations in Contemporary Bulgaria

Edited by
Ger Duijzings

ANTHEM PRESS
LONDON · NEW YORK · DELHI

Anthem Press
An imprint of Wimbledon Publishing Company
www.anthempress.com

This edition first published in UK and USA 2014
by ANTHEM PRESS
75–76 Blackfriars Road, London SE1 8HA, UK
or PO Box 9779, London SW19 7ZG, UK
and
244 Madison Ave #116, New York, NY 10016, USA

First published in hardback by Anthem Press in 2013

British Library Cataloguing-in-Publication Data
A catalogue record for this book is available from the British Library.

Library of Congress Cataloging-in-Publication Data
The Library of Congress has catalogued the hardcover edition as follows:
Global villages : rural and urban transformations in contemporary
Bulgaria / edited by Ger Duijzings.
pages cm
Includes bibliographical references.
ISBN-13: 978-0-85728-073-2 (hardback : alk. paper)
ISBN-10: 0-85728-073-2 (hardback : alk. paper)
1. Bulgaria—Rural conditions. 2. Urbanization—Bulgaria. I.
Duijzings, Gerlachlus, 1961–
HN623.5.G56 2013
307.72—dc23
2013031035

ISBN-13: 978 1 78308 351 0 (Pbk)
ISBN-10: 1 78308 351 4 (Pbk)

This title is also available as an ebook.

CONTENTS

PREFACE AND ACKNOWLEDGEMENTS

This book is based on a collection of papers presented at a workshop entitled 'The "Urban" and "Rural" in Present-Day Bulgaria', which took place at the School of Slavonic and East European Studies, University College London, on 29 and 30 May 2008. The aim of the workshop was to investigate urban–rural transformations in Bulgaria after the end of socialism. The workshop's key idea was to focus on how the urban and rural have been reconfigured, in socioeconomic as well as political, ideological and cultural terms. The participants were practically all anthropologists, except for one human geographer and one sociologist, and most attention was given to rural contexts. One overarching theme crystallized: that of globalization in the Bulgarian countryside. As all case studies presented at the workshop showed, it is no longer possible to speak of 'traditional' Bulgarian villages as they have transformed into 'global villages' – that is, they are directly affected by global forces and influences. Almost all the papers that were presented during the workshop have been included in the present volume, apart from two, which were published elsewhere or did not fit the overall concept of the volume. I would like to thank Dr Iliya Nedin, who co-organized the event and was involved at the early stages of editing this volume. I also gratefully acknowledge the financial support of the Centre for East European Language-Based Area Studies (CEELBAS), the British Academy, the Bulgarian Embassy in London, and the Centre for South-East European Studies at the School of Slavonic and East European Studies, University College London, which made the workshop possible.

Ger Duijzings

NOTE ON TRANSLITERATION

а	a		п	p
б	b		р	r
в	v		с	s
г	g		т	t
д	d		у	u
е	e		ф	f
ж	zh		х	h
з	z		ц	ts
и	i		ч	ch
й	y		ш	sh
к	k		щ	sht
л	l		ъ	a / u
м	m		ь	y
н	n		ю	yu
о	o		я	ya

Chapter 1

INTRODUCTION

Ger Duijzings

This book explores the multiple and combined effects of globalization on urban and rural communities, providing case studies from postsocialist Bulgaria. As globalization has been studied largely in urban contexts, the aim of this volume is to shift the attention to the countryside and analyse how transnational links are transforming the destinies of and relations between cities, towns and villages. Very few scholars have systematically studied the effects of globalization in the countryside. As one of them, Michael Woods, writes, place-based studies that show how rural localities are remade under globalization are lacking (2007, 486–7; see also 2011, 270). Theorists of globalization in anthropology such as Arjun Appadurai (1996) and Ulf Hannerz (1996) have failed to explicitly anchor their analysis in rural sites, while the widely used *Anthropology of Globalization* reader makes almost no reference to the countryside (Inda and Rosaldo 2008; see also Appadurai 2001). A notable exception is Anna Tsing's book *Friction* (2005), which combines a keen theoretical interest in globalization with an ethnography of what she calls 'awkward, messy and unpredictable encounters' in the rainforests of Indonesia, where foreign investors meet local communities and entrepreneurs, as well as environmental movements and other actors. The present volume attempts to make a contribution to this emerging debate, providing ethnographic accounts of global processes in specific rural places without losing sight of urban contexts.

The case studies are from postsocialist Bulgaria, providing examples of the effects globalization has had in a range of specific localities. This geographical focus brings unity and coherence to the book. In addition, drawing attention to a postsocialist country is fruitful since the impact of globalization has been particularly abrupt and dramatic here. After the fall of the Iron Curtain, the global has quickly asserted itself: towns and villages are exposed to global flows and inequalities, resulting in the rescaling and remaking of places, and triggering new cultural and ideological engagements with the notions of 'urban' and 'rural' in public discourse. The links that previously existed between town and countryside, within the framework of the socialist nation-state, have been supplanted by new transnational connections and global 'shortcuts', which have been made possible by the opening of Bulgaria's borders (1989) and EU accession (2007).

Some localities are winners and others losers of these rapid restructurings, their fortunes depending on their 'positionality' (Kaneff this volume) and other factors (Creed this volume). This has produced great diversity in the Bulgarian countryside, leading to the emergence of globalized villages, but also to forms of rural marginalization. Thus, one of the aims of this book is to challenge undifferentiated notions of the 'countryside' and the 'rural community', calling for a greater awareness of the economic disparities and social divisions which we normally associate with urban contexts. It questions the notion of the stable and undifferentiated rural community as denoted in Ferdinand Tönnies's notion of *Gemeinschaft* (community), as opposed to *Gesellschaft* (society). As Woods has argued, there is no such thing as a static and homogenous rural community; there are many rural communities which overlap, interact and compete with each other (2011, 178–9).

As my anthropological expertise does not cover Bulgaria as much as the former Yugoslavia and Romania, this introduction will primarily offer comparative and theoretical perspectives complementing the local insights provided by the other contributors. The first part will offer a brief history of rural conditions and urban–rural relations in Bulgaria, starting with the Ottoman period followed by subsequent transformations (independence, collectivization under socialism, and restitution and privatization since the 1990s), not only as background to the case studies presented here, but also as a reminder that the Bulgarian countryside has never been immune from outside influences. The second part of the introduction will elaborate on certain key themes and concepts of the book, most importantly globalization, neoliberal restructuring, the transformation of urban–rural relations and the global countryside. It will also explore aspects of rural diversity and marginalization. The third and final part of this introduction will provide a summary of chapters.

A Brief History of Rural Conditions and Urban–Rural Relations in Bulgaria

Many have reiterated that Bulgaria has been a 'small nation of small peasants' for most of its history. Even if reflecting particular realities on the ground, this is primarily a political and ideological statement derived from a post-Ottoman national (or nationalist) frame of mind that ignores forms of economic development and cultural diversity, which has always been part and parcel of social life in Bulgaria. In the immediate postsocialist years it was a key slogan for Bulgarian politicians who wanted to turn the clock of history back and restore the land to its presocialist owners. It is clear, however, that Bulgaria has ceased to be a country of peasants: thanks to socialism, it is the most urbanized country in Southeastern Europe. With 70 per cent of inhabitants living in urban settlements, Bulgaria is the only Balkan state that can compare with countries in Western Europe, where urbanites make up between 70 to 95 per cent of the population. So even if some authors continue to depict Bulgaria as a 'traditionally rural country' (see for instance Abadjieva 2008, 8), it is more urbanized than Serbia and Romania, where just over half of the population lives in cities, or even Greece, which has a reputation of being far more advanced and developed (Duijzings 2010, 105; see also Angelidou and Kofti this volume).

Before achieving autonomy (1878) and independence (1908), Bulgaria was at the centre of the European section of the Ottoman Empire, close to the imperial capital Constantinople (Istanbul). Whereas Ottoman territories in the Western Balkans were positioned at the empire's periphery, Bulgarian lands commanded the military and trade routes into Europe and formed part of the protective zone around the capital. They constituted an agrarian hinterland, supplying and provisioning Constantinople and other major cities such as Adrianople (Edirne), Philippopolis (Plovdiv) and Sofia with a variety of agricultural and artisanal products (Crampton 2005, 34). Bulgarian merchants were more dependent on Ottoman markets than their Greek or Serbian counterparts, who were directing their trade towards Central Europe (Lampe and Jackson 1982, 151). Being close to the empire's centre also meant that the Bulgarian lands were under stricter control, with a higher concentration of Ottoman troops present than elsewhere. They were colonized and densely inhabited by Turks and remained under Ottoman control longer than other parts of the Balkans.

During the Ottoman period, most Bulgarians lived in small villages, cultivating the land as sharecroppers for feudal *timar* holders besides having their own vineyards, orchards and vegetable gardens.[1] This agricultural regime is what made Bulgarians into a 'small nation of small peasants'. Villages were run by family elders who chose representatives from among themselves. Ottoman officials rarely visited these villages other than to collect taxes. Some villages were exempted from paying taxes in return for offering goods and services, like protecting bridges or guaranteeing safe passage, or providing cities with specific items such as wool, leather and water (İnalcık 1994, 175; Adanır 1989, 136–7; Crampton 2005, 35). From the end of the seventeenth century Ottoman *timars* passed increasingly into private and hereditary 'ownership', facilitating the development of commercial tax farming, which in some parts of the Balkans (especially Macedonia, Thrace and Thessaly) led to the emergence of the so-called *chiflik* estates. These estates were worked for profit, often at the expense of peasants who were subjected to exploitation in the form of rising taxation and corvée duties. Adanır, however, argues that their role should not be overstated, certainly in Bulgaria where large *chiflik* estates almost did not develop. One of the problems here was the recruitment of a labour force from a peasant population that was relatively free and well-off (Adanır 1989, 154). The Ottoman state also aimed at thwarting the development of *chiflik* estates in areas closer to the centre, since tax revenues from these estates tended to be low (Lampe and Jackson 1982, 135). Small peasant farms were better cultivated and comparatively more productive than farms employing labourers.

During the eighteenth century the Bulgarian population increasingly settled in towns due to growing artisanal and commercial activity, and because life in the countryside became more insecure. Small towns were established in the protected environment of the hills, which were dominated by Bulgarians, while cities located in the plains or along the Danube or Black Sea coast (such as Sofia, Plovdiv, Ruse and Varna) were Ottoman cities typically inhabited by Turks, Greeks and other groups such as Armenians and Jews, although Bulgarians too started to form an important element here (Crampton 2005, 53; see also Lampe 1986, 20–22). After the Porte re-established peace and security during the 1820s, many upland towns entered a period of economic expansion driven by the Ottoman demand for livestock products (such as meat and wool). In this respect, Bulgaria, being close to the centre, was susceptible to the influence of what Karen Barkey has called the 'provisionist mentality' (2005, 142) of the Ottoman state, geared to supply urban populations with sufficient food and other items. The local crafts and trade centres that blossomed during the nineteenth century were catering primarily for internal Ottoman markets. An example is Gabrovo, a town located high on the northern slopes of the Balkan range, where the Ottoman army was one of the largest buyers of local products such as meat, leather and shoes, as well as raw wool and woollen garments. Another example is Koprivshtitsa in central Bulgaria (Mellish this volume), where the local economy was dominated by long-distance sheep trade and textile manufacturing. It created a close link between local agriculture (especially animal husbandry) and crafts and commerce. As these mountainous areas were short of farmland, the Bulgarian population living here was forced into nonagricultural activities (Palairet 1997, 66–76).

Although rural overpopulation was still not an issue, the doubling of the Bulgarian population in the nineteenth century encouraged such activities.

While the share of the urban population remained at around 20 per cent, the geographical spread over a large number of smaller towns facilitated the growth of commercial networks (Lampe and Jackson 1982, 140–44). The Tanzimat reforms (1839–76), an attempt to modernize the empire, gave a further boost to these activities as Bulgarian merchants received the right to trade freely in Ottoman lands. Because of their growing wealth, the mountain towns became the breeding ground for an emerging national elite, which played an important role during the national revival period (Crampton 2005, 53; Lampe 1986, 20–22). The reforms also entailed a change in land tenure, which enabled Bulgarian peasants to acquire almost complete ownership over their land, including the right to sell. The second half of the nineteenth century was thus characterized by a transfer and sell-out of land by Turkish owners and officials to Bulgarian peasants. As the primary aim of the reforms was to improve the state's fiscal position, they did little to modernize agriculture – 'small peasants' continued to cultivate the land in traditional ways (Lampe and Jackson 1982, 136–7). Yet they did boost production – one of the effects was a dramatic growth of agricultural exports (Adanır 1989, 151). Bulgaria became the most productive and dynamic region of all the Ottoman territories, and fared well compared to Serbia, which had experienced a process of economic decline after independence (Palairet 1997, 2).

The historical trajectory outlined above does not warrant the position held by some that the changes introduced in the nineteenth century began with a pristine patriarchal stage, lasting for at least five centuries, in which peasants were tied to the land and 'land possession was in every respect undividable and not for sale' (Giordano and Kostova 2000b, 162). As Todorova (1990) has argued, it is difficult to be certain of this since we lack demographic data, and the information we do have suggests that the patriarchal extended family (*zadruga*) never existed as a stable reality, as it was constantly prone to forms of fissure. We may also challenge the stereotypical notion of a 'small nation of small peasants' because it ignores the presence of a relatively large urban population. Even if we accept that a substantial part of the population was based in the countryside, many centres of craft and commerce existed, inhabited by an active and mobile population consisting both of Bulgarians and non-Bulgarians.[2] The economic 'renaissance' of the mid-nineteenth century led to the diffusion of an indigenous enterprise culture that set the Bulgarian lands apart from most other parts of the Balkans (Palairet 1997, 2).

As Giordano and Kostova write, the 'small nation of small peasants' trope can be widely encountered in the writings of domestic politicians and foreign travellers and observers between 1850 and 1945. It became a cornerstone of Bulgarian national identity, which drew on the ethnically homogenous rural, as opposed to the mixed urban, population. It is true that after Bulgaria achieved autonomy, with the loss of the Ottoman markets and the arrival of cheap industrial goods produced in the West, the class of artisans declined noticeably and the country's population had to rely again on quasi-subsistence agriculture (Lampe and Jackson 1982, 142). Bulgaria entered a period of economic decline, leading to rural overpopulation and no industries to absorb the surplus populations from the countryside (Palairet 1997, 2; Brunnbauer and Höpken 2007, 9). This was a period of failed modernization, in which 'Europeanization' and the introduction of modern laws regarding land inheritance led to fragmentation of agricultural land, producing a truly 'small nation of *smallest* peasants' (Giordano and Kostova 2000b, 162; see also Hristov this volume).[3]

The homogenous mass of impoverished peasants embraced an extreme egalitarianism harnessed by Aleksandar Stamboliyski, who from 1919 until his assassination in 1923 led the first agrarian government (Bell 1977). As the country's leader he exacerbated the problem of land fragmentation by introducing redistributive land reforms, achieving an even more equal distribution of land and establishing the small peasant farm as the idealized and dominant form of land property (Crampton 2005, 148–53).[4] The huge popularity of radical populist ideas in the countryside was part of a Southeast European trend, where nationalist elites idealized the traditional peasant community and embraced the rural past as the source of true national values, against the culturally diverse cities which had been the centres of foreign domination (see for instance Giordano 2003).

With Stamboliyski, Bulgaria produced one of the most powerful peasant movements in the Balkans, which tried to dissociate itself from modernization and the penetration of Western capitalism (Giordano 2003, 265; see also Mouzelis 1976). Indeed, the class suffering most from the impact of capitalist penetration was the peasantry, which, strapped for cash (to pay taxes and buy Western products), was forced to abandon subsistence agriculture and produce for the market under conditions of extreme land fragmentation and lack of technological progress. The main political cleavage in the country took the form of 'peasant masses versus urban elite' (Mouzelis 1976, 102). Stamboliyski's Bulgarian Agrarian National Union was radically antiestablishment, antibourgeois and antiurban, embracing a bipolar view of society in which the village was seen as possessing moral superiority over the town. This world view had an ethnic dimension too, as it drew on the opposition between peasants and foreign (particularly Greek) merchants. Bulgarian rural virtues were contrasted with the corrupt habits of the 'Greeks', a category which also included merchants of (Hellenized) Bulgarian and/or other ethnic origin (Mouzelis 1976, 93).[5]

After the turbulent years of the Great Depression and World War II another transformation occurred with socialism, which was particularly radical in the case of Bulgaria. Within one generation the country was converted into one of the most industrialized states of the world. As Ray Abrahams has pointed out (1996, 2–3), agrarian reforms are certainly not a socialist invention, but what happened in Bulgaria after the revolution was certainly a sweeping instance of such policies. The socialist regime implemented one of the fastest programmes of collectivization: in 1958, Bulgaria declared itself to be the first socialist country after the Soviet Union to have carried out a full collectivization of agriculture. It completely transformed the social and economic make-up of the country, leading to a rural exodus and a reduction of the rural population by almost half (Conte and Giordano 1997, 28). Around 2 million peasants left their villages, and at the end of the 1960s more people in Bulgaria were living in cities than in the countryside (Giordano and Kostova 2000b, 165; Brunnbauer and Höpken 2007, 10). Collectivization brought an end to the family farm, in contrast to neighbouring Yugoslavia where the policy was abandoned because of strong popular resistance (Kovách 1994, 369). By the end of the socialist period Bulgaria achieved the highest level of urbanization in the region, with 70 per cent of the population living in urban settlements.

Collectivization and mechanization pushed the remaining rural population out of subsistence agriculture into wage labour, transforming peasants into workers. Even if families were allowed to keep small plots to grow their own vegetables, fruits and raise livestock, traditional agricultural know-how and the rural way of life were obliterated and largely relegated to folklore festivals and museums controlled by the regime (Mellish this volume; see also Giordano 2003). From the start of the 1970s, collectivization went one step further with the creation of huge agro-industrial complexes (APKs), which formed a key element in the socialist attempts to reduce the differences between urban and rural areas, and between Bulgarians and ethnic minorities such as the Pomaks, who had been reluctant to move to the cities (Nahodilova this volume). The APKs proved not to be successful, causing shortages and forcing the authorities to rely on family farming for the labour-intensive cultivation of fruits and vegetables, as was the case in most other socialist countries (Kovách 1994, 370).

Most young Bulgarians moved to the cities, whereas older Bulgarians typically stayed in villages, often joined by members of minority groups (such as Roma, Turks and Pomaks) who were employed in the agricultural collectives (Kaneff 1997, 18–19). Tight connections continued to exist between family members living in the cities and countryside. In effect these became bilocal or neoextended family households, sharing agricultural and other resources obtained from the urban economy (Smollett 1989; Konstantinov and Simić 2001, 21–2). It was common for urbanites, even members of the

educated classes, to spend part of the week in the village to cultivate their or
their parents' gardens. Rural and urban lifestyles went hand in hand, which
was also visible in the new socialist cities. Even though these cities were meant
to be showcases of socialist modernity, rural values persisted (Roth 1985;
Guest 2003; for Serbia see Simić 1973). In Bulgaria's most iconic socialist
city, Dimitrovgrad, small-scale subsistence farming was practiced in parks
with inhabitants carving out private parcels; it was only in the 1960s that the
authorities succeeded in suppressing these 'backward' practices (Brunnbauer
2005, 109–10). Dimitrovgrad was also Bulgaria's main producer of fertilizers,
which demonstrates how industrialization and agricultural modernization
went hand in hand (Brunnbauer 2005, 95). Notwithstanding the promise of
a bright future, the reality in the new socialist city was often dismal. In many
cases there was not sufficient accommodation available for workers, who had
to commute back to their villages.

It has been pointed out by anthropologists such as Hann (2003) and
Kaneff (2004) that the rural population benefitted from socialism, as many
features of modern life (electricity and roads, healthcare and education)
were introduced in this period. Hence, in the Bulgarian countryside,
socialism was not bitterly resented – elections during the 1990s showed
wide support for the old regime (Creed 1995a and 1995b; Leonard and
Kaneff 2002, 3), with rural inhabitants resisting the imposed changes
introduced during the postsocialist period. These changes entailed first and
foremost the privatization of agricultural assets and restitution of land,
which were implemented by government-led commissions carrying the
ominous name 'liquidation committees' (Creed 1995b, 31–2).[6] As in other
former socialist countries, these measures – the intention of which was to
bring back the land to its original boundaries of 1946 and transform the
large-scale collective and state farms into small family farms – were largely
counterproductive. It came down to a process of 'peasantization' rather
than 'farmerization' (Kichorowska-Kebalo 2000, 153). Instead of creating
efficient family farms, the result was the virtual collapse of agricultural
production, mass unemployment and the demise of the rural communities
that had emerged under socialism. These policies were supported by World
Bank and International Monetary Fund (IMF) advisers, who preferred
family farms to collective enterprises (Heinonen et al. 2007).

With hindsight it is perplexing to see that so much emphasis was put on
the creation of small family farms in the light of the difficulties experienced
by small farming units elsewhere. In the case of Bulgaria it led to the
extreme fragmentation – if not 'pixilation' – of ownership of agricultural
land, but without the 'peasants', who had become urbanized, returning to
the countryside (for similar processes in Romania see Thomson 2003, 5).

Giordano and Kostova speak of a process of 'reprivatisation without peasants': the wholesale restitution of small parcels to people who were not capable or willing to cultivate the land (2000b, 166–8). There was widespread reluctance to return to agriculture, even though some used it as a temporary safety net, including young people who became unemployed and returned to the village of their parents in the immediate aftermath of the land restitution (Ivanova 1995, 222; for Romania see Thomson 2003, 2; Mungiu-Pippidi 2010, 3). Most landowners preferred to put their property into the newly created cooperatives, which were run by people who had the necessary managerial skills and agricultural know-how, and who often had control over equipment and machinery as well. They preferred to share the risk in this unpredictable situation, as social support and agricultural credit were unavailable (Meurs and Spreeuw 1997; see also Cellarius 2003 and 2004 for the restitution of forests with similar outcomes). In addition, restitution proved to be a slow and complex process where (often conflicting) claims on property had to be adjudicated, leading to prolonged legal insecurity (see for instance Hann 2003). It allowed for all kinds of abuses and questionable appropriations of land, especially by the former socialist managers and local party bosses, who became managers of the newly established cooperatives and reinvented themselves as agricultural entrepreneurs. They were able to resist the 'sharks with their Mercedes and mobile telephones' coming from the big cities (Giordano and Kostova 2000b, 172; see also Abrahams 1996, 20; Giordano and Kostova this volume). Ordinary people whose land was returned typically had no effective control over it and very little income from it.

Katherine Verdery's book *The Vanishing Hectare* (2003) gives a good idea of the disruptive character of the privatization process in neighbouring Romania, opening up a world 'filled with deep longings, antagonism and revenge, shady dealings, prideful accomplishment, toil, constant squabbling and tension, devious speech, violence and threats of it, determination, ingenuity, and rage' (Verdery 2003, xiii–xiv). Differentiating between 'private property creation' (of objects that had never been privately held) and the 're-creation of private property' (restoring private ownership over pre-existing goods and objects such as land and houses), she argues that privatization is best understood as a process of *transforming* socialist property, where the old structures of power reinvent themselves in radically changed circumstances. The old hierarchies are reproduced 'with state farm directors at the top, collective farm staff below them, and village households at the bottom, holding very few resources for surviving in the new environment' (Verdery 2003, 11). As Verdery argues, some see this process as a neoliberal success story – unproductive social categories (the elderly and inefficient) are marginalized, and agriculture is made far more efficient by new agrarian entrepreneurs and market-oriented super tenants.

The shadow side is that many villagers lose their jobs and live destitute lives below the poverty line. Whereas Verdery is critical of this process, Giordano and Kostova (this volume) throw a more positive light on the role of these entrepreneurs as the rescuers of the rural economy (see also Kichorowska-Kebalo 2000, 155).

It is undeniable that decollectivization has had dire consequences for the rural population, leading to high rates of rural unemployment (up to 50 per cent or more in Hungary, Romania and Bulgaria). The unemployed are the unskilled and semiskilled workers of the dismantled collective farms, many of whom have been unable to claim land (Kichorowska-Kebalo 2000, 155; Giordano and Kostova 2000a, 32–3). They lack the business and farming skills needed to build up a new existence in agriculture and there are no jobs for them in the urban sectors (Unwin et al. 2004, 112). Rural unemployment is coupled with a decline in social benefits, which means that there is little assistance available for workers displaced from agricultural employment. Those who have the opportunity, primarily young people, move to the cities or abroad. As Koleva writes (this volume), the net result has been a continued exodus from the countryside. The restitution process and the economic hardships of postsocialist rural transition have not reversed the process of outmigration to the urban centres; on the contrary, they have only exacerbated it. Not all rural regions are equally affected – villages in developed agricultural regions, satellites of urban or tourist centres and villages inhabited by ethnic minorities are not losing populations as much as other villages.

As Kaneff (1997) has shown, decollectivization has disproportionally affected members of the minority communities, who were previously employed in the socialist agricultural collectives (with most Bulgarians migrating to the cities). As they were often unable to reclaim land during the restitution process, they have remained landless, while elderly Bulgarian villagers and their urban relatives now own the land.[7] As a result, the countryside has seen a substantial increase in access inequality (to economic and other sources) and employment exclusion for minorities such as the Roma, Turks and Pomaks, but also for other vulnerable categories such as people with little education and women (but see Ghodsee 2005 for a counterexample). Unemployment is worse in regions where minorities are concentrated, such as in the northeast or the Rhodope Mountains. As Abadjieva writes, 'pockets of extreme destitution persist in the country', whereby ethnicity is one of the clearest correlates: 60 per cent of the poor belong to ethnic minority groups and many of them are living in the countryside (46.2 per cent of Roma and 63 per cent of Turks) (Abadjieva 2008, 11–12). Whereas conditions in cities have improved, the rural poor have not benefitted from rising living standards. The Roma are worst off; the most intractable problem is long-term rural unemployment, which is most acute in villages with compact Roma populations (Abadjieva 2008, 18). Roma are ten times (Turks four times) more likely to be poor than Bulgarians, and they are much poorer on average than their poverty-struck non-Roma counterparts. Poverty among the Roma is multidimensional, encompassing substandard housing conditions, low education levels and poor health, all compounded by forms of social exclusion and discrimination (Abadjieva 2008, 19; Stewart 2002, 135; Giordano and Kostova 2000a, 34–5).

Key Themes

Bulgaria's twentieth-century trajectory illustrates the points made by Abrahams that land reforms are not exclusively a socialist or postsocialist phenomenon and that it is possible to trace a historical movement back and forth between small family farms and larger (usually more efficient) farms (1996, 3). In a series of transformations, the small family farm which Bulgaria had inherited from the Ottoman past was replaced by the Soviet model of mechanized and collectivized agriculture, which was again superseded by an abortive movement back to the idealized small family farm. After this historical overview, I will shift the discussion to contemporary issues and make a number of theoretical points relating to the key themes of the book, most importantly the topics of globalization, neoliberal restructuring, the transformation of urban–rural relationships and the global countryside, also exploring aspects of rural inequality and marginalization.

Globalization and Europeanization

The first important (but also rather unoriginal) point I would like to make is that most of the literature on globalization has exaggerated the degree of its novelty, ignoring the parallels with similar processes in recent or more distant pasts (Smart and Smart 2003; Berend 2006). The previous section showed that Bulgarian villages were never cut off from wider trends and ongoing political and economic transformations, over which peasants usually had little control. Bulgarian lands were close to the centre of the empire, with clear effects on their economy and demography. The Ottoman attempts to modernize the empire changed the land tenure system, giving peasants property rights and boosting agricultural production. After Bulgaria gained autonomy the process of 'Europeanization' began (see Katsikas and Siani-Davies 2010), which had the combined effect of inclusion into Western markets and peasant resistance against capitalist penetration and modernization. Finally, the socialist revolution once again overhauled the social and economic make-up of the country. Even if these changes cannot be subsumed under the term 'globalization', it is clear that they originated elsewhere, in places close to or further removed from Bulgaria.

Alan and Josephine Smart write that globalization particularly affects urban settings (2003, 263), by which they seem to suggest that rural settings are immune to or actively resist these processes. There are grounds to question this: in the Bulgarian context for instance we may recall Irwin Sanders's classic monograph on the 'tranquil village' of Dragalevtsi (1949), located close to Sofia, which was clearly affected by wider events – the intrusion of the national state, the advent of World War II and communism. Even though peasants kept their distance from new developments introduced by 'people from the outside world' and 'did not yet want to have a hand in what went on in Sofia, in Berlin, or Washington' (177–8), they were perfectly conscious of these outside forces. Most villagers (especially men) were literate and some read the newspaper in the local tavern. Between 1937 and 1944 the radio made its entry into the village, opening it up to news reports, jazz music and cultural influences from abroad.[8] Urban fashion entered the scene, as 'all self-respecting village women possessed a pair of cheap western shoes' (16). Soon Dragalevtsi was to become part of Sofia and in the postsocialist period it grew into a favourite residence for the city's nouveaux riches.

In spite of the village opening up, the world had become in fact a less global place after World War I – this was the era of the nation-state, or more precisely of a modern 'interstate system' which introduced much tighter controls on the movement of people, capital and goods through the establishment of borders (Smart and Smart 2003, 265; Tsing 2000, 333; Graeber 2002, 1225). Then, after World War II, due to the Cold War, the world became ideologically divided, cutting off countries such as Bulgaria from inclusion into the global economy and integrating them into a rival 'internationalist' political and economic system (that is, of state socialism), which led to instances of deglobalization or delinking (Hannerz 1996, 18). The overarching characteristic of this period was that most European states, including countries behind the Iron Curtain, were new nation-states in the process of consolidation, far from immune from nationalist tendencies. Nowadays, many theorists tend to argue that globalization has reduced the role of the nation-state, but the break-up of Yugoslavia has shown that the nation-state is still an important force and model to be emulated in the region (Duijzings 2004).

Seen from a long-term perspective, contemporary globalization is just another stage in a protracted history of ongoing exposure of localities to external movements and forces. What is different nowadays is the intensity and immediacy of these global connections – that is, the volume and velocity of these global flows (Woods 2007, 500; Tsing 2000, 346).[9] So one can ask (as Creed does in this volume) to what extent the new wave of 'globalization' studies is not old wine in new bottles, having in mind the old world-system and political-economy approaches inspired by Immanuel Wallerstein's work (1974) and influenced by neo-Marxist theories *en vogue* during the 1970s and 1980s.[10] It can be argued that Eastern Europe, trying to escape its peripheral position under socialism, has again become the periphery of the capitalist world (see for instance Berend 1996). It is no coincidence that globalization started with the end of the Cold War – it unchained capitalist global ambitions, which became free to roam the world (Tsing 2000, 331; Ritzer 2007, 22).

Woods calls contemporary globalization 'neoliberal' or 'second-wave' globalization (2007, 487) – he and others have defined it as a dynamic and multifaceted process of integration which involves the 'rescaling', 'stretching' and 'deepening' of social relations across borders, so that activities and interactions in particular localities are increasingly influenced by events and forces operating on a global scale. It enrols localities into 'networks of interconnectivity' organized globally, facilitating the circulation of capital, commodities, services, people, representations and ideas. Many of these processes are not truly global but rather transnational or translocal (Woods 2007, 487; Smart and Smart 2003, 265). Most authors also emphasize that globalization reduces the role of the state, and in economic terms leads to the concentration of capital, the replacement of manufacturing by finance, and growing influence of international financial organizations such as the IMF and the World Bank (see for instance Verdery 2003, 4).

The bulk of the literature on globalization deals with cities, with Saskia Sassen's (2001) work being the main point of reference. It is commonly understood that globalization is most visible in cities such as London, Tokyo and New York, whereas other cities and smaller localities are not or only partially affected. Rural areas are a forgotten world in the literature on globalization, and, if at all, only partially covered in specialist and isolated subfields such as rural sociology and geography. Overall, theoreticians presume that cities are the motors or transmission belts of globalization, and if such processes occur in the countryside then they are the result of rural inhabitants adopting urban lifestyles and villages becoming urbanized (Lefebvre 2000, 3–4). Several chapters in this volume illustrate this, for instance by describing the introduction of Western brands and the inclusion of rural places into global commodity chains (Ermann), the linking of the rural economy with urban centres and elites (Giordano and Kostova), the growth of tourism and the commoditization of rural culture (Mellish), and of entrepreneurial and urban to rural migration across national boundaries (Ermann, Kaneff,

Koleva, Angelidou and Kofti). Bulgarian villages have indeed acquired the trappings of urbanity in terms of increased mobility, connectivity and social fragmentation and exclusion.

Contemporary globalization is often treated in tandem with neoliberalism (see for instance Berend 2006, 275–8). The end of socialism was a triumph for the neoliberalist project – an alternative future was eliminated, and 'history came to an end', as Fukuyama famously claimed (see Giordano and Kostova this volume). Eastern Europe became an arena for neoliberalist restructuring, with the IMF and the World Bank in leading roles. Some key principles, such as deregulation, took their purest form in the former socialist countries, amplified by popular resentment against any state interference, especially in countries where communist interventions had been most dramatic and painful, such as Romania. Yet the rhetoric of the 'withering' of the state disguises some of the realities of neoliberal restructuring, which was never meant to be a free-for-all; it is facilitated by a proactive state – that is, a state which is at the service of global capital – its role being to legislate in such a manner that the neoliberal model of the perfectly functioning market is realized in practice, for instance through property guarantees and the legal enforcement of contracts (Busch 2010, 331–2; Tsing 2000, 354; see also Creed this volume).

As Pierre Bourdieu (1998) and Loïc Wacquant (2012) have argued, neoliberalism can be best understood as a political project – that is, a complex of social governance technologies which result in the freedom to operate and a reduction of state interference. This is equally true in the case of Eastern Europe, where members of the former socialist elites who controlled the state bureaucracies (or parts of it, such as the Securitate in Romania) are among the most important beneficiaries of neoliberal restructuring. The state has not withered away, but has facilitated a path-specific postsocialist form of neoliberal restructuring, where the *nomenklatura* have used their control over the state bureaucracy to privatize assets, partly by selling them off to foreign investors, enriching themselves in the process and allowing new spatial interconnections to occur across national boundaries (Angelidou and Kofti this volume, Ermann this volume). In the countryside, some members of these old socialist elites have managed to retain power, leaving peasants in a position of economic and political dependency (see for instance Mungiu-Pippidi 2003 for Romania). What they have achieved is not a genuine liberalization or free-for-all situation with appropriate legal guarantees but an informal and impenetrable market, where local political and business interests are closely intertwined. In that sense the trajectory has been different from that in other parts of Europe where economic restructuring has been mitigated by pre-existing legal and regulatory frameworks and controls which protect the most vulnerable (Busch 2010, 345).

International organizations such as the World Trade Organization (WTO), the World Intellectual Property Organization (WIPO), the World Bank and the IMF have had an important role in terms of introducing neoliberal principles to the East European economies. These have been extended to the agricultural sector, where it is not land ownership but intellectual property rights over seeds, fertilizers and pharmaceuticals that offer the most lucrative business opportunities. The situation is characterized by the privatization of agricultural research (resulting in patents), the rise of financialization (of speculation and the growing tendency of financial markets to dominate agricultural production) and a shift away from local cultural practices in agriculture. Corporate seed producers profit most as they capitalize on the development of genetic and genomic technologies, while local farmers and processors may only benefit from intellectual property rights in terms of geographical indicators and appellations (Busch 2010). As Verdery writes, land has become 'a medium for absorbing manufactured inputs', 'a platform for chemical products' so as to grow crops (2003, 7). Before Bulgaria's accession to the EU, seed producers such as Monsanto and Pioneer, not hindered by European legislation, introduced genetically modified crops such as tobacco and maize into Bulgarian agriculture, which led to protests by local NGOs accusing these corporations of transforming the country into a playground for genetically engineered crops.[11] Clearly there is a tendency for finance-driven agribusinesses to override environmental and community concerns, especially in countries such as Bulgaria where these concerns are less vocal.

In this context it is helpful to distinguish between globalization and neoliberal restructuring on the one hand and European integration on the other hand. These are parallel but different processes which are potentially at odds with each other. EU agrarian policies were initially aimed at maximizing output, but during the 1990s a shift occurred from agricultural to rural policies, from a productivist to a postproductivist agenda ensuring the prosperity of the wider rural population and sustainability of the environment (Shucksmith and Shapman 1998). The aim has become to support and revitalize rural economies, taking into account the changing aspirations and priorities of people living in the countryside. EU policies are aimed at the diversification of rural economies, tackling rural poverty and social exclusion, and integrating agricultural practices into more broadly defined economic and environmental objectives (Unwin et al. 2004, 114; see also Symes 1992).[12]

Some analysts nevertheless argue that the neoliberal agenda of capital accumulation remains the overriding purpose of EU agricultural policies, causing poverty and social exclusion. They point out that, even though the Common Agricultural Policy aims to preserve rural communities and further welfare in the countryside, most EU subsidies go to large farms at the centre, whereas a myriad of small farms struggle for survival at the peripheries of the EU (Symes 1992, 195). In this context of increased competition, rural areas are forced to adopt an entrepreneurial logic just like cities (Harvey 1989); local authorities, agricultural producers and local businesses collaborate in order to attract investment and carve out niches for their products. One way of doing this is to create distinctive local and regional, as well as rural and agricultural, identities to counterbalance the homogenizing effects of food globalization. The importance of these entrepreneurial forms of 'governance' is growing since local and regional authorities can no longer rely on state subsidies (Creed this volume).

The global countryside: Urban–rural transformations and rural inequality

As a consequence of globalization and European integration, new transnational links have started to complement the traditional nexus between town and countryside (Kaneff this volume). From the perspective of rural communities, these links (or 'shortcuts' as I would like to call them) effortlessly bypass adjacent urban centres and cross national borders. They do not follow the logic of parallel 'wiring' previously imposed by the nation-state. As some chapters in this volume show, villages develop direct connections with other places, reorienting themselves towards new centres of economic power abroad instead of nearby Bulgarian cities, many of which (except for Sofia) have fared badly in the postsocialist period. These new connections play a key role in 'rescaling the locality', linking it to a hierarchy of wealth and power that extends globally (Kaneff this volume). These connections have led to the emergence of the 'postpeasant subject' – that is, the rural inhabitant who tries his luck elsewhere and adopts a transnational identity (Kearny 1996; see Levitt 2001 for a vivid ethnographic example). A growing number of ruralites move abroad in search of jobs, breaking down the old spatial and occupational dualisms that structured images of the 'peasant' in the past (Kearney 1996, 8). There are, for instance, villages in Romania and Bulgaria, inhabited by Roma, where inhabitants have no chance of getting jobs locally and hence travel abroad to find work there (see for instance Tomova 2011). Other villages, again, become a destination for migrating Britons looking for property in the Bulgarian countryside (Kaneff this volume). As Kaneff suggests, this situation of transnational or translocal links can be best understood using Sheppard's concept of 'positionality' (2002), which implies a certain degree of randomness and variety. In this increasingly competitive landscape, some rural places manage to wire themselves more effectively into global networks than others.

Unsurprisingly, this raises the issue whether the traditional urban–rural binary is still relevant (Kaneff this volume). It can be argued that postsocialist transition and globalization have indeed led to the blurring and partial collapse of spatial categories such as 'centre' and 'periphery', 'rural' and 'urban'. These distinctions have become fuzzier and continue to fade as travel and communication become easier. As Zenner (2002) has argued, the urban–rural distinction has become largely irrelevant as that which was specific to the city can now be found everywhere (see also Kearney 1996). Yet it is going too far to conclude that the urban–rural divide has become irrelevant (Creed this volume). It is transforming itself from a spatial or geographical split into a political and ideological divide. So instead of seeing the urban and rural as two distinct 'locations' between which we can physically travel, we now may regard them as constituting a 'fractal' distinction which may operate in any given location.[13] They form 'categories of thought' with which people try to understand, construct and represent their own realities and other aspects of life (Koleva this volume). In geographical terms the boundaries may be less clear, but in cultural and ideological terms the 'urban' and 'rural' still trigger strong feelings: people clearly differentiate the two, contextualizing each category within their own lives (Woods 2011, 8). As I have been able to observe in Zheravna, one of Bulgaria's well-known museum villages, urbanites build 'traditional' houses combining vernacular and rural architectural form languages with modern materials and sanitary conditions. As Woods argues, there is scope for collaboration between rural and urban research, 'in teasing out the messy entanglements of the rural and the urban' (2011, 293).

Woods has developed the notion of the 'global countryside' as a deliberate allusion to the 'global city' without arguing, however, that features of the global city can be straightforwardly mapped onto rural localities. He rather suggests that rural contexts have been brought in line with the configurations that constitute urban space and society (2011, 292). Until recently, the 'rural' was excluded from the imaginary of globalization as it was part of that residual sphere existing outside the global city. However, as Woods indicates, the global city 'command centre model' has made us realize that globalization takes place everywhere, in the form of cultural diffusion (experienced for instance by rural inhabitants) and microprocesses of place making, which apply to urban and rural contexts alike (2007, 491–2). Clearly, the reconstitution of rural places under the impact of globalization cannot be understood as a linear narrative: 'There is no pre-existing stable and uniform "rural place" upon which globalization can act, but neither is there a single unidirectional force of globalization' (495). Globalization is not simply an imposition from above; it also includes processes of negotiation, hybridization and co-constitution that involve both global and local actors. As such it never obliterates the local (497–500; see also Tsing 2005).

Woods defines the 'global countryside' as a hypothetical space that is transformed by a combination of globalizing processes, which only find partial expression in specific rural sites. It includes dependence on global commodity networks, corporate concentration, labour migration, tourism, property investment, commoditization of nature and commercial exploitation of natural resources, changes in the landscape, social polarization, the 'scaling up' of political authority, and the resulting global contestation of rural sites (Woods 2007, 490–94). Current research on the global countryside includes work on the globalization of commodity chains, food regimes, rural development and disinvestment, depeasantization and the commercialization of agriculture, and a wide range of other issues such as poverty and social exclusion (487–90; see also Woods 2011, 266–75). Anna Tsing's work on the effects of globalization in the Indonesian rainforests is a rare example of such an analysis in anthropology. She shows how globalization encompasses contradictory political, economic and cultural tendencies and movements, providing opportunities for 'predatory business practices' as well as 'local empowerment' (Tsing 2005). Globalization means different things in different places, and its dangers, threats and promises are often closely connected: 'There is a lot going on, and it does not all match up' (2000, 336; see also Graeber 2002, 1228). Core to Tsing's understanding is that globalization is not a single programme driven by a transnational capitalist logic, but rather a complex entanglement of multiple, overlapping, unstable and contradictory globalisms 'rubbing up against each other awkwardly', which she calls 'friction'. This notion of 'friction' undercuts the idea of unimpeded 'flow' which is so dominant in the literature on globalization (2005, 6).

This brings us to the differential impacts and uneven effects of globalization on rural areas. As Dingsdale has pointed out, small towns and rural areas have faced the most serious problems of structural adjustment: 'They have the widest spectrum of success or failure because their fortunes can rest on a single major investment or disinvestment' (2001, 183). This means that in spite of the shared neoliberal environment the fortunes of rural places may vary considerably – 'every village a different story' as Creed writes (this volume). Creed points out that rural diversity existed under socialism (see also Stewart 1997, 67), but it has increased as the redistributive mechanisms of the socialist state have been removed. Some localities have succeeded in reinventing themselves in a situation in which agriculture is often not sustainable any more by engaging in alternative economic activities, while these options may not be available to other villages (Dingsdale 2001, 180; Hann 2010, 196). The examples in this book (see Kaneff and Mellish) show that tourism may be one of the most successful ways in which rural localities can survive.[14] The winners of transition are often those villages that manage to attract urbanites, foreign tourists and second-home owners. Bulgarian villages have seen the arrival of Britons in search of a rural idyll, as well as retirement migrants and pensioners, for whom life in the countryside is less expensive. These emerging forms of counterurbanization create tensions between part-time (foreign) and full-time (Bulgarian) residents. Overall, as Woods indicates, there is a rise of mobile and transitory rural inhabitants, whose attachment to the place is limited (2011, 163).

Counterurbanization conceals some of the harsher realities of rural life in Bulgaria, such as poverty and social exclusion.[15] For some, living in the countryside is a lifestyle choice, for others it means social deprivation, inequality and discrimination (Woods 2011, 163). Even though research has shown that rural poverty may vary hugely in terms of severity and duration (Shucksmith and Chapman 1998, 236–7), in postsocialist Bulgaria rural poverty and social exclusion are often extreme, structural and multidimensional, with few chances for those affected to escape it (Nahodilova this volume). Poverty in rural Bulgaria is twice as high as in urban areas, and is exacerbated by an ageing population, out-migration and depopulation (especially in border regions), chronic unemployment, poor and deteriorating infrastructure, low levels of agricultural productivity, and limited access to basic services (water, sanitary, health and so on). Subsistence plots prevent people from starving, but nevertheless the impression one gets is that Bulgaria is a country of 'dying villages', of stagnant 'rural backwaters' and 'rural ghettos' (Tomova 1995, 65). Ethnic minority groups suffer most from these circumstances – as Bulgarians have moved en masse to the cities, the countryside has been left to them (Bates 1995, 149). Roma, Turks and Pomaks tend to congregate in ethnically homogenous rural communities, motivated by the distrust that has existed between them and the Bulgarian majority after the Bulgarization campaigns of the 1980s and the Turkish exodus in 1989. As Konstantinov and Simić have argued, minority groups seek safety in tightly knit rural communities, refusing to move to the cities as Bulgarians have done. They rely on residential proximity, on neighbourhood solidarity and self-imposed segregation, preferring to stay in the countryside among themselves. They lack basic trust in the public life of 'Bulgarian' cities.[16] Even though the socialist state tried to modernize some of these communities by building new settlements (see Nahodilova this volume), many of them are currently suffering from poverty and unemployment, although the situation is complex and not clear cut (see Valtchinova this volume).[17]

Summary of Chapters

Apart from this introduction, the first two chapters written by Deema Kaneff and Gerald Creed provide theoretical reflections on the topic of globalization from a Bulgarian context. Kaneff proposes 'positionality' as a key concept; she argues that in the global age bipolar distinctions and spatial dichotomies such as urban versus rural and centre versus periphery have collapsed. They functioned within the hierarchy of the nation-state, where interactions occurred in the form of standard binary flows between town and countryside. Now villages are globally connected through 'wormholes' that 'leapfrog' across space, linking them to localities and places that once existed as separate worlds, and to hierarchies of wealth and power that extend transnationally. Trying to make sense of these new spatial configurations that bypass the nation-state, Kaneff (following the geographer Sheppard) proposes the notion of 'positionality', denoting the shifting and path-dependent ways in which locations are tied up with other places. She uses the example of British citizens from economically marginal areas such as the Midlands, Scotland and Wales, who buy property in rural Bulgaria. Both buyers and sellers experience downward social mobility, and through these transactions they attempt to gain social security and financial stability. Whereas Bulgarian sellers pay off their debts, the British buyers try to establish a retirement base and regain a sense of community, which they feel is lacking in the UK and still extant on the Bulgarian countryside. Both try to escape the negative effects of globalization and neoliberal restructuring, using the opportunities created by EU enlargement. This process is mirrored by a parallel movement of wealthier Britons from England's Southeast buying property in Black Sea resorts.

Gerald Creed continues with an investigation of what positionality exactly means in the context of the Bulgarian countryside. He portrays the diversity of postsocialist destinies of Bulgarian villages, which makes it difficult, if not misleading, to speak generically about the 'rural condition'. The latter seemingly emerges from the homogenizing and averaging effects of rural statistics, but also from ethnography, which is usually based on a single village, as a result of which differences between villages remain unobserved. Rural variation no doubt existed under socialism, but the state's emphasis on progress for all led to interventions that constrained it. The postsocialist period has seen an increase in this diversity – the state has withdrawn, even if it still plays a key role in facilitating neoliberal reforms, allowing global connections to emerge and keeping them 'open' through legal provisions. Creed distinguishes several variables determining rural fortunes: region, demographic profile, proximity to urban centres and kinship relations, as well as social and political connections, property arrangements that have emerged out of the varied restitution and privatization processes, and individual initiative and leadership. He proposes a broader conceptual understanding of positionality, which links ideas about the 'rural' to other related cultural and ideological notions such as the 'urban', 'nature', 'agriculture' and 'modernity'.

These theoretical introductions are followed by case studies which explore the destinies of different rural, semirural and urban localities in the postsocialist period. Galia Valtchinova focuses on the shifting position of border towns due to political regime changes and international developments. Her chapter deals with the town of Tran, located at the border with Serbia, which has seen shifts in its 'positionality' as the porosity of the border has fluctuated over time. Under socialism it was a marginal town, where communist functionaries were sent in 'exile', but during the 1990s it became a more dynamic place, thriving on the cross-border trade with Serbia (under international embargo at the time). The chapter explores how Tran's changing role has had an impact on local social divisions and cultural hierarchies. Whereas under socialism the urban ethos of the town suffered because of pauperization and ruralization, the postsocialist period saw a reversal of this situation: new status groups emerged, associated with capitalist entrepreneurship, validating the Roma-dominated shadow economy and cross-border trade that had previously been deemed 'illegal'. Smuggling became a survival strategy for all, even though Roma outperformed Bulgarians. From being associated with rural poverty and marginality, Tran developed into a symbol of postsocialist affluence, blurring the old cultural hierarchies between urban and rural, rich and poor, and Bulgarians and Roma.

Lenka Nahodilova's chapter illustrates the opposite trend of rural decline at the Greek–Bulgarian border. It focuses on a socialist model village built in the 1970s in the Rhodope Mountains. Instead of moving peasants into cities, the authorities transferred the inhabitants of several Pomak villages into a modern settlement in the valley, hoping to improve and modernize the lives of the Muslim population and erase the urban–rural divide in line with Leninist utopian ideals. In the fight against 'rurality, tradition and backwardness', the Rhodopes were a key target for the regime because of their location at the border with capitalist Greece, matching old presocialist perceptions of the area as the frontier between civilization and wilderness, and Christianity and Islam. Competing with their Greek neighbours, the socialists vied to bring modern infrastructure and amenities such as electricity, but despite these efforts, the settlement never achieved a truly urban character. In the postsocialist period it became a prime example of rural decline, suffering economic collapse and mass unemployment. Survival strategies have relied heavily on informal trade. Poverty, apathy and time wasting have begun to dominate everyday life. Most importantly, there is no going back to the presocialist situation; the process of socialist modernization is irreversible.

In juxtaposition, Christian Giordano and Dobrinka Kostova describe a case of successful postsocialist rural transition in the Dobrudzha region in the northeast of the country, where socialist collectivization produced the preconditions for new forms of capitalist farming. The chapter shows how the restitution laws of the 1990s led to the phenomenon of the so-called *arendatori*: the former managers of socialist agricultural collectives turning into agribusinessmen in the postsocialist period. They rent plots from urbanites unable and unwilling to work the land that was returned to them. Often living in towns and commuting to the countryside, they have filled the agricultural vacuum, reinventing themselves as capitalist farmers, mobilizing their families and building upon extensive informal networks created during socialism. Even if informal practices and personalized trust are seen as immoral and abhorrent, they represent the best way for all the parties involved to protect themselves from the dangers and traps of the postsocialist system. The most successful *arendatori* have good connections with the city: they are patient negotiators with urbanites who own the land and have to agree to long-term leases, as well as with officials who allocate agricultural subsidies. Even though the *arendatori* are seen as remnants of the socialist elite who managed to enrich themselves, they have proven to be useful in terms of creating jobs and accumulating social capital. This case is used to question Fukuyama's (neoliberal) thesis that wealth and prosperity can only be achieved in high-trust societies; it shows that low-trust societies can develop successful forms of economic cooperation, based on personalized networks.

In line with previous contributions, Petko Hristov's chapter demonstrates the irreversibility of certain social processes wrought under socialism; it looks at changed gender patterns, which have had an impact on the restitution process, the backdrop of the previous chapter. Hristov shows how gender patterns established under socialism have transformed inheritance norms with clear implications for the process of restitution. It looks at the gap between traditional social attitudes and customary practices, and modern state legislation which allows women to reclaim land. It raises the question: what happens when, after fifty years of socialism, land is returned to the previous owners? Do kin slip back into traditional inheritance patterns or is modern gender equality acknowledged? The conclusion is the latter, proving wrong those politicians who claimed (and hoped) that the countryside is returning to tradition. This is clearly not the case, although the postsocialist period has indeed seen conflicts between relatives, in which traditional norms clash with the modern legal ones. The author shows how socialism contributed to gender equality: people who lost land as a result of collectivization ended up in cities, adopting modern and urban attitudes, and their female descendants are now asserting their right to inherit the land, in spite of relatives who try to exclude them.

Overall, since the nineteenth century, the gap between the law and everyday social practices has narrowed, and socialism has played an important role in this.

The second cluster of chapters deals with newly emerging cultural hierarchies and notions of the 'urban' and 'rural' in the global age. Daniela Koleva employs statistical data and a local case study to trace changing perceptions, whereas the following three chapters provide ethnographic examples of these changes in villages and cities undergoing processes of Europeanization and globalization. Koleva's chapter analyses attitudes towards the 'rural' and 'urban' among rural residents and first generation rural–urban migrants in Bulgaria. She engages with Creed and Ching's notion of 'rusticity' (1997), arguing that it fails to capture the complex dynamics of urban–rural interaction and misses the ruralites' point of view. The data are taken from a United Nations Development Programme (UNDP) survey carried out in 2003, in which most rural respondents place themselves outside of the unattainable and undesirable 'modern and urban' category, expressing discomfort and even antagonism to it, and confirm the traditional opposition between the 'modern and urban' and 'traditional and rural'. Yet the rural is not perceived as negative – the respondents display a clearly positive self-image and not an interiorized negative one, as projected by urbanites. The survey also shows that urbanites have positive (even if idealized, romanticized or aestheticized) notions about rural life. Through an ethnographic account of an annual village festival, Koleva demonstrates that in most people's minds the 'rural' is not opposed to the 'urban', but is rather complementary, whereby the countryside is regarded as providing food and space for recreation. The festival draws people from cities and abroad, creating a complex interaction with villagers resulting in a positive assessment of village life. In short, notions of 'rurality' and 'urbanity' are continuously under construction through the practices and discourses of various social actors. The chapter also shows that urban–rural mobility, either seasonal or as part of a life cycle (pensioners going back to the villages where they were born), complicates attempts to distinguish between 'ruralites' and 'urbanites'.

Liz Mellish provides an example of a truly 'global village' event: she traces the development of the National Festival of Bulgarian Folklore, taking place every five years in (and in the hills above) the museum town of Koprivshtitsa. From being a national state-funded festival under socialism, primarily serving a cohort of Bulgarian participants and visitors, it has now evolved into an event attracting tourists and folk enthusiasts from all parts of the world. A decrease in state funding and the insertion of the festival into global markets has led to its commercialization, as well as to the transformation of 'authentic' performances from old-style socialist 'mini spectacles' (theatrical sets in Bulgarian) with an emphasis on the spoken word to the enactment of spectacular rituals which cater for spectators with no knowledge of the language. Foreign folk enthusiasts participate in informal dance activities, fostering an international *communitas* which replaces the national one that predominated under socialism. In the process, 'traditional' Bulgarian culture is globalized, becoming a repertoire that can be appropriated and performed by foreigners. The town provides not only a 'heterotopic' site for folk tourists looking for the authentic experience, but also for wealthy urbanites from Sofia, who want to escape the postsocialist city and buy traditional houses in what they regard as a 'rural idyll'.

Ulrich Ermann's contribution looks at brands and the new consumer culture introduced in Bulgaria after the end of socialism. Consumerist ideals and norms are driven both by global and local brands, the latter of which emulate Western models and standards. Bulgarian companies fix their brands to global lifestyles, separating them radically from the local production context (as the 'Made in Bulgaria' label is tied up with backwardness), reinforcing the semiperipheral position of the country in the global economy. However, there is an irony in the fact that global brands are manufactured locally, in small Bulgarian towns with textile plants built under socialism. Ermann develops the idea of 'brand geographies', building on the notion that the production, marketing and consumption of brands is embedded in spatial relations, adding value through spatial references. The anchoring of brands in global fashion centres such as New York, Milan or Paris, or in high-profile shopping outlets in the main Bulgarian cities, helps them to acquire a certain prestige. They allow consumers to link up with 'the West' and break with their peripheral position in the symbolic geography of Europe. Ermann shows that rural environments are also increasingly sign and consumer oriented, meaning that 'urban lifestyles' are now consumed in the countryside. A high brand awareness among youth in small towns leads to forms of conspicuous consumption and brand addiction, reinforcing the idea that ruralites lack the refined tastes of urbanites. The unsophisticated use of brands transforms them into 'peasants' or 'East Europeans', depending on the context. In response, alternative 'rural' or even 'antiurban' lifestyles have developed, which counter Western brand hegemony. Antibrand tendencies are linked to the 'East', the 'local' or the 'socialist past', but nevertheless follow the same business logic, whereby companies cater for different 'audiences' or consumer 'communities'.

The final chapter deals with Greek expats living in Sofia, forming a close-knit community or enclave of managers and businessmen. This expat community emerged after communism's collapse, triggering entrepreneurial mobility towards the ex-socialist countries. Seeking to advance their careers, Greek businessmen enter a process of steep upward mobility as soon as they accept a job in Bulgaria, enjoying higher salaries and prestige than they would have in Greece. Forming part of the Western business community, they refuse to integrate into local society. Aliki Angelidou and Dimitra Kofti argue that this has led to a strengthening of cultural boundaries, reinforcing power relations and symbolic hierarchies between Greeks and Bulgarians. The former regard themselves as 'pioneers of progress', frustrated by unwilling and undeserving Bulgarians, who are viewed as obedient but lazy and unintelligent and in need of deep cultural training because of their perceived lack of business mentality. Greek domination is expressed through forms of conspicuous consumption and privileges (such as expensive cars and apartments). They prefer the term 'expatriates' as their self-designation, having connotations of power and wealth, whereas 'emigrant' is avoided as it signifies economic struggle.

Notes

1 The *timar* system was a feudal arrangement whereby the sultan owned the land, giving military men (*sipahis*) control over it and providing peasants with secure tenure. It was an arrangement whereby the *timar* holder did not own the land but only took part of the revenues (a share of the harvest), collected taxes and administered the land. The *timar* holder was also given parcels for him to cultivate to provide for himself and his family (the *chiflik*). For a general description of conditions in Ottoman villages, see İnalcık (1994, 173–8).

2 Malanima and Volckart (2007) give a historical overview of processes of urbanization in different parts of Europe. In the eighteenth century, urban populations accounted for more than 12 per cent of the Balkan population, which was above the European average and substantially higher than in Scandinavia, Germany, Austria, Poland and Russia. This figure is distorted by the fact that more than half of the urban population in the Balkans lived in Constantinople, one of the largest European cities at the time; without it the percentage of the urban population in the Balkans was a mere 6 per cent, similar to Germany but still higher than Austria and Russia (Malanima and Volckart 2007, 4–6).

3 The situation in Romania was quite different in terms of the existence of large estates or *latifundia* owned by a 'predatory elite' of *boyars* or agricultural capitalists living in the cities, imposing corvée duties on and creating land shortages for peasants (see Stahl 1969; Mungiu-Pippidi 2010).

4 The Muslim minorities (Pomaks and Turks) did not benefit from these land reforms, as many migrated to Turkey after Bulgaria's independence. Entire Turkish and Pomak villages were abandoned and resettled by Bulgarians (I am grateful to Lenka Nahodilova and Petko Hristov for providing me with this information).

5 Greek was the language of commerce and 'culture' all over the peninsula. Bulgarian and other merchants identified themselves or were identified by others as 'Greeks' and they were generally Hellenized by 1800 (Mouzelis 1976, 90–91). This ethnically marked opposition between town and countryside is reminiscent of urban–rural antagonisms in many other parts of the Balkans, for instance along the Adriatic coast, as described by Giordano (2003).

6 See Kovách (1994) for an early overview of the slow pace and difficulties of the process of privatization in different Central and Eastern European countries.

7 See Dorondel (2007) for the exclusion of Rudari (an ethnic category considered to be Roma by the majority population, although they themselves claim a separate identity)

from the forest restitution process in Romania and Bulgaria, which is particularly salient, as they have always depended for their livelihood on the forest. See also Tomova (1995, 29).

8 For a graphic example of how Western and urban musical influences entered village life in Serbia in the middle of the 1960s, see Želimir Žilnik's documentary film *Žurnal o omladini na selu zimi* (Newsreel on village youth in winter) (1967).

9 Woods gives examples of globalization with far-reaching implications for rural contexts and agriculture from the early stages of colonialism (the end of the fifteenth century). At the time, the European farming model was transported globally, for instance to the Americas and New Zealand, and at the same time new crops such as potatoes and maize entered Europe from the colonies (Woods 2011, 18–26).

10 For works within this paradigm that deal specifically with Eastern Europe, see for instance Berend and Ránki (1974), Chirot (1976, 1989) and Stahl (1969).

11 See the report *Bulgaria: The Corporate European Playground for Genetically Engineered Food and Agriculture: A Report Prepared for EcoSouthWest and ANPED, the Northern Alliance for Sustainability* (Sofia, May 2000). Online: http://www.anped.org/media.php?id=23 (accessed 7 October 2012).

12 The Cork Declaration (1996) has been crucial in defining sustainability, combating poverty and improving rural well-being as the main aims of the EU's rural development policies. In 1999, the EU also established the Special Accession Programme for Agriculture and Rural Development (SAPARD) to help the countries in Central and Eastern Europe deal with structural adjustments in the agricultural sector and rural areas, and assist them with the implementation of the acquis communautaire concerning the Common Agricultural Policy and related legislation.

13 The idea of a 'fractal' distinction is inspired by Gal and Kligman's analysis of the divide between the public and private (2000, 37–62, especially 41).

14 Sometimes they attract outside investment, from which the local community does not always benefit. Dingsdale provides examples from Albania, where foreign investment in the tourist industries has created dramatic contrasts in prosperity between sea resorts existing next to dilapidated villages (2001, 184–6).

15 Woods observes that rural poverty is often ignored or invisible in the global north, where cities (especially industrial cities) are the 'natural' sites of poverty. In the global south, poverty is perceived to be more prevalent in rural regions, and it is seen as a key push factor in rural-to-urban migration (2011, 176).

16 As I have written elsewhere, many Balkan cities (which were ethnically mixed in a not-so-distant past) have become increasingly homogenized and 'nationalized', resulting in a reduced presence of ethnic and religious minorities in both absolute and relative terms (Duijzings 2010, 106). Bulgarian cities are no exception.

17 See for instance Ghodsee (2010), who writes about the effects of the collapse of the mining industry in a Pomak town during the 1990s.

References

Abadjieva, Lilia. 2008. *Poverty and Social Exclusion in Rural Areas: Final Report Annex I. Country Studies: Bulgaria.* European Communities.

Abrahams, Ray. 1996. 'Introduction: Some Thoughts on Recent Land Reforms in Eastern Europe'. In *After Socialism: Land Reform and Social Change in Eastern Europe*, edited by Ray Abrahams, 1–22. Providence: Berghahn.

Adanır, Fikret. 1989. 'Tradition and Rural Change in Southeastern Europe During Ottoman Rule'. In *The Origins of Backwardness in Eastern Europe: Economics and Politics from the Middle Ages until the Early Twentieth Century*, edited by Daniel Chirot, 131–76. Berkeley: University of California Press.

Appadurai, Arjun. 1996. *Modernity at Large: Cultural Dimensions of Globalization*. Minneapolis: University of Minnesota Press.

———, ed. 2001. *Globalization*. Durham, NC: Duke University Press.

Barkey, Karen. 2005. 'A Perspective on Ottoman Decline'. In *Hegemonic Decline: Present and Past*, edited by Jonathan Friedman and Christopher K. Chase-Dunn, 135–51. Boulder: Paradigm Publishers.

Bates, Daniel. 1995. 'Uneasy Accommodation: Ethnicity and Politics in Rural Bulgaria'. In *East European Communities: The Struggles for Balance in Turbulent Times*, edited by David Kideckel, 137–57. Boulder: Westview Press.

Bell, John. 1977. *Peasants in Power: Alexander Stamboliski and the Bulgarian Agrarian National Union, 1899–1923*. Princeton: Princeton University Press.

Berend, Iván T. 1996. *Central and Eastern Europe, 1944–1993: Detour from the Periphery to the Periphery*. Cambridge: Cambridge University Press.

———. 2006. *An Economic History of Twentieth-Century Europe: Economic Regimes from Laissez-Faire to Globalization*. Cambridge: Cambridge University Press.

Berend, Iván T. and György Ránki. 1974. *Economic Development in East-Central Europe in the 19th and 20th Centuries*. New York: Columbia University Press.

Bourdieu, Pierre. 1998. 'The Essence of Neoliberalism'. *Le monde diplomatique*, English edition, December. Online: http://mondediplo.com/1998/12/08bourdieu (accessed 8 October 2012).

Brunnbauer, Ulf. 2005. '"The Town of the Youth": Dimitrovgrad and Bulgarian Socialism'. *Ethnologia Balkanica* 9: 91–114.

Brunnbauer, Ulf and Wolfgang Höpken, eds. 2007. *Transformationsprobleme Bulgariens im 19. und 20. Jahrhundert: Historische und ethnologische Perspektiven*. Munich: Verlag Otto Sagner.

Busch, Lawrence. 2010. 'Can Fairy Tales Come True? The Surprising Story of Neoliberalism and World Agriculture'. *Sociologia Ruralis* 50 (4): 331–51.

Cellarius, Barbara. 2003. 'Property Restitution and Natural Resource Use in the Rhodope Mountains, Bulgaria'. In *The Post-socialist Agrarian Question: Property Relations and the Rural Condition*, edited by Chris Hann et al., 189–218. Münster: LIT Verlag.

———. 2004. '"Without Co-ops There Would Be No Forests!": Historical Memory and the Restitution of Forests in Post-socialist Bulgaria'. *Conservation and Society* 2 (1): 51–73.

Chirot, Daniel. 1976. *Social Change in a Peripheral Society: The Creation of a Balkan Colony*. New York: Academic Press.

———, ed. 1989. *The Origins of Backwardness in Eastern Europe: Economics and Politics from the Middle Ages until the Early Twentieth Century*. Berkeley: University of California Press.

Conte, Édouard and Christian Giordano. 1997. 'Sentiers de la ruralité perdue; reflexions sur le post-socialisme'. In 'Paysans au-delà du mur', special issue of *Études rurales*, 138–40: 11–33.

Crampton, Richard J. 1983. *Bulgaria 1878–1918: A History*. New York: Columbia University Press.

———. 2005. *A Concise History of Bulgaria*, second edition. Cambridge: Cambridge University Press.

Creed, Gerald W. 1995a. 'The Politics of Agriculture: Identity and Socialist Sentiment in Bulgaria'. *Slavic Review* 54 (4): 843–68.

_____. 1995b. 'An Old Song in a New Voice: Decollectivization in Bulgaria'. In *East European Communities: The Struggles for Balance in Turbulent Times*, edited by David Kideckel, 25–45. Boulder: Westview Press.

Creed, Gerald W. and Barbara Ching. 1997. 'Recognizing Rusticity: Identity and the Power of Place'. In *Knowing Your Place: Rural Identity and Cultural Hierarchy*, edited by Barbara Ching and Gerald W. Creed, 1–38. New York: Routledge.

Dingsdale, Alan. 2001. *Mapping Modernities: Geographies of Central and Eastern Europe, 1920–2000*. London: Routledge.

Dorondel, Ştefan. 2007. 'Ethnicity, State and Access to Natural Resources in the Southeastern Europe: The Rudari Case'. In *Transborder Identities: The Romanian-Speaking Population in Bulgaria*, edited by Stelu Şerban, 215–39. Bucharest: Editura Padeia.

Duijzings, Ger. 2004. 'Ethnic Unmixing Under the Aegis of the West: A Transnational Approach to the Breakup of Yugoslavia'. *Bulletin of the Royal Institute for Inter-faith Studies* 5 (2): 1–16.

_____. 2010. 'From Bongo Bongo to Boston via the Balkans: Anthropological Contributions to the Study of Urban Transformations in Southeastern Europe'. In *Urbanisierung und Stadtentwicklung in Südosteuropa vom 19. bis zum 21. Jahrhundert*, edited by Thomas M. Bohn and Marie-Janine Calic, 93–132 (Südosteuropa-Jahrbuch, vol. 37). Munich: Verlag Otto Sagner.

Gal, Susan and Gail Kligman. 2000. *The Politics of Gender after Socialism: A Comparative-Historical Essay*. Princeton: Princeton University Press.

Ghodsee, Kristen. 2005. *The Red Riviera: Gender, Tourism, and Postsocialism on the Black Sea*. Durham, NC: Duke University Press.

_____. 2010. *Muslim Lives in Eastern Europe: Gender, Ethnicity, and the Transformation of Islam in Postsocialist Bulgaria*. Princeton: Princeton University Press.

Giordano, Christian. 2003. 'Der Balkan und das Meer: Das südöstliche Europa zwischen Dorfsidylle und idealisierter Urbanität'. In *Historische Anthropologie im südöstlichen Europa: Eine Einführung*, edited by Karl Kaser, Siegfried Gruber and Robert Pichler, 243–68. Vienna: Böhlau.

Giordano, Christian and Dobrinka Kostova. 2000a. 'Introduction: Bulgaria Spanning a Wretched Past, Present Uncertainties and a Future in the Making'. In *Bulgaria: Social and Cultural Landscapes*, edited by Christian Giordano, Dobrinka Kostova and Evelyne Lohmann-Minka, 9–40. Fribourg: University Press Fribourg.

_____. 2000b. 'Understanding Contemporary Problems in Bulgarian Agricultural Transformation'. In *Bulgaria: Social and Cultural Landscapes*, edited by Christian Giordano, Dobrinka Kostova and Evelyne Lohmann-Minka, 159–75. Fribourg: University Press Fribourg.

Graeber, David. 2002. 'The Anthropology of Globalization (With Notes on Neomedievalism, and the End of the Chinese Model of the Nation-State)'. *American Anthropologist* 104 (4): 1222–7.

Guest, Milena. 2003. 'La ruralité des capitals balkaniques: L'exemple de Sofia'. *Balkanologie* 7 (2): 127–50.

Hann, Chris. 2003. 'Introduction: Decollectivisation and the Moral Economy'. In *The Postsocialist Agrarian Question: Property Relations and the Rural Condition*, edited by Chris Hann and the 'Property Relations' Group, 1–46. Münster: LIT Verlag.

_____. 2010. 'Class, Clans and the Moral Economy in Rural Eurasia'. In *From Palermo to Penang / De Palermo à Penang: A Journey into Political Anthropology / Un itinéraire en anthropologie politique*, edited by François Ruegg and Andrea Boscoboinik, 195–204 (Freiburg Studies in Social Anthropology). Vienna: LIT Verlag.

Hannerz, Ulf. 1996. *Transnational Connections: Culture, People, Places*. London: Routledge.

Harvey, David. 1989. 'From Managerialism to Entrepreneurialism: The Transformation in Urban Governance in Late Capitalism'. *Geografiska Annaler* 71 (1): 3–17.

Heinonen, Maarit, Jouko Nikula, Inna Kopoteva and Leo Granberg, eds. 2007. *Reflecting Transformation in Post-socialist Rural Areas*. Newcastle: Cambridge Scholars Publishing.

Inda, Jonathan Xavier and Renato Rosaldo, eds. 2008. *The Anthropology of Globalization: A Reader*, second edition. Malden, MA: Wiley-Blackwell.

İnalcık, Halil. 1994. *An Economic and Social History of the Ottoman Empire, 1300–1916. Volume 1: 1300–1600*. Cambridge: Cambridge University Press.

Ivanova, Radost. 1995. 'Social Change as Reflected in the Lives of Bulgarian Villagers'. In *East European Communities: The Struggles for Balance in Turbulent Times*, edited by David Kideckel, 217–36. Boulder: Westview Press.

Kaneff, Deema. 1997. 'When "Land" Becomes "Territory": Land Privatisation and Ethnicity in Rural Bulgaria'. In *Surviving Post-socialism: Local Strategies and Regional Responses in Eastern Europe and the Former Soviet Union*, edited by Susan Bridger and Frances Pine, 16–32. London: Routledge.

———. 2004. *Who Owns the Past? The Politics of Time in a 'Model' Bulgarian Village*. New York: Berghahn.

Katsikas, Stefanos and Peter Siani-Davies. 2010. 'The Europeanization of Bulgarian Society: A Long-Lasting Political Project'. In *Bulgaria and Europe: Shifting Identities*, edited by Stefanos Katsikas, 1–22. London: Anthem Press.

Kearney, Michael. 1996. *Reconceptualizing the Peasantry: Anthropology in Global Perspective*. Boulder: Westview Press.

Kichorowska-Kebalo, Martha. 2000. 'The Changing European Countryside: Review Essay'. *Sociologia Ruralis* 40 (1): 150–56.

Konstantinov, Yulian and Andrei Simić. 2001. 'Bulgaria: The Quest for Security'. *Anthropology of East Europe Review* 19 (2): 21–34.

Kovách, Imre. 1994. 'Privatisation and Family Farms in Central and Eastern Europe'. *Sociologia Ruralis* 34 (4): 369–82.

Lampe, John R. 1986. *The Bulgarian Economy in the Twentieth Century*. Beckenham: Croom Helm.

Lampe, John R. and Marvin R. Jackson. 1982. *Balkan Economic History, 1550–1950: From Imperial Borderlands to Developing Nations*. Bloomington: Indiana University Press.

Lefebvre, Henri. 2003. *The Urban Revolution*. Minneapolis: University of Minnesota Press.

Leonard, Pamela and Deema Kaneff. 2002. 'Introduction: Post-socialist Peasant?' In *Post-socialist Peasant? Rural and Urban Constructions of Identity in Eastern Europe, East Asia and the Former Soviet Union*, edited by Pamela Leonard and Deema Kaneff, 1–43. Basingstoke: Palgrave.

Levitt, Peggy. 2001. *The Transnational Villagers*. Berkeley: University of California Press.

Malanima, Paolo and Oliver Volckart. 2007. *Urbanisation 1700–1870*. Paper presented at the symposium 'Unifying the European Experience: Historical Lessons of Pan-European Development'. London: Centre for Economic Policy Research (CEPR). Online: http://www.cepr.org/meets/wkcn/1/1679/papers/Malanima-Volckart-Chapter.pdf (accessed 30 August 2012).

Meurs, Mieke and Darren Spreeuw. 1997. 'Evolution of Agrarian Institutions in Bulgaria: Markets, Cooperatives, and Private Farming, 1991–1994'. In *The Bulgarian Economy: Lessons from Reform during Early Transition*, edited by Derek C. Jones and Jeffrey Miller, 275–97. Aldershot: Ashgate.

Mouzelis, Nicos. 1976. 'Greek and Bulgarian Peasants: Aspects of their Sociopolitical Situation During the Interwar Period'. *Comparative Studies in Society and History* 18 (1): 85–105.

Mungiu-Pippidi, Alina. 2010. *A Tale of Two Villages: Coerced Modernization in the East European Countryside*. Budapest: Central European University Press.

Palairet, Michael. 1997. *The Balkan Economies c. 1800–1914: Evolution without Development*. Cambridge: Cambridge University Press.

Ritzer, George. 2007. *The Globalization of Nothing 2*. Thousand Oaks: Pine Forge Press.

Roth, Klaus. 1985. 'Großstädtische Kultur und dörfliche Lebensweise: Bulgarische Großstädte im 19. und 20. Jahrhundert'. In *Großstadt: Aspekte empirischer Kulturforschung*, edited by Theodor Kohlmann and Hermann Bausinger, 363–76. Berlin: Museum für Deutsche Volkskunde.

Sanders, Irwin T. 1949. *Balkan Village*. Lexington: University of Kentucky Press.

Sassen, Saskia. 2001. *The Global City: New York, London, Tokyo*, second edition. Princeton: Princeton University Press.

Sheppard, Eric. 2002. 'The Spaces and Times of Globalization: Place, Scale, Networks, and Positionality'. *Economic Geography* 78 (3): 307–330.

Shucksmith, Mark and Pollyana Chapman. 1998. 'Rural Development and Social Exclusion'. *Sociologia Ruralis* 38 (2): 225–42.

Simić, Andrei. 1973. *The Peasant Urbanites: A Study of Rural–Urban Mobility in Serbia*. New York: Seminar Press.

Smart, Alan and Josephine Smart. 2003. 'Urbanization and the Global Perspective'. *Annual Review of Anthropology* 32: 263–85.

Smollett, Eleanor Wenkart. 1989. 'The Economy of Jars: Kindred Relationships in Bulgaria – An Exploration'. *Ethnologia Europaea* 19 (2): 125–40.

Stahl, Henri H. 1969. *Les anciennes communeautés villageoises roumaines: Asservissement et penetration capitaliste*. Bucharest/Paris: Editions de l'Academie de la République Socialiste de Roumanie, Editions du Centre National de la Recherche Scientifique.

Stewart, Michael. 1997. '"We Should Build a Statue for Ceaucescu Here": The Trauma of De-collectivisation in Two Romanian Villages'. In *Surviving Post-socialism: Local Strategies and Regional Responses in Eastern Europe and the Former Soviet Union*, edited by Frances Pine and Susan Bridger, 66–79. London: Routledge.

———. 2002. 'Deprivation, the Roma and "the Underclass"'. In *Postsocialism: Ideals, Ideologies and Practices in Eurasia*, edited by Chris Hann, 133–55. London: Routledge.

Symes, David. 1992. 'Agriculture, the State and Rural Society in Europe: Trends and Issues'. *Sociologia Ruralis* 32 (2/3): 193–208.

Thomson, Kenneth J. 2003. 'Introduction: The Context for Reform and Accession'. In *Romanian Agriculture and Transition toward the EU*, edited by Sophia Davidova and Kenneth J. Thomson, 1–14. Lanham, MD: Lexington Books.

Todorova, Maria. 1990. 'Myth-Making in European Family History: The Zadruga Revisited'. *East European Politics and Societies* 4 (1): 39–76.

Tomova, Ilona. 1995. *The Gypsies in the Transition Period*. Sofia: International Center for Minority Studies and Intercultural Relations.

———. 2011. 'Transnational Migration of Bulgarian Roma'. In *Global Connections and Emerging Inequalities in Europe: Perspectives on Poverty and Transnational Migration*, edited by Deema Kaneff and Frances Pine, 103–24. London: Anthem Press.

Tsing, Anna. 2000. 'The Global Situation'. *Cultural Anthropology* 15 (3): 327–60.

———. 2005. *Friction: An Ethnography of Global Connection*. Princeton: Princeton University Press.

Unwin, Tim and Judith Pallot and Stuart Johnson. 2004. 'Rural Change and Agriculture'. In *East Central Europe and the Former Soviet Union: The Post-socialist States*, edited by Michael J. Bradshaw and Alison Stenning, 109–36. Harlow: Pearson Education.

Verdery, Katherine. 2003. *The Vanishing Hectare: Property and Value in Postsocialist Transylvania*. Ithaca: Cornell University Press.

Wacquant, Loïc. 2012. 'Three Steps to a Historical Anthropology of Actually Existing Neoliberalism'. *Social Anthropology* 20: 66–79.

Wallerstein, Immanuel. 1974. *The Modern World-System: Capitalist Agriculture and the Origins of the European World-Economy in the Sixteenth Century*. New York: Academic Press.

Woods, Michael. 2007. 'Engaging the Global Countryside: Globalization, Hybridity and the Reconstitution of Rural Place'. *Progress in Human Geography* 31 (4): 485–507.

_____. 2011. *Rural*. London: Routledge.

Zenner, Walter P. 2002. 'Beyond Urban and Rural: Communities in the 21st Century'. In *Urban Life: Readings in the Anthropology of the City*, fourth edition, edited by George Gmelch and Walter P. Zenner, 53–60. Prospect Heights: Waveland Press.

Chapter 2

RURAL–URBAN RELATIONS IN A GLOBAL AGE[1]

Deema Kaneff

A couple of years ago I was asked by a Bulgarian friend, who was selling his village home and needed a translator present, to attend the house inspection. The prospective buyers were an English couple – a solicitor and her retired husband from Manchester. The house was located in a village close to Talpa (where I have carried out the vast majority of my research since the mid-1980s) and some forty kilometres from the attractive provincial capital of Veliko Turnovo in north-central Bulgaria. I was intrigued as to what the prospective British buyers were intending to do in the village. With its declining and elderly population, a large percentage of empty houses, and run-down public infrastructure and facilities, the village, and the region more generally, has become in the last decade or so a rural 'backwater'.

When the Manchester couple arrived to view the property, they walked through the home commenting, as one might expect, on the presentation of the rooms, their size and so on. But for me the memorable moment came when they reached the first floor. The man walked onto the small terrace and said, 'This must be the balcony.' And then he looked out across the landscape and added, 'It's a nice view.' 'There's a view?' I thought as I stepped out after him to look for myself. I had been familiar with the landscape for twenty years, yet it had never occurred to me that there was a 'view'. What was for the British buyers a 'balcony', where, no doubt, they pictured themselves sitting in the summer evening twilight sipping cool drinks, was a space that for locals had a practical function. It was the place where crops were laid out, protected from the rain, where chillies strung into a necklace were hung under the eaves, and walnuts were spread out to dry in their shells on a newspaper on the floor. As for the so-called 'view', the landscape of ploughed vineyards and a small forest (which provided the source of winter firewood for village households) may have been a potential place of leisure for the Britons, but from the villagers' perspective, it was a site of agricultural labour. This anecdote (for the fuller version see Kaneff 2006) reinforces a point made by Akhil Gupta and James Ferguson (1992, 11; see also Rodman 1992, 640) that the experience of space is socially constructed. For the British couple, one of hundreds who in the last few years have sought to buy property in rural Bulgaria, the space was imbued with potential meanings relating to the property's ultimate purpose for them as a place of leisure – a second holiday home.[2] For the villagers (and me) the same place represented a site for labour. Such discordant meanings attributed to the same space are emblematic of this 'global age'.

Globalization, we are told, entails a tectonic shift in temporal and spatial ways of categorizing the world, where it apparently no longer makes sense to think of space as existing in distinct and distinguishable units (Kearney 1995, 549) such as 'centre' and 'periphery', or 'urban' and 'rural' (see also Appadurai 1990, 296). Transnational migration, the global economy and new communication technologies have brought about an implosion of peripheries into centres, and possibly also, as the above anecdote suggests, of centres into peripheries. This reconfiguration of time and space is given different labels: David Harvey (1990) speaks of 'time–space compression', where space has apparently less importance than time, and speed has become a central metaphor for contemporary globalization – time has accelerated and space has collapsed (Sheppard 2002, 309). Deterritorialization is seen as further evidence of the decreasing importance of space – production, commodities, communities and identities have lost their 'spatial moorings' (Nadel-Klein 1995, 127) and become detached from local places, while at the same time new hyperspaces are created, such as airport lounges and international hotels (Kearney 1995, 552). In Marc Augé's terms, the latter are 'non-places', places which are not localized in social time and space (1995, 34) and which 'cannot be defined as relational, or historical, or concerned with identity' (77–8). I shall say more about some of these processes below, but for now I simply wish to make the point that in this age of deterritorialization and reconfiguration of space and time, there has been a blurring of spatial categories that were once dominant (Gupta and Ferguson 1992, 10; Nadel-Klein 1995, 127). Place is now viewed as less bounded (Kearney 1995, 549).

At the same time, globalization processes are seen as attributing to *particular* cities a crucial role in the expanding global economy (Sassen 2004; Brenner and Theodore 2002). Much has been written about these new centres of power, of their privileged position and their increasing importance (e.g., Sassen 2004; Brenner and Theodore 2002). Cities such as Frankfurt, London, New York, Sydney, Beijing and others have gained economic prominence, making less relevant the core–periphery relationships that once characterized both capitalist (Sheppard 2002) and socialist (Kaneff 2004) development. But relatively little has been written about 'the rural' in this new configuration, despite recognition that globalization and localization must be considered together (Sheppard 2002, 315). Contemporary work by economic geographers, anthropologists and other social scientists on globalization and the importance of cities seems to have left 'the rural' out of the equation. Lack of scholarly attention is particularly surprising considering the ongoing importance of rural regions – a large proportion of the world's population is still resident or dependent on these areas, and in Eastern Europe rural areas retain economic importance in terms of agricultural production. Furthermore, the post-1989 reforms – privatization and cuts in the public sector (resulting in high levels of unemployment and economic hardship), deregulation of the economy, the creation of new markets and EU membership – have led to increased mobility across the region with significant implications for rural–urban relations. Thus, more than ever before, rural spaces need to be considered globally. This, then, provides the general framework for some of the questions I consider in this chapter: If space is indeed 'compressing' as a consequence of globalization, then does this mean that 'the rural' is disappearing in importance and in the face of increasingly dominant cities? Is it still valid to speak about the rural–urban relationship or distinguish between the two spaces? I will suggest that globalization processes require us to rethink this relationship and question the relevancy of rural–urban concepts. Below I begin by saying more about the neoliberal restructuring of space, before moving onto a case study of my field site in the region of Veliko Turnovo.

The Neoliberal Restructuring of Space

Capitalism is characterized by systematic contradictions – 'creative destruction' denotes the periodic restructuring of the social relations of production through the (re)organization of labour, of space, of state institutions, of military power and governance (Harvey 1990, 103–12). Market competition necessitates technological and organizational changes, as well as the opening up of new markets in order to increase productivity and profits. Such innovation, however, devalues (or destroys) past investments, and makes certain specialized labour skills and sectors of production obsolete. This ultimately leads to instability, insecurity and periodic crisis (Harvey 1990). It is 'as capital is restructured during periods of sustained economic crisis [that] the scale-configurations upon which it is grounded are likewise reorganized to create a new geographical scaffolding for a new wave of capitalist growth' (Brenner 1999, 434). We can trace such periodic restructurings – characterized by global expansion followed by contraction periods – through the history of capitalism. The last global expansion, before the present one, occurred between the end of the nineteenth century and the early part of the twentieth century (1880–1914), when European imperialism drew much of the planet into its orbit. Interestingly, approximately 'the same levels of capital export and trade were reached in that period' as in the present (Turner 2004, 84).

However, there is one important difference between the previous period of globalization and today (apart from the development of new communication technologies): in the past the nation-state was the fundamental economic unit – the dominant scale at which economic relations were organized and governed (Sheppard 2002, 313; see also Swyngedouw 1997, 152–4). This dominance of the nation-state was eroded in the 1970s, when neoliberal policies initiated another restructuring of capitalism (Brenner 1999, 435), which did not necessarily disempower the state as much as transform its relative position (Swyngedouw 1997, 156–7). The spatial configuration of economic relations, rooted as they were in the nation-states of the nineteenth and twentieth centuries, were usually conceptualized as being grounded in sharply bounded categories, such as between 'peripheries' and 'centres'. Urban–rural divisions, a core way in which the centre–periphery distinction was expressed, increased with industrialization and modernization. Apart from the spatial grounding of production, the urban–rural relationship also served an ideological and political function in that 'the rural' was depicted as part of Europe's internal 'other'. Much like 'the Balkans' and 'the Irish' in other contexts of analysis, the rural was represented as being in opposition to the modern, technologically and culturally sophisticated urban centre. In other words, 'the rural' was a cultural anachronism. As Jane Nadel-Klein (1995, 110) writes with respect to Western Europe, 'The notion of anachronism is a powerful element in the cultural construction of what we call "the West", one that looks to images of rural, marginal, or "backward" society to create an internal other that validates [...] technologically driven "progress".' She continues to say that the rural–urban dichotomy is part of an 'essentialised vision of western society as having "margins" that harbour pre-modern ways of life' (125). This rural–urban relation was one of opposition and at the same time a *hierarchical* arrangement that denied the rural periphery full access to political and economic inclusion (Nadel-Klein 1995, 126; see also Ching and Creed 1997; Leonard and Kaneff 2002).

The political and ideological function of the rural–urban distinction is not only a characteristic of capitalist modernity; it has also featured prominently in socialist modernization projects. In Bulgaria, for example, an internal rural 'other' has existed over a long period of time, since well before the foundation of state socialism in 1944. Nevertheless, the perceived cultural, political and economic backwardness of the rural population was an important ideological tool in establishing socialist notions of progress centred on the desirability of urbanization. It also helped inform socialist development policies designed to redress inequalities between rural and urban areas. These inequalities were often the source of, and fuelled further, internal divisions and resentments. While the rural–urban relationship is always loaded in favour of 'the urban', 'the rural' was not always seen in purely negative terms (Nadel-Klein 1995, 110). Often 'the rural' provided a cultural resource for nation builders – the idealized and romanticized locus of 'true' national identity and the repository of folkloric and traditional practices (Kaneff 2004). As such it has offered a position from which to critique, for example, values and lifestyles that are a consequence of urbanization, industrialization and modernization. As Laslett has pointed out with respect to the Western rural other, 'The English still seem to want to live in the structures of the pre-industrial world, prizing the thatched cottage and the half timbered house as the proper place for the proper Englishman to dwell in' (cited in Nadel-Klein 1995, 119). Seeking the advantages of rural life is certainly one reason given by British migrants buying property in rural Bulgaria in the contemporary period. The couple from Manchester, mentioned at the beginning of this chapter, spoke about the higher quality of life they were seeking in terms of social contacts and a stronger sense of community.[3]

The 1973 oil crisis and global recession (which were the results of overproduction and capital accumulation) provided a backdrop to neoliberal reforms that were first introduced in Britain during the late 1970s, later to varying degrees in Western Europe, and then finally in Eastern Europe after 1989. Importantly, neoliberal policies included the deregulation of markets allowing free movement of capital between territories. The result, as we all know, has been an explosion in the volume of capital flow transnationally, and the destabilization of national economies. These processes were aided and reinforced by the development of new information and communication technologies that allowed financial transactions to take place virtually and instantaneously. Therefore, when speaking of this new era of 'globalization', I refer to the neoliberal restructuring of capitalism where the nation-state is no longer the primary organizational economic force, a situation lubricated by new communication technologies. Such restructuring has changed the relationship between territory and production (Glick Schiller and Çağlar 2009, 179). New configurations of space have emerged creating a new hierarchy or 'global system of domination' (Gupta and Ferguson 1992, 9), where the juxtaposition of times and places presents spaces quite differently from the pre-neoliberal period (17).

There has been widespread agreement that contemporary globalization, involving the loss of (certain forms of) power at the national level, has increased the importance and influence of *subnational* territorial economic and political units (Sassen 2004, 168; Sheppard 2002, 310). This, I suggest, has been especially true in postsocialist states where restructuring involved a sharp loss of power at the national level. For while a socialist state, with its hierarchically organized central administration, necessitated strong urban–rural connections, postsocialist incorporation into the global economy has resulted in a decline in standard binary flows – between rural and urban centres – as other regions within and outside national borders have become directly engaged in rural spaces (Kearney 1995, 1996). No longer can it be assumed that villages, towns and cities exist in a modernist hierarchy framed by the nation-state (Glick Schiller and Çağlar 2009, 188; see also Brenner 1999). The new spatial configurations have produced a situation in which the bipolar or dichotomous conceptualizations of space such as 'rural' and 'urban' no longer appear to hold the same relevance or importance. Space is now seen as more unbounded and often discontinuous; that is, people may be living in close proximity but do not necessarily share a common culture, instead interacting with dispersed others (Kearney 1995, 557).

I follow Eric Sheppard, who has suggested that the notion of 'positionality' may be a more useful way of conceptualizing these new spatial configurations (alongside other notions such as territoriality, scales and networks), in order to describe 'how different entities are positioned with respect to one another in space/time' (2002, 318). Two places, we are told, should not be measured in terms of physical distance but 'by the intensity and nature of their interconnectedness' (324). So positionality is a relational construct, where places are reliant on their interdependencies with other places and are embedded in power relations, as some positions and relationships are inevitably more influential than others (318). Further, the concept of positionality tries to capture 'the shifting, asymmetric and path-dependent ways in which the futures of places depend on their interdependencies with other places' (308) and has the advantage of being attributable to agents at a wide range of scales, from local to global (322). Thus positionality breaks down the dichotomy between rural and urban, recognizing the specific connections of a place with other localities. This, then, is the essence of positionality as used in my chapter, where I focus on one rural region and examine its present global position by analysing both its history (temporality) and its horizontal spatial relations.

Nina Glick Schiller has developed such an approach in terms of transnational migration. She reminds us that migration should not be treated as a national phenomenon, where national borders define the unit of study and analysis, thereby confusing common origins with shared identities and cultures (2009, 2010). Migrations are not national processes, but movements of people from *specific* regions and places to other *specific* regions – migrants do not settle in an entire country, they settle in particular localities. Glick

Schiller and Ayse Çağlar (2009; see also Glick Schiller 2010) thus emphasize the importance of recognizing particular localities in shaping global migration processes, making it more apt to speak of translocal migration rather than transnational migration. I adopt this perspective in the example below with respect to British property buyers in Bulgaria. These buyers come from *particular* places in the UK, have a *specific* 'structural' location with respect to neoliberal reforms, and go to a *particular* region in Bulgaria. The notion of positionality is especially useful in understanding my case study. It can also help us make sense of the new global positions of other regions in Bulgaria discussed in this book, as well as provide a fresh perspective from which to examine contemporary rural–urban relations.

My concern in this chapter is to explore what happens to rural regions in the context of processes of neoliberal restructuring where the nation-state is no longer dominant and subnational spaces have gained more prominence. We hear much about global (and globalizing) cities and surrounding metropolitan areas, their concentration of wealth and corporate power, and their strategic importance in the global economy (Sassen 2004; Brenner and Theodore 2002, 349), 'unmoored from the nation-states in which they were geographically located' (Glick Schiller and Çağlar 2009, 181).[4] Far less attention has been paid to locating rural places globally, with a few notable exceptions such as a number of anthropologists working on deindustrialized and nonagricultural towns (e.g., Glick Schiller and Çağlar 2009; Kideckel 2002, 2011). Overall, deindustrialized agricultural regions, especially those that lie outside the urban centres of capitalism, have been largely ignored in the literature on globalization. In the following section I will try to address this gap by turning to a case from my own research in rural Bulgaria.

Rural–Urban Relations: The Case of Talpa and Its Surroundings

In Talpa, a village 35 kilometres from the provincial capital of Veliko Turnovo, mobility and movement – between rural and urban areas – has been central in shaping the local economy and social structures over a long period of time. Migration is one way in which we can talk about such movement. I am living proof of a long history of migration from Talpa, as my own grandmother left the village soon after World War I to join her husband in Australia (who was originally from a neighbouring village). This first wave of international migration of Bulgarians leaving for various destinations in Europe (Austria, the Czech Republic and Hungary), Australia and North and South America was followed by two other waves in the twentieth century – after World War II and more recently in the 1990s. During earlier migration waves, ties were maintained and helped shape life in the village through letter writing, occasional visits, material support and so on. Recent communication technologies have given more contemporary waves of migration a renewed intensity, creating new possibilities for continued participation in both sending and receiving countries.

Internal migration also shaped rural life. While this form of migration is associated with the socialist modernization project, it is by no means a recent phenomenon, especially in rural sites located relatively close to towns and cities. We may recall Irwin Sander's (1949) early ethnography of what was then the village of Dragalevtsi near Sofia (now a suburb of Sofia), where trading and other exchanges with the city ensured constant movement between the two. However, by far the greatest level of migration occurred during the socialist period, when industrialization resulted in a massive movement of rural populations to urban centres. Gerald Creed (1998), for example, writes about the importance of rural–urban migration from Zamfirovo (northwestern Bulgaria), and this was equally true for my area of study in north-central Bulgaria, where the migration of children to cities such as Sofia, Varna and Veliko Turnovo provided significant connections for the rural locality. Established networks between Talpa's residents and their migrant children were important to the community and used strategically to bring resources and privileges to the region. Such a network helped the village elite bypass formal bureaucratic and administrative structures, and gave the community privileged access to limited resources controlled by the capital (such as funds for the asphalting of roads or the construction of new public buildings). The village's history – its involvement in antifascist fighting during World War II – was another asset used strategically by the local elite to emphasize their ideological alliance with the socialist state and enhance connections to the state centre. Local ambitions to develop the village were furthered by government policies of collectivization and mechanization of agriculture, as well as the generous allocation of state resources to rural areas, which contributed to the urbanization of rural regions. The development of the village in such a way as to reflect conditions and services more typically found in urban areas was a sign of Talpa's success and inclusion in the socialist state, a situation officially reinforced in 1987 when the village was awarded the nationally acclaimed title of 'model village' (see Kaneff 2004). The model village status, largely a result of good connections with the state centre, was of vital importance for the community's self-representation as a shining example of progressive socialist modernization. This in turn enhanced its capacity to access various resources and services. As with capitalist states, socialist development was driven by goals of modernization and urbanization; urbanity stood for 'civilization', 'progress' and 'technical achievement', and this was an objective to which rural settlements were assumed to aspire. The model socialist village of Talpa was positioned favourably in terms of the state's centre and was relatively successful in its pursuit of 'urbanity'.

Yet its success was relatively short lived; neoliberal reforms after 1989 represented a turning point in rural fortunes. Decentralization and the withdrawal of state support from the public, industrial and agricultural sectors led to the region's economic marginalization. The subsequent decline in infrastructure and services, and the rise in unemployment as a result of the closure of factories and restructuring of agriculture, has contributed to a further loss of population through migration. Resources for the maintenance of buildings, infrastructure and services have dried up and the area has taken on a dilapidated appearance. Talpa, and the region generally, seems more isolated and disconnected than ever from the main urban centres of power. The previously privileged connections to Sofia have not only been disrupted, but also the lack of new communication technologies has exacerbated the region's isolation from economic centres. In this sense the region has become a rural backwater.[5]

Throughout this long history of rural–urban mobility, relations between Talpa and urban centres have seen significant shifts. Antagonisms between village and city inhabitants are recorded in Talpa documents from the late 1800s onwards. Archival documents reveal that villagers resented the fact that city inhabitants had material and educational benefits which gave them certain exploitative advantages. It was only during the socialist period that these antagonisms were reduced, although never entirely removed. The elimination of urban–rural differences (considered to reflect class antagonisms) was seen as a necessary condition for the realization of an egalitarian, classless (that is, communist) society. Therefore the state gave considerable attention to equalizing educational opportunities and reducing other social inequalities and discrepancies between regions. The socialist state brought real material benefits and improvements to rural inhabitants: running water, electricity, health care and educational opportunities. As a result the gap between 'rural' and 'urban' lifestyles decreased.

This situation was reversed after 1989 and the relationships between Talpa and associated urban centres became once again fraught with tension. Expressions of open hostility were common during the 1990s as urban-based reformers pushed ahead with the restructuring and closure of institutions that were highly valued by rural inhabitants. Such acts essentially transferred resources and power away from rural localities. The tensions were particularly strong at the time of the liquidation of the agricultural cooperatives (see for instance Creed 1998; Kaneff 2002).[6] In Talpa, various strategies were adopted as a response to the dire post-1989 circumstances; the predominantly elderly inhabitants cut back on their expenses in order to transfer as many resources (for example, money and food) as possible to their children and grandchildren in the cities. The use of household resources to help children and grandchildren remain in the city (or move to the city, in the unusual cases where this had not already happened) was another strategy. In some instances the preferred solution was to migrate to another country.

However, it was the opening up of new markets across the former socialist world, foreshadowing Bulgaria's increased involvement in the global economy and strengthened by the anticipated entry into the EU, which proved to have the most dramatic implications for the global repositioning of the Veliko Turnovo region. The arrival of foreigners – primarily British citizens looking to buy rural holiday or retirement homes, or first homes for permanent settlement – represents an important new development.[7] To my knowledge it is the first time in the region's history that a transnational movement of migrants has moved *into* the region. The media played an important part in these events. All British buyers with whom I spoke identified the source of their original interest in Bulgaria to one British TV programme: Channel 4's *A Place in the Sun*, screened in 2001, which fuelled other media reports on TV and the print media. The Internet also became an important resource for follow-up information (see Kaneff 2009, 61–2 for further details). Whether British buyers were seeking vacation, retirement or first homes, the role of communication technologies in the establishment and development of the foreign property market cannot be underestimated.

While privatization and the establishment of a property market were part of a broader neoliberal agenda that transformed the entire country, such policies were played out differently in local contexts, and to understand the nature of British migration to the Veliko Turnovo region – as opposed to other regions in Bulgaria – we must look more closely at who the British were and from where they were coming. As I have suggested elsewhere (Kaneff 2009), British property buyers in rural Bulgaria are usually small investors from economically marginal areas of Britain – the Midlands, Scotland and Wales. These buyers come from regions that have experienced the greatest negative effects of neoliberal restructuring, where sometimes entire communities have been disrupted and destroyed. They do not come from the most privileged global elite, nor are they from the most disadvantaged and excluded lower social classes who do not have the option of relocation. Instead these buyers are part of a downwardly mobile British middle class which is struggling to maintain living standards and economic security.[8] They buy in Bulgaria because they recognize that neoliberal reforms in Britain have left them in a vulnerable position and because they believe that they can live a much better life in Bulgaria. Thus these British property owners are escaping the negative effects of neoliberal restructuring in their native country. For those who move permanently to the region of Veliko Turnovo – the number is estimated to be around one thousand (Egginton 2007, 37), plus many more who are temporary or seasonal residents – relocation offers more than just economic benefits. These people are dissatisfied with life in Britain: they feel increasingly disenchanted and talk about the disruption and alienation of their relationships at home, in the neighbourhood and at work, they are resentful of the declining welfare system that cannot guarantee them a secure retirement, and they express concern about the deterioration of the health services and the educational system. Relocating to the Veliko Turnovo region is an attempt to reverse these negative developments and secure one's retirement or gain financial security (through property ownership), as well as obtain opportunities to strengthen social contacts and develop a sense of community and rootedness either with other Britons or with the local population. In this way the move is also about gaining social security in the widest sense of the term.

At the same time, the sellers come from an increasingly impoverished and vulnerable sector of the Bulgarian population. From my observations, those selling in the region of Veliko Turnovo are people living in towns and cities who own second houses in the villages which remain unused. Loss of employment, or low pensions and salaries, combined with lack of state assistance for medical, educational and other services which were once free, have resulted in the escalation of personal debt. Selling the village house provides a quick, although often only temporary, route out of debt for those strapped for cash. Such sales indicate the increasingly precarious and vulnerable position of Bulgarian sellers as they shed assets in order to stave off increasing poverty in the new market economy.

The inevitable reduction in state welfare provision, which has led to a diminishing degree of social protection for citizens both in Britain and Bulgaria, as well as the neoliberal doctrine that demands individuals take responsibility for their own welfare, are fundamental factors in understanding why Britons are buying, and Bulgarians selling, property. Both groups are affected by downward mobility, a part of the global reconfiguration of class relations that involves the middle classes shrinking in size and an increasingly large rift emerging between the new global elite and the vast majority of the middle class who are sliding down the ranks into the lower classes (see Friedman 2004; Thornton 2004; Turner 2004). Buying property for the British and selling for the Bulgarians engages both groups in 'market forms of social security' (Benda Beckmann 2000, 10), where the effects of neoliberal policies have implications that reverberate transnationally (Kaneff 2009).

While the property market in the Veliko Turnovo region is driven primarily by the shared experience of decline in terms of economic and social security, the presence of the British is nevertheless reconfiguring the positionality of the region. This is happening economically; that is, old businesses are being revitalized and new local businesses are being established and supported by tourists and visitors who follow in the footsteps of the British migrants, houses are being renovated and improved, and there are clearly financial gains – at least for the individual Bulgarian families selling their properties. The British migrants are also seen as bringing with them the symbolic power of 'the West', with their transnational links that add prestige and status to the area, as well as connections, resources and assets from a relatively wealthier part of the world. Their presence signals local success in the growing competition between places. With this comes also the hope for a reversal of postsocialist decay. In the same way that migrants are important for the global city – and contribute to a city's profile (Glick Schiller and Çağlar 2009) – so foreign residents in rural areas bring a certain amount of prestige and status to the region, which can result in important material and immaterial benefits. As during socialist times, when personal connections to the state centre (through children or relatives having prestigious jobs in the capital) were a sign of success for a locality, so now the presence of foreigners is attributed a similar value. The foreigners play a transformative role in 'rescaling' the locality, linking the region to a hierarchy of wealth and power that extends globally (Glick Schiller 2010, 118, 126–7). This changes the parameters of the region's connections, repositioning it globally, nationally and/or regionally. Using Eric Sheppard's (2002, 324) metaphor, the British–Bulgarian link constitutes a 'wormhole' that 'leapfrogs' across space, connecting two distant places and in the process changing the positionality of the rural Bulgarian region (possibly also of particular British places, although this requires further research).[9]

While the above historically based exploration of positionality reveals the Veliko Turnovo region to be positively placed in the new global hierarchy, a (spatial) comparison with other rural regions in Bulgaria, which also receive foreign migrants (seasonally or permanently), adds further complexity to the picture. It is not possible to provide details here, but I simply wish to make a few cursory notes. Besides British migration to the Veliko Turnovo region, there is a parallel movement of British citizens buying property in more expensive and lucrative places such as the Black Sea or mountain ski resorts. Buyers in the latter cases appear to come from very different backgrounds: they come from less marginal areas of Britain, or even from what was, at least until a few years ago, an economically booming Ireland. These buyers are wealthier and have much more capital to invest; they are also more likely to buy property purely for investment purposes. In other words, unlike the situation in Veliko Turnovo, British buyers in other regions are more 'attractive' transnational connectors, as they are able to link, for example, the Black Sea area to the wealthier and much more advantaged regions in Britain (especially London and Southeast England). One must therefore suspect that somewhat different rural and urban configurations, both at the national and global scales, would be evident in these other regional locations, with the Veliko Turnovo region being relatively disadvantaged compared to other Bulgarian regions.

When viewed from the perspective of areas of even greater advantage – for example, the global cities described by Sassen (2004) and others – Veliko Turnovo's positioning appears different yet again. Its status and comparative advantage appears to be based, paradoxically, on the fact that it is *not* a strategic production site of globalization. The region, unlike more privileged global places, is marginal in terms of the range of services it has, in terms of access to investment capital and in terms of the range of its networks. As in the case of the Manchester couple with whom I began this chapter, the significance of 'the rural' is that it represents a new home and new way of life, one that is more grounded in locality, in social relationships and the community, and one that offers a quality of life that is unaffected by global pressures, a reprieve from the fast pace and pressures of global cities. Indeed, such 'successful' rural sites 'compete' on the basis of their *distance* from the leading economic and financial sectors of global cities and centres.

While undoubtedly a catchment area for those disenfranchised or excluded from economic centres of power, rural areas also provide an alternative site to global cities and places more integrated into the global economy. Indeed, rural areas remain, as they were during the period of industrial capitalism, a refuge to which, it seems, a growing number of Britons (and others) wish to escape. In an era of greater mobility, the rootedness, stability and relative peace of such rural places seems even more attractive than ever before. It is precisely because the rural region is perceived as everything that the global city is not, and is valued in terms of distance from city life, that Britons find such areas appealing. It offers a sanctuary from urban centres of command and control, an oasis from the pressures of finance, a space of insignificance to most investors and businesses. Rural spaces are deemed attractive or sought after because they are perceived as marginal from the lifestyle associated with global cities and centres. (Ironically, the presence of Britons serves to connect the region globally, exposing it to the very conditions from which the migrants are seeking to escape.) From the perspective of the more advantageously positioned localities, 'the rural' is therefore not so much a place of opposition to globally successful localities as much as a place that offers a sanctuary from it.

Conclusion: Globalizing Rural–Urban Relations

Space does not appear to be diminishing in importance as a consequence of globalization, nor is it less important than time, as some authors writing about globalization have suggested. It is clear, however, that the position and value of particular places are being reconfigured. In this contribution I have not given much attention to rural–urban relations in Bulgaria itself – a topic addressed in some of the other chapters in this volume. Undoubtedly exchanges between rural and urban Bulgaria still exist and need to be researched. However, such relations are increasingly being shaped and transformed by neoliberal globalization processes, and as such need to be accounted for on this basis. Further, while to date most work on globalization and space has focused on cities, it seems to me that we cannot talk about 'global' processes unless we recognize the different ways in which rural areas remain significant – as places of leisure and tourism, as locations of food production and as sites of refuge from the global economy. Cities may be strategically important global centres, but rural areas are also bound up with the global economy and their place in this scheme must be examined.

As Sheppard (2002) and others have noted, rural and urban places should be considered primarily in terms of positionality rather than as bipolar oppositions. Positionality, I have suggested, can be traced through time (looking at the history of a locality) and analysed spatially (comparing one locality to other 'competitors' at various scales). The Talpa example allowed me to examine the historical positionality of the village largely through showing how it and the region have experienced a number of shifts over time, sometimes appearing more disadvantaged (as a backwater) and at other periods more privileged. The recent movement of British citizens into the area is a factor in turning around its fortunes, allowing the region, once more, to gain some advantages following post-1989 decline. The shifting position of the region is also evident spatially. It is experiencing certain benefits as a result of the recent 'wormhole' that has opened up between parts of Britain and the Veliko Turnovo region. However, viewed from the vantage point of other more privileged nonurban regions that are the tramping ground of more advantageously connected Britons, or from the perspective of global cities or other centres where wealth and power are now concentrated, the picture is not so rosy. Veliko Turnovo, with its relatively cheap property prices, is targeted by downwardly mobile Britons who have found greater economic security in a rural region that has itself been caught in a spiral of economic decline. Since migrants contribute to the way in which a locality is repositioned within global hierarchies (Glick Schiller 2010), the attractiveness of the region to those who have experienced the downscaling and negative consequences of neoliberal restructuring is significant. An analysis that compares the Veliko Turnovo region with other regions in Bulgaria indicates that the former is not particularly high on the ladder of competitive success and prosperity.

Such an examination of positionality reveals the region at present to be less dependent on, or connected to, national urban centres than at other times in its history. Partly this is because, as they sell their village homes, urban-based Bulgarians effectively sever their final links to the rural regions. This has the effect of reducing urban–rural interaction. Partly, it is a result of the fact that the new British residents – whether permanent or seasonal – have little interest in connecting to Bulgarian urban centres beyond Veliko Turnovo. Permanent residents make serious attempts to integrate into the local community (learning the language, etc.), while seasonal migrants create networks among themselves, made up almost exclusively of expatriates living in the province, which are held together through email/Internet exchanges.[10] In neither case do links to Sofia or other centres of power and production in Bulgaria seem important.

At the same time, as associations to the national urban centres become less prominent, translocal connections are becoming much more visible. The presence of the British gives the region a transnational orientation, something it has always had but with an important difference: the new connections are based on incoming rather than outgoing flows. These inflows potentially connect Talpa and the region to provincial Britain (and to other parts of Europe). The region's points of reference have shifted away from the national urban centres towards new translocalities (Appadurai 2003, 338–9). Further, the contemporary connections established by British residents are more 'present' than those from previous periods of transnational migration because of the role of new communication technologies and the physical immediacy of the migrants (for at least part of the year).

Therefore, rural–urban relations no longer have the same importance they once had. They are one connection among a number of others that link the region to various centres of power and wealth. New networks provide new forms of connectedness; horizontal networks extend across provincial Veliko Turnovo between British citizens (and sometimes between Bulgarians and the British), and vertical translocal networks connect Veliko Turnovo directly to provincial Britain (rather than to London or Southeast England). These intra- and interprovincial networks provide new scalar positionalities for the Veliko Turnovo region. With the development of these networks, the links to Sofia or other national urban centres are not necessarily eliminated, but they are becoming less important. Instead, local spheres of interaction have expanded to include translocal communities which have incorporated Veliko Turnovo into the global economy. The region is becoming, to use Sassen's (2004, 175) phrase, a 'microenvironment with a global span'.

Globalization needs the 'rural other'. To this extent 'the rural' is still a valid concept, but the once strong rural–urban connections formed during the height of the nation-state and the era of industrial capitalism are being transformed. 'Wormholes' are opening up that create new connections between places that once existed as 'separate' social worlds, and this shifts their global location as well as their positionality across a variety of other scales. Although there are important differences between regions (see Creed this volume), at least in my area of study, the connection between rural and urban appears to be weakening, as the Veliko Turnovo region develops a new translocal positioning through its migrant population and the numerous other tourists and visitors who follow in their path. In this way the region is increasingly incorporated into a global economy, connecting it with other transnational localities, although not necessarily to global centres of power. The question as to how this serves to reinforce or even work against new hierarchies of uneven development that are a feature of the global economy remains to be explored. But any such exploration must always take into consideration 'the rural'.

Notes

1 I would like to thank Kelly Askew, Ger Duijzings, Rainer Hillebrand, Iliya Nedin and Frances Pine for their critical readings of earlier versions of the chapter.
2 As I have not carried out fieldwork in the last couple of years, I am unable to say if and how the global financial crisis has influenced foreign buyers in the region.
3 Increasingly, too, rural places are gaining similar significance for some urban Bulgarians who retreat to such areas during holiday periods.
4 Not all cities are 'global', in the sense that some have fared better than others in attracting capital and becoming world centres of wealth and power. Such variations are also evident for rural regions.
5 Indeed some commentators have gone so far as to say that the decollectivization of the 1990s was 'equivalent to de-modernisation' (Kozhucharova and Rangelova 2001, 38). While such a characterization may be a simplification of the situation, the increasing decline and isolation of the areas in question make it easy to see why such terms might be applicable.
6 Not all urbanites were proreform and many ordinary city workers suffered economic hardship as much as their rural counterparts. Nevertheless, at least in the early years following 1989, perhaps more than in most other East European countries, the Bulgarian anti- and proreform alliances were split along territorial and political lines: rural and prosocialist versus urban and anticommunist, respectively.
7 In 2007, approximately one third (35 per cent) of all financial investments in Bulgaria were property related (see http://www.chambersz.com/a/content/view/10303/109, accessed 10 October 2012), with foreign investment playing a prominent role (30 per cent of all property deals are with foreigners according to http://ww.sunnyvillas-bg.com/bg/faq.php, accessed 25 July 2008). During this period British citizens dominated the foreign market, making up 67 per cent of all foreign deals, the Irish another 13 per cent (ibid.).
8 More research needs to be carried out concerning the background of these buyers as to whether they are from the middle class who can no longer afford second homes in

more expensive parts of Western Europe, or from those who can no longer enter the British property market at all. However, my (admittedly limited) data do not suggest that we are witnessing the emergence of a newly upwardly mobile class, at least not in this region of Bulgaria.

9   According to Sheppard, a 'wormhole' is 'when two relatively isolated places become closely connected, meaning that their positionality becomes closely interrelated' (2002, 323).

10 Seasonal migrants use email to link up with other Britons in order to arrange social events such as drinks at the pub or a barbecue.

References

Appadurai, Arjun. 1990. 'Disjuncture and Difference in the Global Cultural Economy'. In *Global Culture: Nationalism, Globalization and Modernity*, edited by Mike Featherstone, 295–310. London: Sage.

_____. 2003. 'Sovereignty Without Territoriality: Notes for a Postnational Geography'. In *The Anthropology of Space and Place: Locating Culture*, edited by Setha M. Low and Denise Lawrence-Zúñiga, 337–49. Malden, MA: Blackwell.

Augé, Marc. 1995. *Non-places: Introduction to an Anthropology of Supermodernity*. Translated by John Howe. London: Verso.

Benda-Beckmann, Franz von and Keebet von Benda-Beckmann. 2000. 'Coping with Insecurity'. In *Coping with Insecurity: An 'Underall' Perspective on Social Security in the Third World*, second edition, edited by Franz von Benda-Beckmann, Keebet von Benda-Beckmann and Hans Marks, 7–31. Indonesia and the Netherlands: Pustaka Pelajar and Focaal Foundation.

Brenner, Neil. 1999. 'Globalisation as Reterritorialisation: The Re-scaling of Urban Governance in the European Union'. *Urban Studies* 36 (3): 431–51.

Brenner, Neil and Nik Theodore. 2002. 'Cities and the Geographies of "Actually Existing Neoliberalism"'. *Antipode* 34 (3): 349–79.

Ching, Barbara and Gerald W. Creed, eds. 1997. *Knowing Your Place: Rural Identity and Cultural Hierarchy*. New York: Routledge.

Creed, Gerald W. 1998. *Domesticating Revolution: From Socialist Reform to Ambivalent Transition in a Bulgarian Village*. University Park: Pennsylvania State University Press.

Egginton, Jane. 2007. 'Bulgaria'. *Guardian*, 'Weekend' section, 27 January, 37. Online: http://www.guardian.co.uk/theguardian/2007/jan/27/weekend7.weekend7?INTCMP=SRCH (accessed 4 October 2012).

Friedman, Jonathan. 2004. 'Champagne Liberals and the New "Dangerous Classes": Reconfigurations of Class, Identity and Cultural Production in the Contemporary Global System'. In *Globalization: Critical Issues*, edited by Allen Chun, 49–82. New York: Berghahn.

Glick Schiller, Nina. 2009. 'Theorizing About and Beyond Transnational Processes'. In *Caribbean Migration to Western Europe and the United States: Essays on Incorporation, Identity and Citizenship*, edited by Margarita Cervantes-Rodriguez, Ramon Grosfoguel and Eric Mielants, 18–42. Philadelphia: Temple University Press.

_____. 2010. 'A Global Perspective on Transnational Migration: Theorising Migration Without Methodological Nationalism'. In *Diaspora and Transnationalism: Concepts, Theories and Methods*, edited by Rainer Bauboeck and Thomas Faist, 109–30. Amsterdam: Amsterdam University Press.

Glick Schiller, Nina and Ayse Çağlar. 2009. 'Towards a Comparative Theory of Locality in Migration Studies: Migrant Incorporation and City Scale'. *Journal of Ethnic and Migration Studies* 35 (2): 177–202.

Gupta, Akhil and James Ferguson. 1992. 'Beyond "Culture": Space, Identity, and the Politics of Difference'. *Cultural Anthropology* 7 (1): 6–23.

Harvey, David. 1990. *The Condition of Postmodernity: An Enquiry into the Origins of Cultural Change.* Cambridge, MA: Blackwell.

Kaneff, Deema. 2002. 'Work, Identity and Rural–Urban Relations'. In *Post-socialist Peasant? Rural and Urban Constructions of Identity in Eastern Europe, East Asia and the Former Soviet Union,* edited by Pamela Leonard and Deema Kaneff, 180–99. Basingstoke: Palgrave.

———. 2004. *Who Owns the Past? The Politics of Time in a 'Model' Bulgarian Village.* Oxford: Berghahn.

———. 2006. 'Holiday Location or Agricultural Village? British Property Owners in Rural Bulgaria'. *Eastern European Countryside* 12: 79–92.

———. 2009. 'Property and Transnational Neoliberalism: The Case of British Migration to Bulgaria'. In *Accession and Migration: Changing Policy, Society and Culture in an Enlarged Europe,* edited by John Eade and Yordanka Valkanova, 59–74. Surrey: Ashgate.

Kearney, Michael. 1995. 'The Local and the Global: The Anthropology of Globalization and Transnationalism'. *Annual Review of Anthropology* 24: 547–65.

———. 1996. *Reconceptualizing the Peasantry: Anthropology in Global Perspective.* Boulder: Westview Press.

Kideckel, David. 2002. 'The Unmaking of an East-Central European Working Class'. In *Postsocialism: Ideals, Ideologies and Practices in Eurasia,* edited by C. M. Hann, 114–32. London: Routledge.

———. 2011. 'The End of Politics in Romania's Jiu Valley: Global Normalisation and the Reproduction of Inequality'. In *Global Connections and Emerging Inequalities in Europe: Perspectives on Poverty and Transnational Migration,* edited by Deema Kaneff and Frances Pine, 125–44. London: Anthem Press.

Kozhucharova, Veska and Rossitsa Rangelova. 2001. 'Rurality and Late Modernity in Transition Countries: The Case of Bulgaria'. In *Food, Nature and Society: Rural Life in Late Modernity,* edited by Hilary Tovey and Michel Blanc, 19–43. Aldershot: Ashgate.

Leonard, Pamela and Deema Kaneff. 2002. 'Introduction: Post-socialist Peasant?' In *Post-socialist Peasant? Rural and Urban Constructions of Identity in Eastern Europe, East Asia and the Former Soviet Union,* edited by Pamela Leonard and Deema Kaneff, 1–43. Basingstoke: Palgrave.

Nadel-Klein, Jane. 1995. 'Occidentalism as a Cottage Industry: Representing the Autochthonous "Other" in British and Irish Rural Studies'. In *Occidentalism: Images of the West,* edited by James G. Carrier, 109–34. Oxford: Clarendon Press.

Rodman, Margaret C. 1992. 'Empowering Place: Multilocality and Multivocality'. *American Anthropologist,* n.s., 94 (3): 640–56.

Sanders, Irwin T. 1949. *Balkan Village.* Lexington: University of Kentucky Press.

Sassen, Saskia. 2004. 'The Global City'. In *A Companion to the Anthropology of Politics,* edited by David Nugent and Joan Vincent, 168–78. Oxford: Blackwell.

Sheppard, Eric. 2002. 'The Spaces and Times of Globalization: Place, Scale, Networks, and Positionality'. *Economic Geography* 78 (3): 307–30.

Swyngedouw, Erik. 1997. 'Neither Global nor Local: "Glocalization" and the Politics of Scale'. In *Spaces of Globalization: Reasserting the Power of the Local*, edited by Kevin R. Cox, 137–66. New York: The Guilford Press.
Thornton, William H. 2004. 'Civil Antiglobalism and the Question of Class'. In *Globalization: Critical Issues*, edited by Allen Chun, 1–11. New York: Berghahn.
Turner, Terence. 2004. 'Shifting the Frame from Nation-State to Global Market: Class and Social Consciousness in the Advanced Capitalist Countries'. In *Globalization: Critical Issues*, edited by Allen Chun, 83–119. New York: Berghahn.

Chapter 3

EVERY VILLAGE, A DIFFERENT STORY: TRACKING RURAL DIVERSITY IN BULGARIA

Gerald W. Creed

Over the decade between 1997 and 2007, I carried out intermittent research in Bulgaria examining ritual activity, specifically winter masquerade rituals referred to generically as *kukeri* and *suvakari* (Creed 2011). This research, unlike a prior decade of work in the village of Zamfirovo in the northwestern part of Bulgaria (Creed 1998), required me to visit numerous villages in different parts of the country, in some cases more than once. In all, counting a few villages I visited for other reasons, I visited over fifty villages, and passed through multiple towns to get there. I also collected material from a few of those towns, although I spent much less time in urban locations because – with the exception of festivals in which the targeted rituals are performed for an urban audience, and some neighbourhood-based masquerade traditions in towns mostly in the southwestern part of the country – the rituals are more vital in the countryside.

In these travels I became almost as fascinated by the diversity of rural conditions I encountered as by the ritual activity I was going to observe. For a relatively small country the variety of conditions in the Bulgarian countryside is amazing, suggesting that it is distorting to even speak generically of a rural condition without noting the axes and extent of variation. This is certainly not a novel perception. Rural diversity is evident and acknowledged in the work of ethnographers across the postsocialist terrain (e.g., Lampland 2002; Mandel and Humphrey 2002). Still, the rural ethnographer's grounding in one, or at most a few, villages privileges a single area or location. There is usually an effort to situate this location vis-à-vis the country as a whole, but these assessments are often based on national-level rural statistics, so evaluations of typicality and distinction still reference and reflect a homogenized vision of a very varied landscape. Rural ethnographers may be aware of differences across villages, but concerted multisited ethnography has been pursued more popularly in urban locations, or perhaps in combining research in different types of locales, such as a rural and urban location integrated through migration, rather than across multiple villages.

Other social scientists look at large numbers of villages, but are primarily interested in the general profiles that emerge from the combined statistics, not particular differences. Such homogenized results are ultimately justified by the general disadvantage of the rural compared to the (pre)dominant urban situation. Put differently, the situation in the countryside generally is only relevant in its comparison or relation to the dominant urban context, not in the rural context itself, which makes the differences between villages less fascinating. In sum, then, rural researchers who privilege particularities tend to focus on one or a small number of villages, while those with the purview to map the dimensions of difference across a large number of villages tend to focus primarily on generalities and aggregate statistics rather than particulars. The ritual focus of my own research limits how far I can go in filling this analytical gap, but it does provide a basis for thinking about the factors that make a difference. In this chapter, I discuss the factors that seemed particularly consequential to the quality of life in the villages I have visited.

This effort articulates with the suggestion of Deema Kaneff (this volume) to look at what geographer Eric Sheppard (2002) terms the 'positionality' of places. Positionality focuses on 'the shifting, asymmetric, and path-dependent ways in which the futures of places depend on their interdependencies with other places' (308). This effort attempts to draw the attention to inequality and asymmetry central to earlier vertical models of globalization, such as core–periphery and dependency frameworks, within more recent horizontal models of globalization, such as network frameworks.

While this is useful, my analysis suggests that it is still not enough. Relations between places are important, but some important variables are not relational. One needs to appreciate life in rural locations as a reflection of various issues. Postsocialism and globalization have combined to produce a context in which variation is the essence. There are no independent variables – everything is dependent, and the connections between them are varied as well. This makes binary distinctions unhelpful and modelling of any sort limited. In what follows I describe a collection of factors that clearly affected the conditions of the villages I visited: regional location, demographic profile, urban proximity, employment opportunities, social relations, property arrangements and individual action. This is certainly not an exhaustive list, but a necessary first step in recognizing the complexity of forces shaping life in the Bulgarian countryside. Even an exhaustive list, however, would be insufficient to understand the rural situation, because the very notion of the rural itself is a complex dependent construct. Its relation to the notion of the urban is commonly recognized, and indeed provides the theme for this volume, but the idea of the rural is implicated and embedded with other culturally loaded categories. So we must work in both directions, not only specifying the particular qualities and positionalities that impact on rural locations, but also looking at how the understanding of rurality is shaped by its articulation with other analytical and cultural categories, what might be called a conceptual positionality of the very idea of 'the rural'. I pursue this in a concluding section, focusing on the important related terms of 'nature', 'agriculture', 'community' and 'modernity'.

Vectors of Village Variation

Not surprisingly, given the considerations mentioned above, the most recognized variable differentiating rural conditions in Bulgaria is the most general: the region of the country where a village is located. Parts of the country are better situated and/or better provisioned than others. As colleagues and friends always remind me, the northwestern part of the country where I conducted much of my prior research is one of the most disadvantaged regions, lacking either agricultural or mineral resources, bordered by Romania and Serbia rather than richer neighbours such as Turkey and Greece, and lacking tourist attractions such as the Black Sea or Alpine-like mountains.

As Galia Valtchinova (this volume) points out, this location did emerge as having a competitive advantage during the wars of Yugoslav dissolution, when an international embargo of Serbia made smuggling petrol to Serbia lucrative for residents in this region. Yet the option was relatively short-lived and a good example of how fleeting some kinds of regional advantages can be in the context of globalization. Still, some villagers did get wealthy smuggling petrol, and some parleyed these savings into other profitable and legal investments after the embargo ended, in some cases providing employment for other villagers. So a short-term advantage had longer-term influence in some villages, but for most the effects were rather limited.

Rural locations in more economically or geographically advantaged parts of the country have a more enduring advantage, both in terms of their own economic resources and their attraction to potential foreign investors such as the British expatriates described by Kaneff (this volume), who are buying property and revitalizing Bulgarian villages as retirement and vacation destinations. This foreign real estate boom thus amplifies differences that were already extant, but less consequential, prior to the options for foreign investment.

Regional geography is crucial, then, but it is clearly not destiny defining. I often found villages in the same part of the country with very different fortunes. In general, these differences reveal two other important vectors: demographic profile and urban proximity. The differences between two villages near the city of Sliven are illustrative. Topolchane and Gorno Alexandrovo are no more than seventeen kilometres apart, and both are located off the main highway connecting Sliven to points east. Both have large populations of Roma. While Gorno Alexandrovo was always smaller than Topolchane, since 'the changes' it has suffered much more significant out-migration than Topolchane, making the village experience radically different.

Out-migration from villages to towns (as well as abroad) has been extensive throughout rural Bulgaria, driven partially by economic policies after 1989 that ignored the countryside and actually 'liquidated' rural economic resources (Creed 1998). This decimation exceeded that in some other postsocialist countries where the viability of agriculture attracted unemployed urbanites back to the countryside for survival. Bulgarian villagers and townspeople repeatedly reported the opposite: rural residents depended upon support and money from relatives in town, reversing the flow of family support characteristic of socialism, when villagers commonly provided rural produce to relatives in town. Extensive out-migration erodes other dimensions of village vitality in a cascade of effects American journalist Osha Grey Davidson (1996) describes as the rise of a 'rural ghetto'. Similarly, greater out-migration made Gorno Alexandrovo seem like an unattractive place for Bulgarians, while Topolchane still seems vital.

This difference is easily explained by proximity to Sliven. Topolchane is right outside the city limits and city buses serve the village with some degree of regularity. In addition, many of the other buses that leave Sliven for locations east stop at an intersection on the way out of town that is at easy walking distance from the village. Gorno Alexandrovo in not very far away at all, and is on the main highway, but a declining frequency of bus services, and more importantly the increasing cost of bus tickets along with rising costs of petrol for car travel, have all made what was in the past a somewhat minor difference between Topolchane and Gorno Alexandrovo in terms of their distance from Sliven much more significant and consequential. The upwardly mobile citizens of Gorno Alexandrovo, still small in number, who might be able to afford commuting to work in Sliven, prefer to live in the city and perhaps visit their village houses and gardens on weekends. So Topolchane has suffered much less from out-migration because of its closer proximity to Sliven and may have even attracted new residents from more distant villages. The result is a very different experience of village life. This advantage has not turned it into a suburb of Sliven – it is still decidedly rural in character, and still experiencing a population decline, but it remains more vital than many other villages in the region.

Village outmigration, however, can also have a positive effect in the form of remittances, especially from villagers who work abroad. This suggests an interaction with another demographic variable: the age profile of the village. Rural to urban migration was restricted under late socialism, but rural to rural migration was much easier, producing what Bulgarians commonly referred to as 'disappearing' villages populated only by pensioners. These villages were rather depressed under socialism. They have suffered not so much from new outmigration as from natural processes as the older residents die. Villages with significant numbers of younger residents under socialism have been hit harder by out-migration, but they were in a much better situation to start with, and more importantly, some of those migrants have been successful at landing jobs in town or abroad and send money back to relatives, significantly boosting the village economy. Many of those who go to work abroad only do so temporarily and return to the village, bringing the money they have earned back with them, which they invest in their village homes and farming activities. There is an interactive path-dependence here, as other factors interact with the socialist demographic heritage to shape village fortunes.

Urban proximity is an important force for multiple reasons, but central among them is the greater opportunity for employment in the city. So we need to add the related variable of employment options to the profile of variation. Some towns have more options than others, so proximity to those cities is likely to be more consequential than proximity to a city with less economic options. Employment options in the village itself are also extremely consequential. In 2002, the village of Malomir, between Yambol and Elhovo, looked like a disaster area. Obviously abandoned houses dotted the streets and villagers I interviewed complained about depopulation and lack of employment: 'we have no work here', 'life has become too hard', 'there is nothing'. As in other villages, socialist collectivization and mechanization of agriculture had moved most of the village population out of agriculture and into wage labour, sometimes in neighbouring towns, but often in small enterprises established by the collective farm itself. Most of these jobs disappeared with the liquidation of collective farms. As a result there were few people employed in Malomir; the village's two teachers lived in Yambol and commuted to work, and expressed concerns that the remaining young people were becoming criminals or even potential sociopaths as a result of the desperation. There was no policeman in the village to counter these dire outcomes. The village square seemed to confirm the reports, with the windows of administrative buildings missing and the potentially impressive *chitalishte* (cultural centre) looking dismal, as if no one had used the place in years.[1] The masquerade rituals I had come to document had suffered a similar decline, undercutting a festivity that had made village life enjoyable and helped redress village social tensions. Villagers attributed their difficulties to the loss of jobs in various enterprises previously run by the collective farm and the lack of prospects in such a poor region. I left depressed, convinced that the village's remote location in a rather poor region had doomed it to oblivion and misery.

I then headed to the village of Boyanovo, only ten kilometres away on the other side of the main highway and no closer to any town or city. The same complaints I heard in Malomir about the lack of work were common, and the population was even a few hundred less than that of Malomir. There was also clear evidence of economic difficulty, as several older pensioners had gathered at the post office where they waited for overdue pensions to be delivered. They complained that they could not buy bread until they got their pensions and they were so hungry they chose to wait there to be on hand immediately when the funds arrived. They had spent the previous day there as well. But the impression here was radically different. While their desperation mirrored that of Malomir residents, other aspects of the village could not have been more distinctive: it was clean and well maintained, and while it hardly bespoke prosperity, it did not suggest abject prostration either. The administrative offices were functioning efficiently and were fully staffed. Interestingly, their masquerade rituals were also vital, and posters from various festivals village ritual groups had attended, as well as awards they had won there, decorated the mayor's office. Since the *chitalishte* often helped coordinate such folk performances in Bulgarian villages, it is probably no coincidence that the Boyanovo *chitalishte* was in good shape and obviously operative, despite being a less impressive structure than that in Malomir. What can we make of this difference between two similarly positioned and provisioned villages? Three additional factors emerge as important here: social relations, property arrangements and individual leadership.

Social relations include a number of different types of relationships between people, including occupational, genealogical, political and economic. This moves people to the centre of our understanding. With this factor we recognize that villages and rural locales with successful migrants abroad are advantaged only because those people maintain important social relations with villagers still in the village. If they did not, the resources they acquired would not rebound to the village. Social relations with successful migrants can provide a means for other villagers to migrate for similar opportunities, amplifying the impact on the village as a whole. Thus social relations determine whether out-migration is a simple loss of population, a net benefit, or something of a mixed blessing. There is a dialectic here, as migrants' commitments and attachments to village locations may attenuate if the other vectors previously discussed continue to erode and depress a village's attraction. But it is not solely about global connections, as relations with people within Bulgaria can also be beneficial. Such social relations, also known as 'connections', clearly advantage individuals or families, but sometimes the bases of an individual's or family's connections can be traced to someone or something about their village, which means that other villagers may also have the same or similar connections, producing a more general impact on the village. Indeed, since relations are thick in a Bulgarian village, if one villager has a kinship connection to someone useful or helpful elsewhere, chances are several other village relatives will benefit as well.

Of course we are talking about Bulgaria, so we must also include political connections centrally among the consequential social relations. Connections between villages and politicians could improve the former's access to state resources. Villagers who reach positions of political significance beyond the village can ease bureaucratic barriers for village leaders seeking governmental assistance or make sure those leaders get useful information in a timely fashion before leaders from other villages. Political power shifted so constantly in Bulgaria after 1989 that this resource might have been available to more villages than would be the case in more stable circumstances. Successful entrepreneurs can also make a difference, as they often locate enterprises or workshops in villages where they have social relations.

The Boyanovo mayor seemed to have some useful connections, but it was the vitality of the village agricultural sectors that seemed to have also been important. Villages had different experiences with the postsocialist processes of property restitution and privatization, which had lasting consequences differentiating village fortunes for many years. We might characterize this variable as different profiles of property arrangements. The laws affecting property restitution and ownership applied to the whole country, but their application varied tremendously. These differences reset the foundations of the countryside significantly and formatively for subsequent years. In some villages the officials in charge of the process managed to protect local resources, sometimes for their own profit, but sometimes for the benefit of broader groups of villages, including both industrious entrepreneurs and reformed cooperatives. In other villages resources were squandered, pilfered, destroyed or fragmented to the degree that they were nearly useless. The different outcomes of the process reflected some of the previously discussed variables, such as regional location and potential value of the natural resources. But these interacted with the different profiles and agendas of village liquidation committees, appointed by political leaders at higher levels, sometimes with local preferences in mind, sometimes in explicit opposition to local interests.

While the interaction of the previously described variables would be enough to produce a distinctive profile for nearly every Bulgarian village, villagers repeatedly privileged another factor that I consistently ignored in my previous research because as an anthropologist I am not well trained in how to deal with it: individuals. Villagers attributed significant impact to the influence of individuals – especially mayors, but also cultural workers and even local volunteer activists and enthusiasts. Inversely, mayors and leaders could also be instrumental in snuffing out the enthusiasm or interest of village activists. In one village, for example, village activists responsible for the active masquerade tradition complained that the event was less vital than it could be because the mayor was disinterested. A carpenter from the same village reported that he volunteered to repair the benches on the village square, but the mayor refused to let him plug his electrical tools into municipal outlets, so the benches remained a broken down reflection of a decrepit village economy. This, then, is an extremely idiosyncratic factor that escapes existing efforts to understand rural diversity.

Of course we can imagine psychosocial factors that might explain the different motives of individuals, but the fact remains that village fortunes sometimes reflect the commitment or disinterest of one or a few individuals. This was evident in the socialist period as well. One of my favourite jokes from the 1980s was one in which two Bulgarians are discussing politics and bemoaning the slow progress of perestroika and glasnost in Bulgaria. 'With bai Tosho (Todor Zhivkov) in charge', one quips, 'we'll never have perestoistvo (perestroika). We need a Gorbachev!' The other counters, 'We'd need thousands of Gorbachevs.' 'Why thousands?' the first asks. To which his friend responds, 'One for every village.'

What's New?

The evident continuity of individual influence in socialist and postsocialist eras raises the question of novelty in regard to all the forces and factors I have examined. Certainly rural variation is not a postsocialist phenomenon. The same forces differentiating postsocialist villages also distinguished socialist ones. Regional variation made a difference under socialism as the villages in the plains and river valleys of south-central Bulgaria and the northeastern 'bread basket' were commonly described as richer than those elsewhere. A village that was the centre or seat of its *obshtina* (municipality) was usually better provisioned than the other villages in the same municipality. A village housing the headquarters for a collective farm was likely to be economically privileged over the other villages making up the farm. Villagers living close to a town could commute daily to a greater diversity of jobs while residents of more isolated villages were limited to economic enterprises in the village or neighbouring villages. Model socialist villages (Kaneff 2004) received many advantages, and they often acquired such designations because they were the natal or ancestral village of communist party luminaries. The same factor might also influence whether a village was chosen as an *obshtina* centre. Even if such links did not earn a village formal distinction, the political or economic success of village natives could definitely improve the fortunes of a village. State enterprises often chose between many desiring and deserving villages in locating their subcontracting workshops, and the rural connections of managers and planners made a difference in these decisions. Consequently, Bulgarian villagers had no illusions of socialist uniformity. Indeed, whenever I responded to a villager's description of some significant practice with the variant practice I had heard about or solicited in another village, he or she would invariably explain, 'Vsyako selo, druga istoriya' (every village a different story). Such difference was also graphically performed and celebrated in the rituals I examined.

A major change, however, concerns the role of the state. As noted by Kaneff (this volume) models of globalization suggest that the displacement of the state as the central actor on the global stage has broken down the determining role of states, granting local relations more consequence, producing more varied positionalities. But we should also be cautious about the extent of this dynamic. While Britons seeking vacation and retirement homes may now go directly to Bulgarian villages, the attraction of Bulgarian real estate for Britons is itself a product of Bulgarian state policies. State and national issues, most obviously property laws and ease of purchase, as well as stereotypes about national culture, figure in the decision of foreigners to buy property in Bulgaria, rather than say Romania or Serbia. This is not a criticism of Bulgaria's neighbours, but a recognition that national and state associations and considerations shape the establishment of the very (local) relations that can then be seen as bypassing state structures. The state structures might not seem as insignificant if we look at earlier steps in the process. Globalization has produced what might be seen as shortcuts to global–local interaction, in which the state is not involved directly, but it keeps those shortcuts open. Likewise, while the European Union has challenged the traditional role of the nation-state, it is itself a parastate organization, with significant power (aiming toward a state-like construction). It should not be understood simply as an example of eroded state control.

In some sense, the idea of a less significant state is nothing more than an element of the current ideology of global statecraft. The notion of a declining state shores up state legitimacy. Still, we cannot overlook the difference created by different ideologies of legitimation and it is here that postsocialism has definitely increased the degree of variation across the Bulgarian countryside. The socialist state's ideology of equality and progress constrained the consequences of rural variation under socialism. Migration was restricted, so the village populations were maintained to a greater degree; but more importantly, the state radically redistributed wealth, so the economic consequences of location, resources and even individual advantages were limited. The advantages were still evident, but their extent was constrained. In the postsocialist context they are less restrained and not redressed, producing more variation.

The variations are then made more consequential by a decline in the degree of interaction between rural and urban locations, making the conditions in the countryside more determinant of the quality of life. A reduction in the degree of urban–rural interaction makes the situation in any particular village more consequential in shaping the overall experience of life there. Interaction has been reduced by numerous factors already mentioned. Jobs in town have been lost, leaving villagers at home, and those with urban employment have moved to town rather than commute, diminishing the daily interaction of rural and urban residents in the workplace. In addition, the rising cost of travel has made it difficult for remaining villagers to visit towns and cities on a regular basis to shop or socialize. The higher rate of international migration has increased global connections for rural family members, but perhaps reduced the intensity of connections to Bulgarian towns. Demography coincidentally abetted this abatement, as the first predominantly urban generation, most of whom still had significant rural connections, died off in the early postsocialist era, and their children had less intense social relations with villagers. Democratization added to the isolation. The rigid communist party structure integrated villages into a political hierarchy, certainly not in an equal fashion or with any political power, but there was a structural integration that provided significant interaction. This is no longer the case, as villagers eschew politics generally and most political parties pay little attention to rural problems.

While variation across villages has become more evident and consequential, it has not eclipsed the overall distinction between the plight of the countryside and the urban situation. This justifies continued discussion of the rural condition generically, despite growing diversification. Indeed, if one of the major factors that helps disaggregate and differentiate the rural category into more specific positionalities is the relationship with urban locations, are we not still left with a relevant category, as always a supplement to the urban? In other words, rural places are indeed very diverse, but if their very diversity is defined partially by different relationships to urban spaces, then does that itself not justify thinking and looking at these (always supplemental) places categorically? Indeed, places that escape this second-class status are often reframed as 'suburbs' or 'resorts', or some other qualification that moves them out of the generic rural category and confirms that the category itself still signifies.

A Conceptual Positionality

How are we to navigate this seemingly contradictory dilemma in which forces seem to be undermining the value of the rural as a generic or analytical category, yet in ways that still invoke or traffic in an overarching rural/urban distinction? Following Sheppard (2002) and Kaneff (this volume), we clearly need to look at places in terms of particular positionalities, but not to the exclusion of broader meaningful categories. Rather than simply replacing categories with particulars, we need to devote similar analytical attention to the categories themselves. We might consider this an exercise in conceptual positionality in which we probe the meaning and content of these categories through their relations to other important signifiers. Therefore, I would argue for a broader notion of 'positionality' that includes multiple intertwined dimensions: economic, social, political, cultural and ideological.

Instead of giving up on the rural as a gross homogenizer of a place's complex positionality, maybe we could look at 'the rural' in relation to other concepts to help us understand what is at stake without reifying a particular image or standard. How does 'the rural' or 'the village' relate in people's world views to other categories? Ethnographic research should not assume these categories, but rather be open to finding unexpected ones. By way of example, I conclude by mentioning a few I have found recurrently important in Bulgaria.

First, it is essential to appreciate how rural notions in particular locales, or for particular people, relate to notions of *nature*. A love or appreciation of nature often grants rural locations value for their proximity to natural beauty. Obviously, if people live and work in the countryside, it is not unspoiled nature, but the rural image or concept often includes unspoiled natural contexts along with the village, and the latter benefits from its association with the former. We need to appreciate how these notions of the rural and nature interact in culturally specific ways.

One primary interaction is the practice of *agriculture*. The relationship between this notion and nature is complex and often contradictory. Food production and processing is about exploiting nature and transforming it into culture, so in some ways it is in opposition to the veneration of nature, but it is still a natural process connecting farmers to nature in an intense way. Moreover, the process of agriculture can enhance or create natural

beauty – to use an iconic American example, 'spacious skies' are paired
with 'amber waves of grain', and 'purple mountain majesties' are linked to
'the fruited plain' to characterize 'America the Beautiful'.

This relationship was at the heart of a story I heard in the village of
Tserevo, located between Sofia and the city of Pazardzhik. A Sofia couple
who had purchased a summer home or villa there went to great effort to
grow a lawn in their village yard. The house has a nice tall wall around
it so few villagers knew about their project, but one house up the hill had
a view of the yard from its windows. After the grass had begun to grow
the well-intentioned neighbour came down from the hill to warn the
newcomers that grass was taking over their yard and if they did not get
it cleared soon it was going to ruin their garden. This is a great example,
not only because of its graphic illustration of distinctive rural and urban
sensitivities, but because the 'lawn' is also a feat of agriculture. In fact,
grass can be very difficult to grow and, depending on the conditions, may
require more attention than some food products. Why are these efforts not
more 'exploitative' of nature than farming activities that rotate crops and
allow fallow times and pasturage for natural soil fertility? So while observers
see radically different visions of a village yard, the differences are partially
cultural constructions that differentiate related and similar processes. Here
it is urban assumptions about a great divide between utilitarian functions
(food production or money making) and aesthetic functions (pleasure or
beauty) that shape the ways we think and conceive of the countryside. I am
not questioning whether these distinctions are valid or real, but insisting we
need to be aware of them when we attempt to make sense of the urban–
rural dynamic. I am also suggesting that they are not as discreet as the
opposition implies. Bulgarian villagers always talked about their connection
to nature as something that made life in the village better than urban living,
and commonly embellished their utilitarian fields or plots with aesthetic
plants and flowers. Investigating this triad of agriculture–rural–nature can
help expose the vectors at work.

Two final concepts that emerge centrally in urban–rural dynamics
are *community* and *modernity*. For urbanites, villages have long provided the
surviving archetype of an imagined romantic 'community' supposedly
lost with urbanization and modernization. This seeming valorization
actually contributes to rural devaluation. The equation of a lost, idealized
community with the contemporary village highlights the latter's premodern
(if admirable) character, while the inability of villagers to live up to the
ideals attached to such a romantic notion brings them derision. Rural places
are in a double bind – escaping this premodern derision may require their
disappearance.

Sheppard (2002) suggests the future of places depends on their interdependence, and Kaneff (this volume) gives a clear illustration of this equation in the way new British property owners sustain and promote Bulgarian villages. But these interdependencies can reshape places in ways that transform rather than sustain the village. The fact that Bulgarian villagers welcome their new British neighbours for revitalizing rural areas does not negate the displacement involved. Villagers have already been displaced by neoliberal policies, and when Britons purchase their land and houses the product is more of a reconstitution than revitalization. Something significant is still lost, made more tragic by the fact that it is not even recognized or acknowledged, but rather celebrated as survival.

Note

1 The *chitalishte* is an indigenous cultural institution that spread throughout Bulgaria in the nineteenth century, reconfigured during the socialist era along the lines of Soviet houses of culture.

References

Creed, Gerald W. 1998. *Domesticating Revolution: From Socialist Reform to Ambivalent Transition in a Bulgarian Village*. University Park: Pennsylvania State University Press.

_____. 2011. *Masquerade and Postsocialism: Ritual and Cultural Dispossession in Bulgaria*. Bloomington: Indiana University Press.

Davidson, Osha Gray. 1996. *Broken Heartland: The Rise of America's Rural Ghetto*. Ames: University of Iowa Press.

Kaneff, Deema. 2004. *Who Owns the Past? The Politics of Time in a 'Model' Bulgarian Village*. New York: Berghahn.

Lampland, Martha. 2002 'The Advantages of Being Collectivized: Cooperative Farm Managers in the Postsocialist Economy'. In *Postsocialism: Ideals, Ideologies and Practices in Eurasia*, edited by C. M. Hann, 31–56. London: Routledge.

Mandel, Ruth and Caroline Humphrey, eds. 2002. *Markets and Moralities: Ethnographies of Postsocialism*. Oxford: Berg.

Sheppard, Eric. 2002. 'The Spaces and Times of Globalization: Place, Scale, Networks, and Positionality'. *Economic Geography* 78 (3): 307–30.

Chapter 4

SMUGGLERS INTO MILLIONAIRES: MARGINALITY AND SHIFTING CULTURAL HIERARCHIES IN A BULGARIAN BORDER TOWN[1]

Galia Valtchinova

Tran is a small town located at the Bulgarian–Serbian border that blends a certain pride of its 'urban' status and past with 'rural' appearances and ways of life. Its border location has impacted hugely on its development and the mentality of its inhabitants, giving it an almost iconic 'peripheral' place in the Bulgarian national imaginary, unsuitable as a site for a 'representative' Bulgarian ethnography.[2] Nevertheless, since the early 1990s, Tran has enjoyed increased ethnographic interest because of its growing reputation as a dynamic place, due to the numerous opportunities offered by transborder petty trade and smuggling. Around 1995, petrol stations mushroomed in all the villages located on the road from Tran to the border checkpoint Strezimirovtsi, while rumours spread about the emergence of local 'millionaires' who had become rich from smuggling petrol to Serbia, a country that was under international embargo at the time. Tran made headlines in the Bulgarian media, first because of the joint Bulgarian–US military exercise Cornerstone in the summer of 1998, and then for the blind bombs falling on Bulgarian territory during the 1999 bombing of Serbia. These events put Tran on the map, as well as on the map of an emerging global ethnography in which locality (or neighbourhood as 'the actually existing social form of locality', see Appadurai 1996, 178–9), relational and contextual as it is, has become an autonomous unit in a network of global flows, unmediated by the state, and transcending national borders (187). On the scale of the Bulgarian nation-state, these events triggered public debates and media reports that replaced the old negative clichés linked to the place, those of 'border', 'poverty' and 'marginality', with more ambiguous ones such as 'enrichment', 'abandonment' and 'the West'.[3]

In this chapter, I will show that this border town is a neighbourhood in Appadurai's (1996, 182–4) sense of the term, and as such it is particularly suitable for observing sociopolitical change, and for producing ethnography that is well attuned to address the major issues in the anthropology of postsocialism and globalization. My case study will investigate the urban–rural division from the perspective of economic and ethnic processes, as well as from the perspective of growing social inequality between 'rich' and 'poor'. Its border location helps us to understand better the central importance of location and positionality in ethnography. In sum, locality, identity and socioeconomic change are the main themes of my contribution, which will particularly look at the ways in which marginality, the border and transborder exchange influence local understandings of what 'urban' and 'rural', as well as 'rich' and 'poor', mean in this postsocialist context.

Tran's Positionality and Location

In providing a focus for both the temporal and spatial analysis of a locality, the concept of positionality (Kaneff this volume) constitutes a magnifying glass when looking at the urban–rural dynamic in a border town like Tran. In the context of my analysis, it helps to better understand the position of a particular place such as this one in the globalizing economy, as well as the role assigned to it from the point of view of the shifting and changing priorities of the nation-state. Here, positionality represents a dynamic relationship in which history and temporality, place and collective belonging are all contributing factors to the process of the making of a locality, which is fundamentally an active and multifaceted social practice. A similarly broad perspective can and should be applied to the term 'location', which is understood here as the inscription of place – at once social, cultural and political – within a real (national or global) space (Gupta and Ferguson 1997a, 5). The notions of positionality and location are important conceptual filters that refract the ethnographer's experience, help to reveal processes that are normally hidden from the observer's eye and make sense of sociopolitical change (as in Marcus's concept of multisited ethnography, 1995; see also Gupta and Ferguson 1997a; 1997b). This double focus also brings to the surface 'the nearly omnipresent cultural hierarchies, often buttressed by political and economic stratification, in which rustic people […] are marginalized and their culture devalued' (Creed and Ching 1997, 5). As Wilson and Donnan (1998 and 2005) have shown, location at an international border may actually shift or subvert common cultural hierarchies, which will be one of the core themes of my contribution.

Tran is part of the cultural-historical region of Znepole, which continuously swung between Bulgaria and Serbia, putting to test the ethnic and national belonging of the local population. The issue of the population's identity and uncertain loyalty was raised after every conflict involving the two countries, including the two World Wars. Even today, Tran's marginalization is still associated with it being part of a contested territory and having a contested history. I carried out my ethnographic fieldwork in the *mahala* (quarter) of Barintsi, located at the town's periphery. It is seen as the poorer 'suburb' and is looked down upon by those living in the centre and the 'posher' parts of Tran. It forms an excrescence along the main road which runs through the town to the border checkpoint. Indeed, people in Barintsi have made a living out of this road connecting Tran with the border, and this dependence gives the place a distinctive microidentity, a result of the road's lively and commercial character. It is the main economic artery and arena of social life and control: shops are located in garages attendant to the road, houses have their façades and windows turned to the road, and people passing by – or getting out of a stopping car – are discretely monitored, which is often a prelude to a volatile or persistent rumour. In this sense, the road determines local people's existence and marks the rhythm of everyday life. Far from corresponding to Augé's definition of *non-lieu* or nonplace (1992), the road organizing the space of Barintsi fully validates Dalakoglou's observation that the road 'emerges as a space […] of the most proximate, visible, and tangible consequences of the otherwise abstract and distant processes of globalization and postsocialism' (2010, 133).

This pivotal importance of the road – and the mobility it allows – is counterbalanced by claims about Barintsi's roots and ancient origins. Local elders like to argue that Barintsi used to be the nucleus of the town, the place from where 'Tran came out' and began to grow. These claims are underscored by religious motifs – a number of legends trace back the foundation of the town to the deeds of two Orthodox saints whose imagined 'presence' is literally written into, or embedded, in the surrounding landscape (Valtchinova 1999). Though anecdotal, local history as told by the people of Barintsi is a resource of symbolic capital for its inhabitants. It is in this local context that I carried out fieldwork and collected life histories (intermittently between 1994 and 2002), exploring the topics of locality, identity and socioeconomic change, which I deal with in this text. Among a group of around thirty-five respondents, a core group of eight people produced multiple (5 to 15) accounts of their lives, engaging in multifaceted interactions with the ethnographer, most of them between 1998 and 2000. These repeated exchanges made me realize that life histories were never simply reproduced – they varied significantly depending on an ever changing context. Recounting one's life was a way to make sense of the ongoing transformations, helping to bridge the gap between people's images of the past and the present in which they were living. It was also a way to put into perspective and reduce the obvious distance between the rural aspects of people's everyday life and their sense of being urbanites.

From *Palanka* to Postsocialist Border Town

Throughout its existence (since the early Ottoman period), the *kasaba* or *palanka* (small town) of Tran experienced numerous shifts in its positionality as a result of the political entities it has formed part of. The town and its surrounding area was twice 'liberated' from Ottoman rule during the Russo–Turkish War of 1877–78 – first by the Serbs and then by the Bulgarians – and with the proclamation of the modern Bulgarian state in 1878 a new border was imposed on a region that had been previously comfortably located within the Ottoman Empire. Tran was one of the 42 settlements in this young modern state that acquired an urban status (*grad*). Shortly after its inclusion into Bulgaria it became the westernmost district centre of the principality, and for the first time in its history white-collar workers appeared in the town. Nevertheless, its urban pride was short-lived as the town was rapidly marginalized due to its border location. Tran was deprived of the status of district centre in 1903 and separated from most of the Znepole villages at the end of World War I. Collective memory holds, however, that the town's decline was primarily due to the 'loss of territory' imposed on Bulgaria by the Neuilly Peace Treaty.[4]

The Western Marshes – the name of the territory 'lost' after 1919 – were again recovered during World War II, from 1941 to 1944. Even if brief in duration, this period restored Tran's urban status as it recovered its centrality within the 'reunited' Znepole area. This was symbolically expressed in the growing importance of the local cult of Saint Petka based in the parish church of Barintsi during the early 1940s. During this brief period, Tran and its rural surroundings became renowned for the highly effective communist resistance, which contributed to its ambiguous reputation in Bulgaria. The networking talents of local partisan leaders (most of whom came from families of traditional seasonal migrants) and their propensity to collaborate with 'foreign agents' were deemed incompatible with Bulgarian communism.[5] In the late 1950s and 1960s the town suffered severe depopulation, and during the 1970s it became a destination for 'unorthodox' communist functionaries who were sent into 'exile' there. In 1999, ten years after the introduction of democracy, my elderly informants still insisted ardently on Tran's marginalization and mistreatment under socialism.

Shaping Tran's positionality, the border was of pivotal importance. Regime change on either side of the border always immediately led to the tightening of border controls. During the interwar period, crossing the border was an almost everyday reality for local people (for both urban and rural dwellers) who owned land close to the border or 'on the other side'. They continued to work their parcels despite numerous incidents (such as humiliations by the border guards, random prohibition of one's access to land, and even skirmishes where accidental deaths were reported) as for many of them subsistence agriculture was the only way of survival. Because they occasionally suffered mistreatment by the Serbs, working one's land across the border also became meaningful as an act of anti-Serb resistance. Since working one's land acquired this political edge, the categories of rural and urban somehow became blurred – 'land' had become 'territory', to use Kaneff's (1998) apt formulation. Land and agriculture were imagined as *loci* of national belonging and political contestation. Even in the 1990s, working a plot of land near the border was seen as an act of political nonconformism.

The border had been 'open' for local people during World War II and in its aftermath. My elderly informants lumped together the war and the first postwar years as the period 'when the border was open', though this covered two periods with rather distinctive and contrasting political regimes, that of Greater Bulgaria and the initial years of the never completed project of the Balkan (communist) Federation. Things changed radically in 1948, when, following the ideological rift within the communist world, ties between Bulgaria and Yugoslavia were severed. The border was closed and crossing it was criminalized by the Bulgarian authorities as an anticommunist act equivalent to high treason. Between the late 1940s and early 1980s, Tran became an isolated place 'where the world ended' (Berdahl 1999). Its very name evoked in people the thought of a heavily guarded border, where police and military did everything to prevent people from escaping the country. This closure of the border contributed to what was locally perceived as a process of 'going rural' (*oseljanchvane*), which paradoxically occurred simultaneously with the rural exodus in the rest of Bulgaria. In time, however, the border controls loosened and forms of ritualized transborder exchange began to occur again regularly. Border gatherings that developed in the 1960s and 1970s gave rise to the town's association with entrepreneurship and the free market, thus reinvigorating its urban condition. In sum, Tran's ever changing positionality over one century produced multiple social, economic and political boundaries which incessantly reconfigured the local identities and ideas of otherness.

Between Urban and Rural: Tran as a Small Balkan Town

Small towns have long since attracted the attention of anthropologists, sociologists and historians. They offered a suitable environment for community studies carried out in the mid-twentieth century (Vidich and Bensman 1968). Also, the anthropology of the Mediterranean focused predominantly on small towns, especially agro-towns. The notion of agro-town implies the existence of an economy organized around agriculture, or more precisely a *latifundia* economy where agricultural workers and wage labourers do not live on the land but in a small town. It is no coincidence that the related concept of the agro-town was coined by anthropologists who were carrying out research in southern Italy and Spain.[6] It may be tempting to use the term also for a site such as Tran, which although featuring some urban social forms, cultural styles and subjective feelings of its inhabitants, does not display all the attributes of a modern urban settlement, even though the question remains to what extent this structural similarity is still applicable to the postsocialist context.[7]

I would like to suggest that without being identical to the Mediterranean agro-town, the small town studied in various Balkan contexts may indeed be called 'agro-town' because of the predominance of agricultural activities and occupations in combination with urban settlement and lifestyles. Most ethnographers depict the Balkan small town as a place where urban status and rural characteristics, in terms of work, speech and everyday life and culture are incessantly negotiated.[8] These assessments come close to my own observations that a small agricultural town such as Tran is a place where urban status is actively promoted in particular to outsiders, while at the same time it is balanced against much more ambiguous notions of the same place having a 'peasant-like' appearance.

Demography, particularly age profile, is one of the clearest indicators of the urban–rural divide in postsocialist Bulgaria. In recent decades, most Bulgarian villages and a number of small towns are inhabited disproportionately by elderly people, the retired and economically weak, who nevertheless dominate the younger generations in terms of social visibility and political influence. This is also the case in Tran, where people aged over 60 remain very active, both in business and local politics, even though economic activities are limited to the transformative economies of survival, including smuggling, in a situation where the town lacks a manufacturing economy.[9] Tran also displays a high level of social cohesion along the traditional lines of kinship and neighbourhood. As Konstantinov (2000, 134) has shown for other contexts in postsocialist Bulgaria, networks based on kinship and locality interweave with political networks, producing strong forms of clientelism in local politics, as was the case in Mediterranean agro-towns (see also Duijzings this volume; Giordano and Kostova this volume). Wider forms of association going beyond particular interest groups are indeed limited, the most notable being religious associations.[10] In both socialist and postsocialist Tran, various informal arrangements based particularly on kinship ties were and still are part of everyday life. For instance, the first large-scale public initiative in postsocialist Tran was the restoration of the rock chapel above the parish church. It led to the formation of a locally based network (in Barintsi) that proved similarly effective in matters other than religious. Until the late 1990s, two religion-based associations remained the only examples of home-grown 'civil society'.[11]

'Culture' and the Ethnicization of the Urban–Rural Divide

'Culture' and talk about 'having culture' helps us to understand the mechanisms and resources of identity formation and status making in Tran. I refer here to a peculiar notion of culture or urban 'civilization' which has been attested in various Balkan ethnographies, and which has been theorized for example by Gilles de Rapper in his study of the Albanian town of Devoll. It encompasses 'ideas and behaviours, practices and artefacts in the spheres of family and gender relations, architecture, food, clothes, and education' which are broadly associated with modernity and the West, especially in the postsocialist period (2008, 35 and 41). Since De Rapper's example bears structural similarities to our place, even in terms of positionality and location, it is all the more suitable to use his categories.

In Tran, everything – from how people dress to the look of their houses, from public hygiene to paved roads, from hospitals to monuments – is captured under the local and totalizing emic category of 'urban culture'. People attach huge importance to dress code and other formal signs associated to 'the urban', and closely monitor each other's appearance and manners (see also Ermann this volume). The town's urban status is tied up with the presence of white-collar jobs and the use of advanced technology in offices, and with the fact that local structures of power, political parties and the municipal council, as well as the recently opened offices administering EU programmes for border areas, are located here. These public institutions, as well as bank offices, which form another defining mark of urbanity, are all concentrated in the town centre. Barintsi has traditionally been denied this urban identity, because it lacks these attributes of 'urban' culture – its communist apartment blocks were only introduced during the 1980s, a decade later than elsewhere in Bulgaria. Neither is it a political and administrative centre, although it has a reputation of being an 'entrepreneurial' place. Tran's first private company (for construction materials) appeared in Barintsi, just off the road, along which several other small shops popped up in the early 1990s.

Another allegedly urban element in the local landscape are the characteristic houses built at the end of the nineteenth and first decades of the twentieth century by the local masons (*djulgeri*), who used to export their skills to other cities and countries.[12] Featuring some Central European architectural elements, these houses gave Tran its Western and urban character in the interwar period. Locals still regard them as a genuine mark of Tran's urbanity, even if the lack of maintenance has reduced most of these houses to partial ruins. During socialism, many of these houses, deserted or abandoned by their owners, were used to house the needy (especially Roma). After the 1992 Restitution Law, the return to their previous owners (or their descendants) became one of the most hotly debated issues of local postsocialist transition. Many houses were simply demolished because of the state of devastation they were in; neither restitution, nor private ownership or public upkeep by the municipality was a viable option. My elderly informants saw their demolition as a sign of 'lack of culture'. Their preservation as part of Tran's cultural heritage was never envisaged by the local authorities, neither under socialism nor after.

One of the most distinctive aspects of 'culture' is speech. The employment of standard Bulgarian is normally considered to be 'urban', while the use of dialect betrays one's peasant condition. One of the reasons for contesting the urban character of Tran was precisely the highly specific dialect, very different from standard Bulgarian and close to Serbian, which the local population spoke and still speaks. As a result, the inhabitants of Tran prefer to switch between the local dialect when speaking among themselves and standard Bulgarian when talking to outsiders, making their identity ambiguous. Also, other elements of local culture, such as the family ritual *svetats*, which is similar to the Serbian *slava*, have been seen as indicative of the ambiguous identity of the local population.[13] Local elderly people have completely internalized the insidious accusations of 'Serbian' identity which deride their speech or devalue their rituals. The elders I interviewed in the late 1990s were very much aware of this, assuring me that their culture 'is ours, not Serbian'.[14]

Even if persisting in jokes and in cultural stereotypes, the nationalist accusations of 'Serbian' identity have almost disappeared now. In recent times another line of division has become more salient: that between Bulgarians and Roma. Even though it is hardly ever rendered explicit in official statistics or political discourse (where the Serbs continue to be the main other), this division has nevertheless become the most salient in everyday interaction and local knowledge, especially when talking about economic fortunes and poverty.[15] This *de facto* ethnic division now permeates everyday life. The Roma, who settled in massive numbers in Tran during socialism, as a result of the town's political and economic marginalization as well as the emigration of a large part of its active population, have rapidly gained visibility. This is reinforced by opposite demographic trends among Roma and Bulgarians in terms of fertility and migration; in the late 1990s the youngest segment of the local population (under 20) was almost exclusively Roma. Many local Bulgarians blame the growing Roma population for what they regard as the disappearance of the town's urban character and the decline of urban culture and lifestyles (or 'culture' *tout court*). This multifaceted process is locally subsumed under the two suggestive terms 'ruralization' and 'Gypsification' (*otsiganchvane*), and it is visually epitomized by Roma children running in and out of derelict or partially ruined *djulgerski* houses located along the road.[16] Such images were regularly convoked by the media reporting about the town in 1998 and 1999, providing arresting images of postsocialist Tran.

The division between Bulgarians and Roma in Tran is reinforced by other lines of division, for example the urban–rural opposition, as well as the division between old-time settlers and newcomers. The latter is cast in terms of rootedness: unlike the old-time settlers, the Roma 'have no roots'.[17] At a deeper level, ideas of rootedness point to a differential understanding of the value of the past and represent a claim to ownership of that past. In declaring they were the old-time settlers, the local Bulgarians not only show their pride in having these urban roots, but also express claims of control over the local past and Bulgaria's national history. They do this either by making references to collective memory or by evoking picturesque details of their families' urban lives. On the contrary, Roma neither claim local roots nor show a particular pride of local belonging. The ethnic divide is still articulated by other elements in the urban fabric, for instance the contrast between privately owned urban-looking Bulgarian family homes and the chaotic housing situation of the Roma, which reinforces the divide in terms of 'property', 'cleanliness' or 'propriety'. Bulgarian houses are privately owned and therefore proper and clean, which cannot be said of the decrepit houses in which the Roma live.

At the end of this series of dichotomous oppositions I would like to point at the category of work, which contrasts the 'work-loving' Bulgarians with 'lazy' Roma. By the standards set by socialism, Roma had no work ethic and were unable to comply with the discipline of work (cf. Stewart 1993). The appearance of massive unemployment in early postsocialism only added a new dimension to this dichotomy. Yet in spite of the growing importance of the division between Bulgarians and Roma, the urban–rural divide remains the most salient, and in that sense all inhabitants of Tran are somehow in the same boat. Despite the urban pretence, which is upheld in the presence of outsiders, among themselves the inhabitants speak about Tran as a 'village' and of the population as 'fellow villagers', which has the effect of minimizing the ethnic divide. The simultaneous occurrence of public and external claims to urbanity in combination with the private and concealed recognition of a reality of village or peasant life and poor living conditions is a perfect illustration of the work of cultural intimacy (Herzfeld 1997).

Border, Cross-Border Exchange and the New 'Capitalism'

The location at the border is an important variable to take into account in case one tries to analyse local identity. My fieldwork has helped me realize that despite official decisions to 'open' and 'close' it, the border has always been much more permeable than the dominant discourses want us to believe. In accordance with Fredrik Barth's understanding of boundaries (1967), the border is a place where ethnic, social and political identities are negotiated and transformed in mutual interaction. The above principle is illustrated by forms of cross-border exchange that have been part and parcel of Tran's social and economic life ever since the establishment of the postwar border. Undoubtedly the most interesting of these exchanges have been the border gatherings or fairs (*granichni sabori*) that flourished in the 1960s and 1970s. They were initiated in the late 1920s to facilitate ritualized meetings of relatives living on both sides of the Bulgarian–Serbian border, whose families had been separated by the 'border of Neuilly'.[18] They quickly transformed into arenas for the expression of mutual rivalries and escalating nationalisms, as a result of which they were cancelled in the late thirties. The border fairs of the interwar period were nevertheless looked back upon with nostalgia by my informants. After a pause of more than twenty-five years they made a comeback in the early 1960s, in the shape of 'brotherly meetings' of Bulgarian and Yugoslav citizens, taking place annually in the narrow strip of no man's land between the two states; the one closest to Tran was at the checkpoint village of Strezimirovtsi, where the Barintsi road (and 'the world') ended. The kinship rhetoric of divided families, characteristic for the previous period, gave way to that of socialist brotherhood.

In the recollections of elderly informants, at that point the fairs were not any more associated with kin behind the borderline, nor did they evoke nostalgia for broken family unity.[19] Instead they became to be perceived as providing an opportunity for interaction with the West, or alternatively as an opportunity to escape to the West, which sometimes happened during the *sabor*.

The common-sense understanding of Bulgarians was that Yugoslavia was a 'free country' closer to capitalism. Having kin in Serbia made one a suspect of trying to cross the border in order to 'escape', and it was not uncommon that a successful 'escapee' would take the opportunity of the fair to meet parents or friends under the cover of the crowd. Yet in most cases the people of Tran used these border meetings as a chance to glance at Western-style illustrated magazines, and to look at or even buy highly desirable Western goods from Serbian traders. As a local postsocialist boss indicated, 'they were damn good traders, these Serbs; evoking that we were kin did not help us very much'. In time, the border fairs started to attract urbanites coming from afar, most frequently natives of Tran living in cities, especially Sofia. Going to a border *sabor* was a fashionable activity for many dwellers of the Bulgarian capital city in the 1970s. Here they could get into direct contact with the attributes of the nonsocialist world; that is, the embodiments of the capitalist West – the behaviours, eating habits, and dress and speech codes associated with it. In the late 1970s, border fairs had become arenas of multiple interactions between the Yugoslav 'West' and Bulgarian 'socialism'. Serbs living across the border (even peasants) became associated with capitalism, 'Europe' and the urban in the eyes of most Bulgarians.

These overlaps are suggestive of the hidden workings of an ideological model that posited the rural and the urban at the opposite edges of the acceptable (communist) world. Whatever the benefits of urbanization and socialist industrialization – and in spite of the Marxist axiom of the working class being the driving social force – in socialist Bulgaria the urban was still seen as potentially more dangerous and less controllable than the rural. Formerly inhabited by the hated bourgeoisie, cities and towns were perceived as complex social aggregates where it was much easier to generate dissent and disorder. Urbanites were also regarded as being more inclined towards emulating 'the West'. In such a mental framework it was easy for Bulgarians to equate 'urban' culture with capitalism and the 'freedom-loving' Yugoslavs – the more socialist, the more 'peasant'.

The regular occurrence of these fairs solidified Tran's association with the border, in which elements of 'freedom' (exchange, meeting the 'other' or simply crossing the border) and 'danger' (related to 'escape' or to suspicious interactions with Yugoslavs, including the purchase of goods) were closely intertwined. These negative political connotations, reinforced by forms of exchange and black market activities led to the disappearance of these fairs in the early 1980s. The Bulgarian authorities saw these increasingly dominant commercial activities as unlawful and immoral. With the regime change in November 1989, this configuration changed once again. Crossing the border became much easier; between 1990 and 1992, the panoply of border control mechanisms was demolished, and in the early 1990s petty trading and smuggling became the dominant survival strategy for major parts of the population suffering from growing unemployment and poverty.

These new forms of local border 'capitalism' and entrepreneurship operated through informal kinship or ethnic networks, which was also attested in the early 1990s at the Bulgarian–Greek (Agelopoulos 2007) or the Turkish–Bulgarian border (Konstantinov, Kressel and Thuen 1998; Pickles 2000). The interaction with Turkey had a further dimension in terms of the proximity of Istanbul as a global city, which formed the main 'globalizing factor' for large parts of the Balkans as the main destination for the petty ('suitcase') trade.[20] Using their ethnic and confessional affinities and their linguistic skills, Turkish and Roma entrepreneurs in Bulgaria dominated the new market economies of small towns and areas close to the border and even in the larger cities.[21] The proverbially 'lazy' Roma showed an incredible adaptability to the new market system and its demands, benefitting from the improvisation skills and informal practices for which they had been stigmatized before. In many places their market activities led to a reversal of ethnic and social hierarchies between Roma and Bulgarians. Though Konstantinov, Kressel and Thuen's (1998) suggestion that Bulgarians were 'outclassed by former outcasts' would go too far in the context of Tran, the Roma largely contributed to the town's changing position from a marginalized into an economically dynamic place.

Between Survival and New Capitalist Accumulation in Postsocialist Tran

The situation as outlined above needs further specification to convey the peculiar state of affairs at the Bulgarian–Serbian border. In a popular joke of the mid-1990s, Tran was notable for having the most Gypsies and millionaires in one place. Indeed, between 1992 and 1995, when the former Yugoslavia was ravaged by wars, cross-border trade and smuggling became a full-time occupation for the majority of inhabitants. Under the combined effects of the wars and the embargo on Serbia, shortages of food and other goods created a practically unlimited market on the other side of the border, attracting Bulgarian entrepreneurs of various kinds. The most lucrative item for this cross-border trade was petrol, which was taken from local petrol stations and carried across the border into Serbia in car reservoirs, canisters and plastic water bottles carried by hand. In this way local Bulgarians and Roma who had no cars could take part in what became a truly massive economic undertaking. For most of the smugglers, however, this was not more than a short-lived episode of profit making, and brought only temporary relief from unemployment – in 1997, Tran had still one of the highest unemployment rates in Bulgaria, affecting primarily its Roma population.

As I started to carry out research on it in 1997, the 'petrol fever' was over and locals refused to talk about the previous smuggling activities of identifiable Bulgarians or Roma. The topic remained largely inaccessible. Needless to say, I did not meet a single 'petrol millionaire', let alone a person admitting to have engaged in petrol smuggling, nor could I verify the figures reported through hearsay or in the national media. The issue of petrol smuggling was swept under the carpet and refuted as gossip of outsiders ('those up there in Sofia'), or at best tacitly acknowledged as a morally deplorable practice carried out by others. People talked more easily about outsiders, such as the petrol-smuggling local priest (the *pop benzindzhiya*), who was said to have come to serve the parish 'just for profit', ending his short stint of service in 1993 in a scandalous manner. On the contrary, the fact that the local church caretaker (*klisar*), coming from a local family, had been involved in the cross-border trade of food was almost never commented upon.

From the local point of view, the predominant justification given for this kind of dubious economic activity was survival. Survival or 'putting aside for hard times' was the key element of local discourse, common to both Bulgarians and to Roma. Any notion of trade being a vehicle for the accumulation of capital was refuted. Two examples will show how these local understandings of capitalism, entrepreneurship and survival were intertwined, and how cross-border trade was harmonized with the image people had of themselves. What follows are excerpts from interviews with well-off Bulgarians in Barintsi.

At the end of the 1990s, one of my informants was locally known as 'the boss' – that is, the person who provided employment to people of his native town. At the time of my fieldwork, he talked about his enterprise with unconcealed pride, deploying a markedly paternalist discourse. He also loved talking about his past experiences of crossing the border and episodes of cross-border exchange. He never mentioned any kin 'on the other side', but he did regularly attend the border fairs. His first experience with capitalism occurred at the end of World War II, when he, still a teenager, was recruited as wage worker in the Western Marshes (now part of Serbia), which was then under Bulgarian control. During socialism, he followed a trajectory typical for a local male youth: he was employed in the construction industry and then moved to Sofia, where he built up an informal network of acquaintances and connections with influential persons. These were of great use when times changed. A few years after his retirement (at the age of 55), he started a private business in his native town, relying on the local population for manpower. By 1999, he employed approximately ten local Bulgarians on the basis of permanent contracts and many more Roma as day labourers. In conversation, he always emphasized that he held family values in high esteem, boasting that his son and daughter-in-law were closely involved in the family business. Yet at the same time he avoided building business networks with wider kin. For him private businesses made Tran truly urban again after decades of economic decline and 'going rural'. He condemned smuggling (especially of petrol) as 'shameful', nevertheless turning a blind eye to such activities when it concerned his own staff – mostly Roma – who supplemented their meagre income through petty trade and smuggling.

My second example is a chief nurse of the local hospital, who had just retired when I met her for the first time. She was typical of the great majority of Bulgarians who never openly acknowledged that they had been involved in petrol smuggling, but nevertheless shared what I have called the 'survival discourse'. Being part of a once important local family and the only daughter of a former mayor of Tran, she never liked the cross-border trade, even though she had close relatives in a nearby Serbian village. She became a trader in 1995, at a relatively late stage of the 'petrol fever'. At the time she was still employed in the hospital, which assured her a high social status. She knew that she was not going to do this for a long time – she was due for retirement and her salary failed to provide for her and her old mother's basic needs. Even though she felt that petty trade and smuggling were deeply 'shameful' activities, she started to carry petrol across the border, taking it in plastic containers from a petrol station some distance from town, in order to disguise her activities from neighbours and acquaintances. With her house opening onto the road, she took particularly care to not be seen carrying identifiable items – every move on the road was watched, and most talk about local smuggler 'millionaires' originated from road rumours. When crossing the border, she and her female companion kept themselves separate from other identifiable smugglers (especially Roma) and well-known profiteers (dalaveradzhii). In her effort to remain a respectable woman, she never linked up with her kinsmen living on the other side of the border, ashamed as she was at the thought that they might be able to see her involvement in petty trade. After having had problems with border guards, she gave up the petrol smuggling ten months later, having put aside a significant amount of money.

Concerns with morality of trade are central to both narratives either centring on entrepreneurial work (as in the first case) or survival (the second case). It is significant that in both narratives, the narrators deny having had any intention of making profit, which is projected onto others, especially Roma. These moral dilemmas are common to all postsocialist societies, as Caroline Humphrey and Ruth Mandel have pointed out (Humphrey 1997; Humphrey and Mandel 2002). In the case of Tran, these dilemmas have been complicated by the proximity of the border and the varying social and political arrangements produced by it over the last century. Yet what is clear from both cases is that shame has been experienced both at the personal and relational level – linked to the fear of 'losing face' and of identification in face-to-face interaction – and at a systemic level, as an essential and inherent characteristic of a particular economic activity such as cross-border trade. The very possibility of being identified as a 'smuggler' was perceived as a threat to both social status and self-esteem.[22]

In the case of the nurse, the experience of 'shame' is connected with a wide range of other issues: from being a female facing male guards, to being Bulgarian with kinship relations 'on the other side' of the border. The woman in question was particularly attentive to the 'border theatre' in terms of keeping up her respectability.[23] Keeping economic interactions with local people to a minimum, and avoiding any contact with relatives 'on the other side', was the price she paid for preserving her face and status, even if it minimized profit. Bribes and talk about survival were other tactics used at critical moments. Whether a border guard was to be bribed or to be told tales of poverty and hardship was a matter of cultural intimacy and part of common knowledge of local life on the border. In all cases, personal interest and gain – the moving force of capitalist market transaction – were deliberately occluded or simply negated.

Smuggling, Roma and the Urban Poor: Pieces of a Mosaic

The vignettes presented in the previous section captured the existence of ethnically coloured social hierarchies which reproduced the mental frameworks of socialism. The 'shamefulness' of smuggling and market activities in general was predicated on the socialist value system and based on a negative vision of wealth acquired not through production but through petty trade, which presented and stigmatized the Roma as *the* smugglers *par excellence*. It is clear that the survival discourse embraced by Bulgarians and Roma alike was strategically used to diminish one's intentionality and deny one's agency.

At this point, we are closer to understanding how cultural hierarchies between Bulgarians and Roma influenced, and were intertwined with, the pragmatic hierarchies of the survival economy. If neither 'kinship' nor 'roots' had the same sense and the same appeal for local Roma, 'shame' as a cultural construct was not meaningful to them in the way it was to Bulgarians. Roma had already been recast by the socialist state as the negative 'other' in the social construction of respectability based on productive work. Low on the social and cultural ladder, having no local roots and reputation for work, the Roma of Tran had little concern for issues such as shame and respectability.

For them, the end of socialism provided new and unprecedented opportunities in the form of an 'open' and easily permeable state border, with a population on the other side of the border experiencing social decline and impoverishment, making the unrestrained pursuit of capitalist practices even more attractive. Some acted on their own account, others however worked for Bulgarians, who saw similar opportunities but also deemed it to be more 'shameful'. In both cases, their activities and involvement firmly established their public image as the essential smugglers, even if Bulgarians were involved in it as well.

Even though the Roma were seen as intentional and self-conscious smugglers, they were systematically denied the kind of agency associated to capitalist business and truly capitalist entrepreneurship. As the two examples show, business is a source of pride – and of public display – only insofar as it is the result of productive or transformative work. Smuggling represents the opposite. Under socialism, smuggling was prohibited and seen as politically disruptive and morally suspect, associated with marginalized populations already stigmatized as lazy or inept. Concomitant with the introduction of market capitalism, the spread of the activity of cross-border smuggling across other ethnic groups in the first decade of the postsocialist period revealed the constitutive ambiguity of this economic activity. As before, smuggling was cast against the category of work, and the only positive justification was that it provided a strategy for survival.

My last point concerns the impact of cross-border trade on social and cultural hierarchies and more specifically the urban–rural dichotomy. With smuggling and cross-border exchange widely practiced by Roma and Bulgarians, developing into a common way of earning a livelihood, the activity lost its association with 'capitalism', at least in the eyes of those who practiced it. In consequence, smuggling had two opposite effects: on the one hand, it helped the mixing of people from different social and ethnic background that were involved in the same practice; on the other, according to the logic of maintaining social difference, it acted to preserve the distinction between Bulgarians and Roma. Yet the overarching effect was the blurring of previously clear-cut differences, for example between occupations, between urban and rural, or between rich and poor. Even if Bulgarians somehow succeeded in maintaining such social differentiations and cultural hierarchies inherited from the past, the Roma more readily accepted the new capitalist principles and postsocialist urban identity associated with it, even if they were still looked down upon by others.

I hope to have demonstrated the elasticity of categories at the border, among them the notion of the poor and the rich. As Tran's positionality changed in the process of postsocialist transformation, categories have shifted. The category of the poor as defined by international agencies may now be applied to diverse categories: the Roma, poor by every standard and mostly unemployed but resourceful in terms of finding temporary work; the Bulgarians with mostly peasant roots but also with a developed urban consciousness; and the economically precarious pensioners who have retained a high degree of social capital. The category of the rich appears to be equally elusive, for another reason: if being poor was previously perceived not as a status but as a claim (especially for access to social assistance), being rich was perceived as a matter of visibility and of a visually recognizable status. The elusive and dynamic character of these categories is comparable to the central role of the road, the epitome of mobility, of exchange and not least of postsocialist globalization.

Notes

1 This paper is based on fieldwork done intermittently between 1997 and 2000, at the end of a period of intense transborder smuggling following the wars in the former Yugoslavia, and peaking with the tensions leading up to the NATO bombings of Serbia (summer 1998–spring 1999). Providing the magnifying glass for most of the processes and phenomena discussed here, the context of military intervention in neighbouring former Yugoslavia forms the unique and crucial context of my research and analysis.

2 In 1998, an anonymous reviewer for the French journal *Balkanologie* challenged my fieldwork as being 'not representative' of Bulgaria because of the town's border location, the proximity of the local dialect to Serbian and the high percentage of Gypsies (Roma) among the local population.

3 For a discussion of these subsequent events, their effects on the local population and other related topics, see Valtchinova (1999, 2003a, 2003b).

4 The Peace Treaty of Neuilly-sur-Seine (concluded on 27 November 1919) settled the postwar status of Bulgaria, imposing severe sanctions on the country and its elite's aspirations to create a Greater Bulgaria – hence the label of 'national catastrophe'. It sanctioned, among other things, the annexation of the Znepole area to the newly created Kingdom of Serbs, Croats and Slovenes. The border near Tran divided villages and even houses, sometimes leaving members of the same family in two different states.

5 After the break with Tito's Yugoslavia in June 1948, the links with Tito's partisan movement and the transborder character of the local resistance became a problem for the new socialist state. As a result local partisan leaders were sent to communist prison camps. Even after they were released in the early sixties they remained an embarrassment for the Bulgarian communist regime.

6 For an overview see Boissevain (1979) and Kenny and Kertzer (1984). The agro-town is a town located in a rural area dominated by large agricultural estates (latifundia), which condition the occupational profiles and patterns of its inhabitants, while at the same time having an urban status (see Blok and Driessen 1984).

7 I am indebted to Ger Duijzings for this idea. Even though one cannot argue that the large socialist estates of collectivized land functioned in the same way as latifundia, they produced similar effects and social patterns. If the latifundia economy forces landless agricultural workers and day-labourers to live in towns, large socialist cooperative estates deprived the peasants of their land, transforming them into agricultural workers who were forced,

through economic and ideological pressures, to become urbanites or project themselves into the urban condition. See Creed (1998) for this interplay of urban and rural.

8 See for instance Santova (2001), which is based on ethnographic work in Bansko, a small town in southwest Bulgaria; cf. Lory 2005 (1996). Another recent study of a small town in a postsocialist context is Chevalier (2000).

9 In 2002 (according to the national census), almost 45 per cent of the population of Tran was aged over 65. For strategies of postsocialist survival, see Konstantinov (2000) and Konstantinov, Kressel and Thuen (1998).

10 Again, this pattern is best studied in Mediterranean ethnographies: see Boissevain (1965, 1977).

11 In the postcommunist Balkans, civil society was assimilated to a dense network of NGOs imported by Western agencies. For some perverse effects of this transference of expertise see Konstantinov (2000, 132–3) and Sampson (2002).

12 Tran's masons were renowned in the late Ottoman period. In search of work, they engaged in seasonal migration travelling in small groups to Istanbul, Serbia (as far as Belgrade) and Romania. After World War I most of them converged on Sofia (see Hristov 2008). In the early decades of socialism, Tran's masons were employed in the socialist construction industry.

13 The ritual, which consists in celebrating the patron saint of Ego's father's lineage by special prayers said during a festive dinner, usually on the saint's commemoration day, has a strong nationalist emphasis. Since the late 1870s, it has been conceptualized as a Serbian national identity marker and any similar practice is interpreted as a 'proof' of Serbian identity. After World War I, assigning national identity to a population on the basis of its practice of the *slava* ritual became a political issue, which strained Bulgarian–Serbian relations for the whole interwar period (see Hristov 2002).

14 See Hristov (2002) for the nationalist propaganda around the *slava* ritual with respect to this area.

15 Hereafter, I will designate these two groups as Bulgarian and Roma (without inverted commas), respectively, even if local Roma recognize an overarching Bulgarian identity and do not claim to be an ethnically distinct group.

16 Keith Brown (2001) has described similar processes in Skopje (Macedonia), where Macedonians regard the influx of Albanians to have led to both the 'Albanianization' of the city as well as the demise of its urban character. Here the urban–rural distinction is established along ethnic lines – Albanians being 'rural' and Macedonians 'urban' – while in De Rapper's (2008) ethnographic account it follows religious lines, with Muslim Albanians viewed as 'peasants' and less 'cultured' than the Christian inhabitants.

17 De Rapper (2008, 3–6) noticed the same reaction of Christian Albanians vis-à-vis Muslim ones. It is worth noting that in Tran the massive involvement of Roma in the Evangelical Church in the early 1990s was taken to be the ultimate proof (if needed) of their lack of 'roots'.

18 On the border fairs of the interwar period see Valtchinova (1999, 131–3).

19 It is worth noting that villagers from the Serbian part of Znepole kept emphasizing this aspect. During interviews I conducted in 2000, people living 'on the other side of the border' depicted the border fairs as joyful encounters dominated by a 'peasant' type of sociability, where 'we used to eat and drink a lot'.

20 For the role of Istanbul as a megalopolis, and of Turkey more generally in the capitalist globalization of the postcommunist neighbour states to the northeast and northwest, see Hann and Beller-Hann (1998) and Tarrius (2007, 17–53).

21 The best known study on trade and smuggling through the Bulgarian–Turkish border by Konstantinov, Kressel and Thuen (1998) focuses on traders of Bulgaria's third city and sea capital, Varna; for areas closer to Turkey, see Pickles (2000, 9–11, 15–21). To my knowledge there are no such studies on the Rhodope Mountains, where the large Muslim minorities were heavily involved in cross-border trade and smuggling with Turkey during the 1990s.

22 According to Pine and Bridger (1998, 8–9), postsocialist 'shame' attached to trade may be closely connected to the characteristic socialist *person*, which is rooted in productive work.

23 McMurray (2001, 112–19) uses the term in a similar context including female smugglers, who had to carefully engineer their appearance, leaving no doubt about their respectfulness, never crossing the thin line separating them from 'prostitutes'. For the uncertain status of female traders see Hann and Beller-Hann (1998, 253–7).

References

Agelopoulos, Giorgios. 2007 (1996). 'The Coca Cola Kashkaval Network: Belonging and Business in the Balkans'. *Anthropology of East Europe Review* 25 (1): 42–52.

Appadurai, Arjun. 1996. *Modernity at Large: Cultural Dimensions of Globalization*. Minneapolis: University of Minnesota Press.

Augé, Marc. 1992. *Non-lieux: Une anthropologie de la surmodernité*. Paris: Seuil.

Barth, Fredrik. 1969. 'Introduction'. In *Ethnic Groups and Boundaries: The Social Organization of Cultural Difference*, edited by Fredrik Barth, 9–38. Boston: Little, Brown.

Berdahl, Daphne. 1999. *Where the World Ended: Re-unification and Identity in the German Borderland*. Berkeley: University of California Press.

Block, Anton and Henk Driessen. 1984. 'Mediterranean Agro-Towns as a Form of Cultural Dominance, with Special Reference to Sicily and Andalusia'. *Ethnologia Europaea* 14 (2): 111–24.

Boissevain, Jeremy. 1965. *Saints and Fireworks: Religion and Politics in Rural Malta*. London: Athlone Press.

_____. 1977. 'When the Saints Go Marching Out: Reflections on the Decline of Patronage in Malta'. In *Patrons and Clients in Mediterranean Societies*, edited by Ernest Gellner and John Waterbury, 81–96. London: Duckworth.

_____. 1979. 'Towards a Social Anthropology of the Mediterranean'. *Current Anthropology* 20 (1): 81–92 (with comments and reply).

Bridges, Susan and Frances Pine, eds. 1998. *Surviving Post-socialism: Local Strategies and Regional Responses in Eastern Europe and the Former Soviet Union*. London: Routledge.

Brown, Keith. 2001. 'Beyond Ethnicity: The Politics of Urban Nostalgia in Modern Macedonia'. *Journal of Mediterranean Studies* 11 (2): 417–42.

Burawoy, Michael and Katherine Verdery, eds. 1999. *Uncertain Transition: Ethnographies of Change in the Postsocialist World*. New York: Rowman and Littlefield.

Chevalier, Sophie. 2000. 'Stratégies d'échanges en Bulgarie'. *Balkanologie* 4 (2) (December). Online: http://balkanologie.revues.org/index332.html (accessed 4 October 2012).

Creed, Gerald W. 1998. 'Agriculture and the Domestication of Industry in Rural Bulgaria'. *American Ethnologist* 22 (3): 528–48.

Creed, Gerald W. and Barbara Ching. 1997. 'Recognizing Rusticity: Identity and the Power of Place'. Introduction to *Knowing Your Place: Rural Identity and Cultural Hierarchy*, edited by Barbara Ching and Gerald W. Creed, 1–38. New York: Routledge.

Dalakoglou, Dimitris. 2010. 'The Road: An Ethnography of the Albanian–Greek Cross-Border Motorway'. *American Ethnologist* 37 (1): 132–49.

De Rapper, Gilles. 2002. 'Grenzen überschreiten: Migration in der albanischen Grenzregion Devoll'. In *Die weite Welt und das Dorf: Albanische Emigration am Ende des 20. Jahrhunderts*, edited by Karl Kaser, Robert Pichler and Stephanie Schwandner-Sievers, 83–106. Vienna: Böhlau.

———. 2008. 'Religion in Post-communist Albania: Muslims, Christians and the Concept of "Culture" (Devoll, South Albania)'. *Anthropological Notebooks* 14: 31–45.

Gupta, Akhil and James Ferguson. 1997a. 'Discipline and Practice: "The Field" as Site, Method, and Location in Anthropology'. In *Anthropological Locations: Boundaries and Grounds of a Field Science*, edited by Akhil Gupta and James Ferguson, 1–46. Berkeley: University of California Press.

———. 1997b. 'Culture, Power, Place: Ethnography at the End of an Era'. In *Culture, Power, Place: Ethnography at the End of an Era*, edited by Akhil Gupta and James Ferguson, 1–29. Berkeley: University of California Press.

Hann, Chris and Ildiko Beller-Hann. 1998. 'Market, Morality and Modernity in North-East Turkey'. In *Border Identities: Nation and State at International Frontiers*, edited by Thomas Wilson and Hastings Donnan, 237–62. Cambridge: Cambridge University Press.

Herzfeld, Michael. 1997. *Cultural Intimacy: Social Poetics of the Nation-State*. New York: Routledge.

Hristov, Petko. 2002. 'The Use of Holidays for Propaganda Purposes: The "Serbian" Slava and/or the "Bulgarian" Săbor'. *Ethnologia Balkanica* 6: 69–80.

———. 2008. 'Trans-border Exchange of Seasonal Workers in the Central Regions of the Balkans (19th–20th Century)'. *Ethnologia Balkanica* 12: 215–30.

Humphrey, Caroline. 1997. 'Exemplars and Rules: Aspects of the Discourse of Moralities in Mongolia'. In *The Ethnography of Moralities*, edited by Signe Howell, 25–47. London: Routledge.

———. 1999. 'Traders, "disorder", and Citizenship Regimes in Provincial Russia'. In *Uncertain Transition: Ethnographies of Change in the Postsocialist World*, edited by Michael Burawoy and Katherine Verdery, 19–52. New York: Rowman and Littlefield.

Humphrey, Caroline and Ruth Mandel. 2002. 'The Market in Everyday Life: Ethnographies of Postsocialism'. In *Markets and Moralities: Ethnographies of Postsocialism*, edited by Ruth Mandel and Caroline Humphrey, 1–16. Oxford: Berg.

Kaneff, Deema 1998. 'When "Land" Becomes "Territory": Land Privatization and Ethnicity in Rural Bulgaria'. In *Surviving Post-socialism: Local Strategies And Regional Responses in Eastern Europe and the Former Soviet Union*, edited by Sue Bridger and Frances Pine, 21–39. London: Routledge.

———. 2002. 'The Shame and Pride of Market Activity: Morality, Identity and Trading in Postsocialist Rural Bulgaria'. In *Markets and Moralities: Ethnographies of Postsocialism*, edited by Ruth Mandel and Caroline Humphrey, 33–51. Oxford: Berg.

Kenny, Michael and David Kertzer, eds. 1984. *Urban Life in Mediterranean Europe: Anthropological Perspectives*. Urbana: University of Illinois Press.

Konstantinov, Yulian. 2000. 'Survival Strategies in Post-1989 Bulgaria'. In *Karl Polanyi in Vienna: The Contemporary Significance of the Great Transformation*, edited by Kenneth McRobbie and Kari Polanyi Levitt, 132–45. Montreal: Black Rose Books.

Konstantinov, Yulian, Gideon M. Kressel and Trond Thuen. 1998. 'Outclassed by Former Outcasts: Petty Trading in Varna'. *American Ethnologist* 25 (4): 729–45.

Lory, Bernard. 2005 (1996). 'Bansko, culture citadine ou culture rurale?'. In *Les Balkans: De la transition post-ottomane à la transition post-communiste*, edited by Bernard Lory, 191–204. Istanbul: Isis.

Marcus, George. 1995. 'Ethnography in/of the World System: The Emergence of Multi-sited Ethnography'. *Annual Review of Anthropology* 24: 95–117.

———. 1998. *Ethnography through Thick and Thin*. Princeton: Princeton University Press.

McMurray, David A. 2001. *In and Out of Morocco: Smuggling and Migration in a Frontier Boomtown*. Minneapolis: University of Minnesota Press.

Pickles, John. 2000. '"There Are No Turks in Bulgaria": Violence, Ethnicity, and Economic Practice in the Border Regions and Muslim Communities of Post-socialist Bulgaria'. *Max Planck Institute Working Papers* 25 (Halle/Saale): 1–19.

Sampson, Steven. 2002. 'Weak States, Uncivil Societies and Thousands of NGOs: Benevolent Colonialism in the Balkans'. In: *The Balkans in Focus: Cultural Boundaries in Europe*, edited by Sanimir Resic and Barbara Törnquist-Plewa, 27–44. Lund: Lund University Press.

Santova, Mila. 2001. *Kultura i traditsiya na malkiya grad*. Sofia: Akademichno Izdatelstvo 'Prof. Marin Drinov'.

Stewart, Michael. 1993. 'Gypsies, the Work Ethic, and Hungarian Socialism'. In *Socialism: Ideals, Ideologies, and Local Practices*, edited by C. M. Hann, 187–203. New York: Routledge.

Tarrius, Alain. 2007. *La remontée des Suds: Afghans et Marocains en Europe méridionale*. Paris: Editions de l'Aube.

Valtchinova, Galia. 1999. *Znepolski pohvali: Lokalna religiya i identichnost v zapadana Bulgariya*. Sofia: Akademichno Izdatelstvo 'Prof. Marin Drinov'.

———. 2003a. 'Entre le "choc des civilisations" et le "choix" de civilisation: Visions bulgares de la guerre, du Kosovo 1999 à l'après-11 septembre 2001'. *Cahiers d'études du monde Ottoman, Turc et Iranien* (Paris: Institut de Sciences Politiques / CERI) 35 (January–June): 175–99.

———. 2003b. 'Znepole, Western Bulgaria, Between "Europe" and "America": The Changing Vision of the "West" in a Balkan Border Area during the Kosovo Crisis'. *Ethnologia Balkanica* 7: 159–80.

Vidich, Arthur J. and Joel Bensman. 1968. *Small Town in Mass Society*, revised edition. Princeton, NJ: Princeton University Press.

Wilson, Thomas and Hastings Donnan, eds. 1998. *Border Identities: Nation and State at International Frontiers*. Cambridge: Cambridge University Press.

———. 2005. 'Territory, Identity, and the Places In-Between: Culture and Power in European Borderlands'. In *Culture and Power at the Edges of the States: National Support and Subversion*, edited by Thomas Wilson and Hastings Donnan, 1–29. Münster: LIT Verlag.

Chapter 5

RURAL DECLINE AS THE EPILOGUE TO COMMUNIST MODERNIZATION: THE CASE OF A SOCIALIST 'MODEL' VILLAGE

Lenka Nahodilova

'Modernization' in terms of state-organized urbanization, industrialization and emancipation was one of the important goals of the communist regimes in Central and Eastern Europe. It became an important measure for the achievements of socialism, epitomizing the degree at which society was approaching the final stage of communism. In every socialist country this process worked out differently, each having its own specific local agendas and dynamics. Yet there was enough common ground to be able to speak of shared patterns and characteristics of socialist 'modernization'. In the immediate postwar decades, for instance, the emphasis was put on fast-track industrialization and urbanization. Then, during the 1970s and 1980s, most socialist regimes in Central and Eastern Europe abandoned this ideologically driven programme of rapid industrial development, reaching a social and political compromise which Creed (1998) has called the 'domesticated revolution' in Bulgaria's case. It is often argued that this compromise between the regime and the population heralded the transformation of socialist society into a consumerist society, by inserting the practice of consumption into the experience of socialist modernity (Brunnbauer and Taylor 2004; Taylor 2006).

Yet in Bulgaria the situation was in many respects specific. In some parts of the country, for instance in the Rhodope Mountains, on which I will be concentrating in this chapter, Bulgarian socialist modernization, even during the 1970s, closely resembled the 1920s Soviet experiment of fast-track modernization, of rapid and forced industrialization and urbanization (Kotkin 1995). I will be looking at the impact on and experience of this process by some of those who were at the receiving end: the Muslim minority of Pomaks, considered to be more 'traditional' and therefore specifically singled out to be modernized 'from above'.[1] Even though similar policies were applied to other Muslim minorities in socialist Eastern Europe (such as the Torbeshi in Macedonia, the Gorani in Kosovo or various groups in the Soviet Union), the Pomaks were exposed to harsher and more radical attempts at assimilation and forced modernization.[2] In the immediate postsocialist period this was followed by the sudden withdrawal of the state and the abolition of its modernization programme, which among other things led to the strengthening of ethnic and religious identities among Muslim minority groups across the former socialist bloc. Again the Pomaks form partly an exception as they lacked an intellectual elite and failed to develop their own nationalist agenda. In many ways they were the 'losers' of postsocialist transition, unable to wire up to global networks and mobilize new resources (Duijzings this volume). Especially in the rural and mountainous parts of the country where the Pomaks are concentrated, the population became socially and economically marginalized, in some cases ending up in harsh and unacceptable living conditions characterized by unemployment, poverty and lack of basic provisions. The following analysis stems from fieldwork research I carried out between 1998 and 2004 in the Pomak (Bulgarian-speaking Muslims) village community of 'Modrava' in southern Bulgaria.[3] The methodology for this research included oral history interviews and narratives collected from both the villagers and the former socialist functionaries who implemented the local modernization programme.

Communist Modernization, Time and Periphery

Modernity heralds a changing semantics of historical time, when the past stops accounting for the present and the future, and constant change and recurring crises become the dominant mode of experience (Koselleck 2004, 2006). Early sociologists such as Georg Simmel (1971) and Ferdinand Tönnies (1955) studied the impact of these changes on individuals in urban contexts, and later generations of scholars continued to focus on societies which were already constituted in terms of possessing long-standing urban forms of social, cultural and political organization, disregarding the potentially disruptive effects on rural societies. An exception is the work of social historian Eugen Weber (1976), who describes the process of modernization as an encounter between rural and urban social organization, in which rural subjectivities are transformed into modern national or citizenship identities as part of the emerging nation-state. In most of the literature, however, modernization is linked with urban society, and described in terms of a process of migration from rural areas to cities, which started in earnest in the eighteenth century. This process of rural–urban migration is seen as one of the preconditions of industrialization and the development of a modern society. Socialist modernization differed to some extent in terms of communist regimes applying many of the features of modernity to traditional rural communities in an attempt to transform them and create urban patterns of social organization in the countryside. This was, for instance, happening in the Bulgarian Rhodopes during the 1970s, a process modelled after the Soviet example of the 1920s and 1930s.

The socialist regimes established in Central and Eastern Europe after World War II were operating on the ideological platform of 'modernity and progress'. They were carrying out their modernization programmes in line with Leninist principles proclaiming that society will only reach the desired stage of 'communism' when the distinctions between 'men and women', 'physical and mental labour' and between 'town and countryside' have disappeared (Tucker 1975). Following these ideological premises, all East European communist regimes, embedded in societies which were still predominantly agrarian in character, were investing huge human and financial resources into dismantling gender, class and social differences as well as the urban–rural divide. Unlike in Western Europe, where modernization was based on movement in the rural–urban direction, in socialist countries modernity was introduced 'from above', not only by moving peasants into cities, but also by spreading urbanity into villages.

The urbanization programmes were partly aiming at inserting 'civilization' and 'modernity' into marginal and peripheral places, introducing it to traditional rural societies and native populations. For instance, in the Soviet Union the socialist modernization mission was first directed towards the frontiers between Europe and Asia in an attempt to civilize the so-called 'small peoples' of the eastern parts of Russia and Siberia (Slezkine 1994). Similar policies were carried out in socialist Mongolia, where, as Caroline Humphrey writes, 'during the socialist period, lasting from 1921 to 1990, the Mongolian cities used to be associated with industrialization and development, and the sparsely populated countryside, home to villagers and nomadic pastoralists, was considered a space to be civilized and urbanized' (Humphrey and Sneath 1999, 301).

Soviet urbanization programmes were a continuation of the Russian colonial agenda, as Slezkine suggests, and they were indeed driven by the idea of creating socialist settlement patterns that were different than the capitalist ones (1994, 265). Scholarship on Central and Eastern Europe, however, points out that in the socialist satellite states, the urbanization process consisted mainly of the movement of millions of 'backward' peasants into urban areas, a process which amounted to the 'ruralization' or 'rurbanization' of the city (Lewin 1994; Rihtman-Augustin 1970, 34; Simić 1982). In Central and Eastern Europe, Bulgaria was the country that followed the early Soviet model most closely by inserting modernity into rural and traditional milieus. Modern conditions were to be brought to peripheries and traditional populations in order to have a lasting effect. During the 1970s, the Rhodopes were targeted specifically: traditional rural settlements were to be transformed by the introduction of electricity, water and asphalt roads, and in some cases to be replaced by new socialist 'urban' settlements, which, as local Communist Party officials promised, would 'twinkle with lights in the night'.

My research (especially the interviews I carried out with former Communist Party leaders) shows that the modernization process in the Rhodope Mountains in the 1970s combined elements of competition with the West, of national homogenization and, similarly to the early Soviet approach, of the dismantling of the distinction between urban and rural social organization. Similarly to Eugen Weber's 'making' of the French, this process was equally an attempt at 'making' the Bulgarians – that is, to bring about national homogenization by transforming Pomaks into Bulgarians or 'modern socialist Bulgarian citizens'. As some former communist politicians indicated to me, this project formed one of the 'flagships' of the Bulgarian socialist modernization programme.

The Rhodopes as the Bulgarian 'Periphery'

The Rhodopes, a mountainous area in the south of the country at the border with Greece, is traditionally perceived as the periphery or 'wilderness' *par excellence* by Bulgarians living in the lowlands of northern Thrace or in the urban centres such as Sofia or Plovdiv. There were sustained efforts to modernize, 'civilize' and 'domesticate' the region and integrate the Muslim population into the corpus of the Bulgarian nation since the early days of Bulgarian modern statehood.[4] Since the last decades of the nineteenth century the border between the Ottoman Empire and the newly emerging Bulgarian state ran through the Rhodope mountain range, making it into a frontier dividing two distinct cultural worlds.[5] Later, it developed into a bridgehead for Bulgarian expansion into western Thrace. During the Cold War, again, the Rhodopes continued to play the part of a 'border zone' between the capitalist and socialist world. From a nationalist perspective, apart from being a territorial border, the Rhodopes also form an internal frontier, the embodiment of the encounter between Christian Orthodoxy and Islam, between the Bulgarian nation and its own internal 'other' or 'national enemy'. As Maria Todorova argues (1997, 2002) the Bulgarian national myth represents the Pomaks as compatriots whose ancestors were forcefully converted to Islam during the Ottoman period.[6] This narrative also formed an important leitmotif behind the socialist modernization campaign.

Yet even if the Rhodopes were the ultimate periphery, in national discourse it was also seen as a source of pure Bulgarian culture.[7] For this reason, the Rhodopes and its Pomak population have attracted the interest of nationally oriented ethnographers from the early period of modern Bulgarian statehood onwards. Their aim was to present the region as part of Bulgarian state territory, naturally, historically and culturally (Konstantinov 1884, 1887; Shishkov 1914; Deliradev 1937).[8] It is not surprising, then, that the agents of socialist modernization, the local Communist Party bosses, also singled out the Rhodopes as a peripheral frontier which was to be brought back into the orbit of (Bulgarian) civilization through a programme of modernization and urbanization. Apart from this being an important ideological goal, there was also an element of competition with the capitalist 'West' located across the border. As one former communist official told me in an interview, 'The policy was that these villages should never be allowed to disappear. We said: We are a border district and we need large villages along the border to show that this is Bulgaria! Elsewhere [in the "capitalist" neighbourhood] the land is empty. One would look at our neighbours and say that there was no one there. The policy was indeed to keep them [the Muslim population] there [in the mountains].' As members of the former communist elites explained to me, the Bulgarian side of the border was supposed to flourish and 'twinkle by light in the night'. This was not just a nice image but also a symbol of modernization, the electrification of the country, electricity being one of the important 'fetishes' of socialist modernization.[9] The modern village settlement was supposed to have not only electricity, but also an urban plan, with proper asphalt streets, schools, medical facilities, clean water and a social centre. Local party officials understood the process as follows: 'As our neighbours were Greece, Yugoslavia and Turkey, it was necessary to keep an eye on the border regions and therefore electricity was task number one. All the settlements were electrified in order to create a contrast. Standing at the border, Greece is in darkness, while Bulgaria lights up. The village was my child. It should twinkle with lights at night.'

The modernization efforts and material improvements were aimed at socially uplifting the Muslim minority, making them into real 'Bulgarians' and bringing an end to their status as 'second-class' citizens as they were seen by the majority of society. The ideological imperative was to increase the living standard of the rural Muslim population, to introduce modern infrastructure in remote mountain villages, and to diminish the rural lifestyle and introduce urban culture. One of the most important priorities was the emancipation of women, which for local political figures such as Communist Party officials, agents of the Fatherland Front, managers of the cooperative farms and other municipal representatives became part of their own personal agendas. Yet these ambitions, echoing official plans and policies coming from the higher ranks of the party, were truly demanding. It was supposed to be achieved through education, through industrialization of agricultural production and (collective) work in newly introduced industries, but most importantly, everything 'had to be done fast'. As a former party official told me, 'We were backward and wanted to be better and faster than the USSR!' Communist bosses and local teachers were personally involved in urging Muslim children to attend school, the industrial production of electronic devices was introduced to employ women, and the construction of water cascades in the mountains was launched in order to give jobs to the men.[10]

What makes the Rhodopes special in the context of these modernization programmes is that the process was accompanied by forms of assimilation, aimed at diminishing the cultural and social distinctiveness of the Pomaks. As part of this effort, during the 1970s Turkish or Arabic first and second names were changed into Bulgarian ones, and religious dress codes (for women) were banned. Everyday traditional and rural practices linked to the transhumant economy, predominant before World War II, were targeted through collectivization and the organized resettlement of Pomaks from their old shepherd settlements located in the higher altitudes of the mountains into newly created urban centres established in the valleys.[11] Local officials conceptualized this assimilation process as a 'fight against rurality, traditions and backwardness', rather than as a fight against 'religion' or the 'capitalist enemy'. Nevertheless, Islam was seen as backward. In the interviews I carried out, some of the officials told how they had been annoyed by the 'peasant dress' (*selski drechi*) of local Muslim women. The expression 'peasant dress' referred to the rural and religious character of female clothing, with Muslim elements such as the *shalvari* and *feredzhe*.[12] Many of them still vividly remember how they disliked the local town, which had been unbearably 'rural' and 'ugly' for them.

Urbanization: Transforming Villages into Cities 'At Any Cost'

The settlement where I carried out my fieldwork was established as a 'model' socialist village in the context of the socialist modernization and urbanization programme. The first settler came to the village in the 1950s after the process of forced collectivization had begun. Listening to Pomak narratives, it is clear that collectivization affected them badly. People had to hand over their numerous livestock and were often forced to leave their homes in the mountain hamlets. The urbanization process gathered full pace in the late 1960s and reached its peak in the mid-1970s, when migration into the new village was accompanied by assimilation measures aimed at making Pomaks into 'proper Bulgarians', for instance by prohibiting women to wear the Muslim veil. During the 1980s, the village grew, extending considerably beyond its original borders; in the modernizers' minds and plans it was meant to become a real 'town'. With the collapse of the communist regime, however, the development of this socialist experiment ended.

The location of this new settlement corresponded with the precepts of modernization – it was to house a mobile labour force meant to meet the demands of the locally developing industry. According to the recollections I registered, the mobile labour force was especially necessary at socialist construction sites such as the water cascades, and for the seasonal agricultural campaigns in tobacco and potato production. Hence the location for the new village was chosen at the intersection of a narrow railway track and transit road. However, in spite of the settlement being promoted as a 'model' village, it was not an ideal place of residence. Located at the bottom of a deep mountain valley it had a cold microclimate, with harsh winds blowing in all seasons and an overpowering skyline composed of the contours of hills and mountain edges. Unlike settlements located at higher altitudes, the soil and the microclimate of Modrava did not offer the conditions for growing fruits or vegetables; they were suitable only for potatoes and beans. Even so, former party bosses talked in positive and aesthetical terms about the settlement being a 'beautiful', 'well-ordered', 'proper' and 'genuine' village. Also, the inhabitants referred to their village as a 'properly ordered place', using the term 'town' (*grad*) for it. As one villager said on the way back from our trip to his former home in the mountain hamlet, 'Here it is better. Here it is like in a town. Up there [in the former settlements] are only bushes.'

Another villager, having bitter memories of the assimilation campaign in the 1970s, recalled the 1980s nevertheless as a period of relative prosperity. At that time he lived in Modrava and he still has good memories of the positive outcomes of the urbanization project:

> And we liked it here; it was nicer. Here they let us build the streets more in a row, not like we used to have in the mountains, one by one. Here the streets are clearly demarcated, on the right and also on the left side. And so on… Another advantage is the transport connections. Before, every time you went somewhere you had to walk to reach some transport connection, but here this is a centre – in one word it is like a town!

In spite of these positive memories, attitudes and opinions about the socialist past continue to be ambivalent; they vary according to the context. Many people, for instance, refuse to visit the hamlets which they abandoned forty years ago, because of emotional reasons. The same people on other occasions refer to their former hamlets as 'proper, nice, clear places to live', which suggests a certain degree of rural nostalgia. They regret the socialist resettlement policies that were driven by the desire to overcome the dispersed dwelling patterns in the traditional hamlets, which prevented children to go to school during winter. As one former party officer told me, 'The most important motive was to lift the standard of living and existence. The policy was to offer economic progress for both groups, Christians and Muslims alike, equalizing their standard of living.' The local party institutions pursued their policies through administrative measures, such as rules preventing the construction of new residential houses in the old settlements in the mountain areas. Inhabitants of the shepherd hamlets were not given building permits for houses to be built at a distance from the village centre, as the goal was to provide all settlements with full infrastructure, electricity, schools, proper communications and water supply. This was not easy to achieve in the remoter areas, and dispersed settlement patterns only made the problem worse. As one party leader and 'father' of the new socialist model village said, 'You cannot introduce electricity around the mountains!'

Hence new houses had to be built within reach of the available communications and infrastructure. Restrictions on building activities in the hamlets, material benefits given in the new settlements, together with the rather oppressive measures of the assimilation campaign, all contributed to people abandoning their houses and moving to the new settlement in the valley. It amounted to a policy of centralization and concentration, creating a new settlement absorbing the populations from a number of surrounding villages at an old intersection of communications crossing the mountains (during Ottoman times an inn (*han*) had been located there, and during the 1920s a military point with a small wood factory nearby). Despite administrative and logistical difficulties, state-sponsored development produced a positive outlook for the new settlement, which meant that it suffered little from the economic crisis in the late 1980s. People were able to build large houses and had a regular income from local agricultural (especially potatoes) and industrial production (electronic devices, the construction of water works and cascades, and mining). This situation of a relative flourishing local economy came to an abrupt end with the collapse of the communist regime.

Postsocialist Transition: The End of a Socialist 'Model' Village

Nowadays, the settlement's economy has completely and utterly stagnated. The asphalt road goes only halfway through the village, and the water is not always running. The socialist project of modernizing the Rhodopes has come to a halt, which means that it is one of the regions in Bulgaria hit hardest by the consequences of the economic and social downturn of the 1990s.[13] Sources of income dried up and industrial production and construction came to an end, which led to an unemployment rate of 80 per cent at the end of the decade.[14] In this final section I will describe how the dramatic economic situation of the 1990s forced people to develop new survival strategies, primarily engaging in the informal economy, seasonal labour and the alleged unregulated trade in natural resources, sold on increasingly globalized markets.

The informal trade in natural resources became an important source of seasonal income for the local population.[15] Natural resources such as herbs and mushrooms were collected, stored, dried and processed into sellable commodities in the spare rooms of the many large houses that had been built as part of the socialist development programme. Thus the spaces, assets and facilities that were inherited from the period of socialist modernization were appropriated and made available for economic activities that emerged in response to its failure. In this respect, postsocialist transition can be seen as an 'epilogue' to communism – that is, the socialist modernization project.

Apart from the trade in natural products, for a limited period there was another source of income in the local milk factory (*mandra*), the only local private enterprise that emerged after the end of socialism. Since the collapse of the local cooperative, there were at least two attempts to turn the remains of a former socialist factory into a running business for the local production of milk. An entrepreneur who was an outsider took the initiative, processing milk supplied by village households. Previously milk produced at home was consumed within the household or processed into home-made dairy products, which were bartered for commodities that were otherwise difficult to produce such as fruits or vegetables. The *mandra* provided an opportunity for the inhabitants, especially for the women, to supplement the household budgets. The *mandra* was started up in the derelict premises of a former socialist enterprise, and it utilized the buildings and parts of the equipment, such as the cellars (used for the maturing of cheese), the electric generators and the pasteurization vessels. During the period of my fieldwork the firm employed five people. Yet the production process, which is complex in terms of logistics and time management, was not well organized. Mostly, the firm's employees simply wasted time waiting for the prerequisite necessities to arrive. People were awaiting either the delivery of milk or the cash to purchase the milk from the producers, or other items which were needed to complete the production process, such as plastic bottles and labels.

The entire process was characterized by bricolage and improvisation, using the equipment inherited from the socialist period supplemented by new pieces which were introduced during the transition period. The milk was pasteurized in two old vessels, and an old rusty wood boiler was used for part of the production process, which requires a stable temperature for a fixed number of hours. Plastic wrapping and a gas fire were used for the packaging of bottles. Every step in the production process was attended by the entire work force. The colouring and flavouring of the final 'fruit milk' product was almost ritually performed by the entrepreneur himself in presence of all members of his staff. They gathered around one of the vessels, while he, smoking a cigarette, ceremonially added drops of artificial flavour and colour (raspberry and blueberry) into the milk. This improvised character of the production process was often a source of what could be called 'postmodern' self-irony on the part of the workers. Making mocking comments on the improvised nature of the *mandra*, people reflected on their own depressed economic situation. The financing of the business went mostly through a lease chain between the boss and one employee. Occasionally cash had to be borrowed from a third person while the employees often backed up the purchase of the milk with their own money just to keep the business running.

Despite these difficulties, the *mandra* performed an important social role in the village community. In a situation where most inhabitants were unemployed, the *mandra* workers managed to improve their social status. In addition, the *mandra* provided an opportunity to socialize, which others lacked during the period of economic collapse. It gave people a sense of purpose, of having a job and a work place, and of being part of a collective. Because of this, working hours were often voluntarily extended to almost literally 24/7, as the *mandra* provided a venue for *moabet* (conversation). In spite of the fact that everybody else knew that those working in the *mandra* received an extremely poor salary, having a job in the *mandra* was regarded with envy. The social status gained through it extended to the members of the entire family – that is, the household of the *mandradzhiyas* (*mandra* workers). It was not necessarily the (almost negligible) economic advantage which caused envy but the social status and prestige, the advantages achieved through that job, and above all the membership of a 'working collective'.

Employees of the *mandra* positively evaluated their work experience. With only a small amount of exaggeration one can say that these people were working for free, exchanging their labour not for money but for social comfort and prestige. During the crisis of the 1990s, when the entire country went through a period of deep decline, in a situation where there was nothing else to do but to engage in selling natural products or sparse possibilities of seasonal migrant labour, a company, as nonprofitable and bankrupted as it seemed, was regarded as offering at least a spark of hope, security and order. In contrast to others, whose activities were limited to the unpredictable seasonal work, they could at least, for a short time, maintain some semblance of a 'normal life', in terms of the everyday rhythm of activities, income, status and social relations. All these were aspects of a 'normal' life people remembered well from the previous socialist times.

The *mandra* stopped working shortly after I finished my fieldwork. The *mandradzhiyas* went back to collecting natural products and to casual subsistence agriculture in their gardens and tiny plots. The entrepreneur left the region. Although the *mandra* never resumed its production, people fondly recalled 'how we used to work together in the *mandra*' two years later when I visited the village again. With hindsight, the fact that Modrava had been a socialist model village may have contributed to the severity of the economic collapse, in terms of the disintegrating social fabric of the village. In comparison with other neighbouring villages, Modrava had not developed the same degree of social or community organization – it lacked the religiously based social cohesion organized around traditional celebrations and rituals, and it did not have grassroots activities which would have provided a vehicle for sustaining social life. Despite receiving support from outside to build a new mosque, the village failed to establish any meaningful religious community life. Although being located near a main road, the village has remained marginal due to the general decline of infrastructure in Bulgaria in the 1990s. All of these elements are exemplary of the place's hybrid character between village and town, tradition and modernity, and development and decline. The region as a whole remained caught halfway in between tradition and modernity, countryside and town, and community and association, as Ferdinand Tönnies (1955) would call it.

Semantics of Time in the Postsocialist Village

Simmel, in his well-known essay 'The Metropolis and Mental Life', explains how the modern city experience fundamentally differs from that of the small town. When talking about the latter, Simmel writes, 'The smaller the circle which forms our environment and the more limited the relationships which have the possibility of transcending the boundaries, the more anxiously the small community watches over the deeds, the conduct of life and the attitudes of the individual' (Simmel 1971, 333). Simmel's description seems to perfectly fit the situation in Modrava. We could argue that 'modernity', as described and defined by Koselleck and Simmel, never really took hold over the village. Despite the modernization of every possible aspect of life, the industrialization of the economy, the emancipation of women, and the urbanization of the landscape and settlements imposed and subsidized by the socialist state, it never lasted. If at all, the socialist goal of taking 'modernity' to the countryside, spreading urban conditions and city culture into villages and towns only partially succeeded. Social structures never gained a truly urban character, even though modernization brought enormous material achievements and an improvement of living standards.

The development of the place was brought to an abrupt halt with the collapse of the socialist system. As part of this, the experience and perception of time has fundamentally changed. High unemployment and general decline has slowed down village life to an extent that it has come to a complete standstill. At the time of my fieldwork, the only events marking some kind of rhythm of the day were the evening *azans* (prayers) from the newly built mosque and the arrival and departure of the train which passed twice a day nearby the village. Unemployment and survival had changed people's daily routines; the sparse agriculture and informal trade required a different type of schedule as most of these activities took place irregularly and only seasonally on a rather unpredictable basis, and hence life during the remaining days was characterized by deep inertia. The situation is well illustrated by the following story, which shows that Modrava somehow missed the 'train' of modernity, in the most literal sense.

On one day during my fieldwork the locals were preparing to go to the weekly market in the town. The only means of transportation was the morning train. Time was fast approaching that my friends and I were supposed to leave the house in order to catch it. But no one took the initiative, as everyone was just waiting for 'the neighbours' to leave. And so it happened that everybody was waiting for everybody else. Finally when the train had arrived at the station people realized what happened and that they were about to miss the train. Everybody started running, the whole village hurried to catch the train, and fortunately the train waited until the last person got on board in spite of the timetable. The situation created a strange atmosphere of shared euphoria. For most villagers it seemed that this running was the only running they ever had done in their lives as the story 'how we ran to catch the train' was told again and again for several weeks to come.

This story is an appropriate metaphor for the socioeconomic situation brought about by the failure of the socialist development project. It also demonstrates the fact that despite being connected to global social and economic flows, 'time' in the village did not gain any new qualities and never really accelerated.

The fast-track socialist modernization failed in the end, and together with that time gained a different dimension, quality and value. It is clear that even though socialist modernization in Bulgaria was modelled (rather unusually in the context of Central and Eastern Europe at that time) on the early Soviet example, with an emphasis on fast social and cultural change achieved through mobilization of huge human and financial recourses, in the case of Modrava the process got stuck halfway: society remained caught between tradition and modernity and the urban and rural. It provides a clear case of halted development (Ferguson 1994), a situation where the dichotomy between rural and urban is blurred, where social structures and experiences form a hybrid between rurality and urbanity. The Pomak inhabitants are not rural anymore, but they are not urban either.

Even though it ended in failure, the socialist period of development had an enormous impact in the Rhodopes, and has left behind an infrastructure on the basis of which, during the transitional period, people tried to build a new or 'normal' society even though it had rather become a rural backwater. As my case study shows, after socialist development ended, people did not return to their original presocialist or 'natural' habitat and economic strategies, but continued to operate in the current ones. Thus, the process of socialist modernization, even though it came to a sudden halt, is irreversible. Seen from this perspective, the period of transition is the last (and sad) chapter in a thwarted history of socialist modernization: not a journey from 'socialism' to 'capitalism', but rather from socialism to its epilogue. Unlike the other cases analysed in this volume, the global connections emerging during the transformations of the 1990s did not bring any major advantages and opportunities to the local community. Although they provided some limited opportunities to develop certain survival strategies and means to overcome a major economic crisis, the process also erected new and reinforced old boundaries. As a consequence, the peripheral character of the region was reinforced and the local communities found themselves again at the margins of global social and economic networks.

Notes

1 The term 'Pomaks' has negative connotations for the members of this minority as well as the majority population in Bulgaria. However, Western scholarship uses it when referring to 'Bulgarian-speaking Muslims'. To comply with this general practice the name Pomaks is used here as well. The Muslim community in Bulgaria comprises three subgroups: the Turks, the Pomaks and the Muslim Roma. Ethnic Turks represent the largest group with around 600,000 people, 8.8 per cent of the population (http://www.nsi.bg/census2011/PDOCS2/Census2011final_en.pdf, accessed 5 February 2013). The Bulgarian National Census 2011 does not acknowledge the Bulgarian-speaking Muslims as an ethnic category; however other sources estimate the number of Pomaks to be at around 200,000, while there are 140,000 Muslim Roma. (Neuburger 2004, 20; for comparable figures, see Daskalov 2005; Eberhardt 1996; Georgieva 1998; Konstantinov 1997; Todorova 1997; Stoyanov 1998; Eminov 1997).

2 For the sake of comparison, see for instance Duijzings (2000, 106–131); Bougarel and Clayer (2001).

3 Throughout the chapter localities have been given pseudonyms in order to grant anonymity to the respondents. For the same reason individuals have not been named in person. I would like to thank my respondents for sharing their life experiences with me.
4 On the assimilation policies applied by the Bulgarian nation-state, see Georgiev and Trifonov (1995); Neuburger (2004).
5 Before the emergence of nation-states in the Balkans the mental maps were markedly different, and the Rhodopes were rather considered a 'suburb' of the capital Constantinople; see Popović (1986). An interesting nineteenth-century image of the Rhodopes from a Central European perspective can be found in Jireček (1888).
6 For a literary classic representing the Turks as a national enemy in the context of the Rhodopes, see Donchev (1964).
7 The novels of Nikolay Haytov (1965, 1974) provide examples of representations of the Rhodopes as 'wilderness' and at the same time as a source of true national culture.
8 See also in Todorova (2002, 187).
9 About the importance of electricity as a symbol of socialist modernity, see Scott (1998, 166). For an extensive study of the cultural and political meanings of electrification in the context of the Soviet Union, see Coppersmith (1992) and Bailes (1978).
10 For a contemporary account of socialist development, which former party officials often referred to in the interviews, see Strandzhev (1971) and Kirova et al. (1984).
11 Transhumant practices were slowly disappearing with the establishment of the new state borders in the late nineteenth and early twentieth century. The final blow to the transhumant economy was the collectivization process carried out in the 1950s. For the transhumant economy of the Pomaks, see for instance Dimitrov and Stoykov (1963), Shishkov (1903, 1936).
12 *Shalvari* is the local name for the specific trousers worn by Pomak women, while *feredzhe* is the name for a long veil covering the Muslim woman's face.
13 For the postsocialist transition in the Rhodopes, see for instance Cellarius (2003); Tomova (2000).
14 On the situation in the Muslim areas of the Bulgarian south during the postsocialist transition, see Neuburger (2013, 232–3) and Ghodsee (2010).
15 On the informal economies with natural products in the Rhodopes see also Kressel (2010, 115–20).

References

Bailes, Kendall. 1978. *Technology and Society under Lenin and Stalin: Origins of the Soviet Technical Intelligentsia, 1917–1941*. Princeton: Princeton University Press.
Bougarel, Xavier and Nathalie Clayer, eds. 2001. *Le nouvel islam balkanique: Les musulmans, acteurs du post-communisme, 1990–2000*. Paris: Maisonneuve and Larose.
Brunnbauer, Ulf. 2004. *Gebirgsgesellschaften auf dem Balkan: Wirtschaft und Familienstrukturen im Rhodopengebirge (19./20. Jahrhundert)*. Vienna: Böhlau.
Brunnbauer, Ulf and Karin Taylor. 2004. 'Creating a "Socialist Way of Life": Family and Reproduction Policies in Bulgaria, 1944–1989'. *Continuity and Change* 19: 283–312.
Cellarius, Barbara A. 2003. 'Property Restitution and Natural Resource Use in the Rhodope Mountains, Bulgaria'. In *The Postsocialist Agrarian Question: Property Relations and the Rural Condition*, edited by Chris Hann et al., 189–218. Münster: LIT Verlag.

Coppersmith, Jonathan. 1992. *The Electrification of Russia, 1880–1926*. Ithaca New York: Cornell University Press.

Creed, Gerald. 1998. *Domesticating Revolution: From Socialist Reform to Ambivalent Transition in a Bulgarian village*. University Park: Pennsylvania State University Press.

Daskalov, Rumen. 2005. *Bulgarskoto obshtestvo, 1878–1939*, vol. 1. Sofia: Gutenberg.

Deliradev, Pavel. 1937. *Rodopite kato selishtna oblast i planinska systema: Istoriko-geografski ocherk*. Sofia: Gladstone.

Dimitrov, Strashimir and Roumen Stoykov. 1963. 'Excerpts from a Register of Fiefs in the Western Rhodopi and the Seres Area'. In *Rhodopi Collection*, vol. 1, 283–324. Sofia: Bulgarian Academy of Sciences.

Donchev, Anton. 1964. *Vreme razdelno: Istoricheski roman*. Sofia: Pisatel.

Duijzings, Ger. 2000. *Religion and the Politics of Identity in Kosovo*. London: Hurst.

Eberhardt, Piotr. 1996. *Między Rosją a Niemcami: Przemiany narodowościowe w Europie Środkowo-Wschodnej w XX w.* Warsaw: PWN.

Eminov, Ali. 1997. *Turkish and Other Muslim Minorities in Bulgaria*. London: Hurst.

Ferguson, James. 1994. *Anti-politics Machine: 'Development', Depoliticization and Bureaucratic Power in Lesotho*. Minneapolis: University of Minnesota Press.

Georgiev, Vasil and Staiko Trifonov. 1995. *Pokrastvaneto na bulgarite mohamedani 1912–1913: Dokumenti*. Sofia: Akademichno Izdatelstvo 'Prof. Marin Drinov'.

Georgieva, Tzvetana. 1998. 'Pomaks: Muslim Bulgarians'. In *Communities and Identities in Bulgaria*, edited by Anna Krasteva, 221–38. Bologna: A. Longo Editore.

Ghodsee, Kristen. 2010. *Muslim Lives in Eastern Europe*. Princeton: Princeton University Press.

Haytov, Nikolay. 1965. *Shumki od Gabar: Kniga za Rodopite*. Sofia: Narodna Mladezh.

———. 1974. *Rodopski vlastelnini: Istoricheski ochertsi*. Plovdiv: Izdatelstvo Christo G. Danov.

Humphrey, Caroline and David Sneath. 1999. *The End of Nomadism? Society, State, and the Environment in Inner Asia*. Durham, NC: Duke University Press.

Jireček, Konstantin. 1888. *Cesty po Bulharsku*. Praha: Matice česká.

Kirova, Krasimira, Atanas Lyutov, Kiril Kiryakov, Dimitar Kehayov, Kolio Kolev, Galab Georgiev, Vasil Vasilev, Kiril Voynov, Violeta Popova, Ivan Ivanov, eds. 1984. *Dinamika na vazchoda. Blagoevgradski okrug*. Sofia: Partizdat.

Konstantinov, Hristo. 1884. 'Obshestevnite zabavleniya i praznenstva u Pomacite v Chepino'. *Slavovi Gori* I (III).

———. 1887. *Nepokornite sela v rodopskite planini*, vol. 1, *1878–1879*. Veliko Tarnovo.

———. 1893. 'Pisma od Rodopite. Pismo XIV. Istoricheski pregled na pokrainata Chepino'. *Svoboda* VII (7 April). Reprinted in Khr. P. Konstantinov, 'Chepino (Edno bilgarsko kraishte v severozapadnite razkloneniya na Rodopskite planini)'. *Sbornik za Narodni Umotvoreniya* 15 (1898): 230–31.

Konstantinov, Julian. 1997. 'Strategies for Sustaining a Vulnerable Identity. The Case of Bulgarian Pomaks'. In *Muslim Identity and the Balkan State*, edited by Hugh Poulton and Suha Taji-Farouki, 33–54. London: Hurst.

Koselleck, Reinhart. 2004 (1979). *Futures Past: On the Semantics of Historical Time*. New York: Columbia University Press.

———. 2006. 'Crisis'. *Journal of the History of Ideas* 67: 357–400.

Kotkin, Stephen. 1995. *Magnetic Mountain: Stalinism as a Civilization*. Berkeley: University of California Press.

Kressel, Gideon, ed. 2010. *Anthropological Studies in Post-Socialist Micro-Economies in the Balkans: Creative Survival Adaptations in Bulgaria and Yugoslavia*. Lewiston: Edwin Mellen Press.

Lewin, Moshe. 1994 (1985). *The Making of the Soviet System: Essays in the Social History of Interwar Russia*. New York: New Press.

Neuburger, Mary. 2004. *The Orient Within: Muslim Minorities and the Negotiation of Nationhood in Modern Bulgaria*. Ithaca: Cornell University Press.

_____. 2013. *Balkan Smoke: Tobacco and the Making of Modern Bulgaria*. Ithaca and London: Cornell University Press.

Popović, Alexandre. 1986. *L'islam balkanique: Les musulmans du sud-est européen dans la période post-ottomane*. Wiesbaden: Harrassowitz.

Rihtman-Augustin, Dunja. 1970. 'Tradicionalna kultura i suvremene vrijednosti'. *Kulturni radnik* 23: 26–45.

Scott, James C. 1998. *Seeing Like a State: How Certain Schemes to Improve the Human Condition Have Failed*. New Haven: Yale University Press.

Shishkov, Stoiu. 1903. 'Rodopskite Pomatsi ot obshstveno: ikonimichesko gledishte i prichinite na izslevaneto im'. *Rodopski napredak* 1 (5): 28–35.

_____. 1914. *Pomatsite v trite Bulgarski oblasti: Trakiya, Makedoniya i Miziya*. Plovdiv: Makedoniya.

_____. 1936. *Bulgaromohamedanite (Pomatsi): Istoriko-zemepisen i narodnauchen pregled v obrazi*. Plovdiv.

Simić, Andrei. 1982. 'Urbanization and Modernization in Yugoslavia: Adaptive and Maladaptive Aspects of Traditional Culture'. In *Urban Life in Mediterranean Europe: Anthropological Perspectives*, edited by Michael Kenny and David Kertzer, 203–24. Urbana: University of Illinois Press.

Simmel, Georg. 1971. 'Metropolis and mental life'. In *On Individuality and Social Forms: Selected Writings*, edited by Donald N. Levine, 324–9. Chicago: University of Chicago Press.

Slezkine, Yuri. 1994. *Arctic Mirrors: Russia and the Small Peoples of the North*. Ithaca: Cornell University Press.

Stoyanov, Valeri. 1998. *Turskoto naselenie v Bulgaria mezhdu poliusite na ethnicheskata politika*. Sofia.

Strandzhev, Kosta. 1971. *Goreshti verchove, ocherki za stroitelite na kaskadata 'Belmeken-Sestrimo'*. Plovdiv: Christo G. Danov.

Taylor, Karin. 2006. *Let's Twist Again: Youth and Leisure in Socialist Bulgaria*. Münster: LIT Verlag.

Todorova, Maria. 1997. 'Identity (Trans)formation among Pomaks in Bulgaria'. In *Beyond Borders: Remaking Cultural Identities in the New East and Central Europe*, edited by László Kurti and Juliet Langman, 63–82. Oxford: Westview Press.

_____. 2002. 'Conversion to Islam as a Trope in Bulgarian Historiography, Fiction and Film'. In *Penser la transition/Rethinking the Transition*, edited by Ivaylo Znepolski, Koprinka Tchervenkova and Alexander Kiossev, 181–205. Sofia: St Kliment Ohridski University Press.

Tomova, Ilona. 2000. 'The Rhodope Mountains in the 1990s: Development Tendencies'. In *Bulgaria: Social and Cultural Landscapes*, edited by Christian Giordano, Dobrinka Kostova and Evelyne Lohmann-Minka, 129–43. Fribourg: Fribourg University Press.

Tönnies, Ferdinand. 1955. *Community and Association (Gemeinschaft und Gesellschaft)*. London: Routledge and Kegan Paul.

Tucker, Robert, ed. 1975. *The Lenin Anthology*. New York: W. W. Norton.

Weber, Eugen. 1976. *Peasants into Frenchmen: The Modernization of Rural France, 1870–1914*. Stanford: Stanford University Press.

Chapter 6

NO WEALTH WITHOUT NETWORKS AND PERSONAL TRUST: NEW CAPITALIST AGRARIAN ENTREPRENEURS IN THE DOBRUDZHA

Christian Giordano and Dobrinka Kostova

At first sight the title of our chapter may seem paradoxical and controversial, especially for a reader familiar with Francis Fukuyama's work. The main thesis of this Japanese American author in his famous book *Trust: The Social Virtues and the Creation of Prosperity* is that, from a socioeconomic standpoint, individual and social prosperity cannot be created on the basis of purely personal trust relationships, as they are essentially located in the private sphere. According to Fukuyama, individual and social prosperity can only emerge in conditions of impersonal and systemic trust anchored in the social organizations and institutions that make up the public sphere. For such organizational structures, the neoliberal thinker Fukuyama focuses mainly on the democratic institutions of civil society (alliances, associations, NGOs, parties, unions, etc.), but also the state's institutions should not be left out as instruments of legitimate authority. Fukuyama's theoretical model posits an ideal-typical division between 'high-trust' and 'low-trust' societies. Although this dichotomy is rhetorically effective and to a degree scientifically plausible, from an anthropological or ethnographic standpoint it should not be received uncritically as it contains obvious as well as hidden ideas of an ethnocentric nature which should not be unquestionably accepted. Despite the undeniable heuristic significance of Fukuyama's theoretic framework, anthropologists ought to be critical of the evident 'Orientalist' (Said 1978) and respectively 'Balkanist' (Todorova 1997) connotations inherent to the dichotomy of high-trust versus low-trust societies.

Next, it could be pointed out that Fukuyama's division between high-trust and low-trust societies has created a limited theory, as he ascribes a moral value to the first social type that is lacking in the second. The positive human and social qualities that make up this moral value, however, are the same ones in which liberal-capitalist models (with the exception of Japan) of occidental and especially Northern European and North American origin are grounded. Fukuyama automatically qualifies all societies which consider the Western way to be either socially not desirable or culturally inadequate, or which follow it only conditionally, as low-trust societies, and as such carrying a stigma. Thus, Fukuyama's ethnocentrism is clearly discernible, since he obviously aims to confirm the occidental model's moral superiority as well as its socioeconomic supremacy because of the presence of specific systemic trust structures that generate wealth. Given the legitimate doubts about the ideological argumentation connected to Fukuyama's above-mentioned theoretic model, from an anthropological standing the question is whether the assumption that low-trust societies in comparison to high-trust societies are generally plagued by mistrust, and therefore less likely to develop forms of cooperation, can be empirically verified. From here, we can define the specific question of whether and to what extent other virtues are important and if other forms of trust, cooperation and eventually the accumulation of wealth are observable in low-trust societies.

In order to counter Fukuyama's thesis, our analysis uses empirical data relating to the socioeconomic activities of successful entrepreneurs in the agricultural sector of the Bulgarian Dobrudzha region to exemplify that socioeconomic prosperity is entirely possible in low-trust societies in which systemic mistrust is undoubtedly present. In contrast to Fukuyama's opinion, here wealth stems from the development of trust and cooperation structures mainly based on personal relationships. We will also show that agrarian entrepreneurs in the Bulgarian Dobrudzha region did not adhere in full to the Western model of modernity, which Fukuyama implies to be the best road to prosperity. In this sense, our case confirms that modernity can and should be considered as a *plurality* in accordance with sociologist Shmuel N. Eisenstadt's concept of multiple modernities (2002).

The Postsocialist Agricultural Reform: A Return to the Future?

The decollectivization of farmable land has been one of the foremost problems of postsocialist governments in Eastern Europe, from Estonia to Bulgaria (Abrahams 1996; Stewart 1998; Creed 1998; Verdery 2003). Even though the process differed and varied in each of these countries, in most cases the new governments enacted the return of the land to the original owners as a necessary act of justice towards the people who had been illegally deprived of their property. These owners were viewed as the victims of a brutal and cruel policy of illegitimate previous (socialist) governments. In many cases the entire process was based on the following two specific agro-political objectives: a) to restore presocialist ownership relationships; and b) to establish family-operated farms as the basis of the postsocialist agricultural sector.

The official intent of providing a necessary compensation for previous suffering conceals the rather covert wish to reverse history. At first, the main idea was to recreate traditional peasant society and the presocialist village community, which had been wiped out by fifty years of collectivism. They were seen as the cradle and guardian of true national values, virtues and customs. After the breakdown of socialism, certain politicians immediately embraced a traditional village ideology, arguing for the restoration of the Bulgarian nation as a 'small nation of small farmers'. Consciously or unconsciously, a part of the political, bureaucratic and intellectual elite, with the support of well-meaning experts from the West, advocated a national-populist agricultural political policy which would take the nation back to the times prior to World War II. Even though the *paysannerie pensée* of this political and ideological programme held hardly any similarities with the actual *paysannerie vécue* that surfaced after socialist times, it was conceived as an abstraction that was to serve as a benchmark for the formulation of the land reform laws.

Bulgaria is an excellent example of how land laws and their application shortly after the fall of the Berlin Wall intended to bring back the presocialist past. The presocialist and primordial notion of inalienable land ownership – praised by famous writers and artists of the interwar period and politically represented by the Bulgarian Agrarian National Union under the charismatic leadership of Alexander Stamboliyski – proved to be a myth which socialism could neither demolish nor outlive. This myth was rooted in the presocialist reality of extremely fragmented land ownership in Bulgaria, in which only 9 per cent of holdings was above 10 hectares. Stamboliyski's 1921 land reforms further contributed to this fragmentation as they required the sale of holdings above 30 hectares to the state, if the family was not cultivating the land itself, after which the accumulated land was given to landless families (*Bulgaria: 20th Century*, 312). However, in the context of an inefficient credit system, bad infrastructure, backward technology and the devastating consequences of lost wars, efficient agriculture could only be realized through cooperatives in the times before socialism and collectivization during socialism.

In the postsocialist period, however, this ideological instrument of small family-based land ownership was powerful, and the 1991 Land Law (Law on Agricultural Ownership and Use of Land) and its numerous amendments (for instance in 1992 and 1995) managed to provide the conditions to dissolve the agricultural collectives which formed the socioeconomic basis of Bulgaria's entire socialist agricultural sector, as well as the subsequent re-establishment of the precarious state of affairs concerning farmland which had existed in 1946. Analogous though not identical policies were introduced in neighbouring Romania, to restore the land to farmers who owned it before the collectivization (Stewart 1998; Verdery 2003). But this meant re-establishing the excessive fragmentation of land property characteristic of those days. The expectation was that the new legal landowners, following the philosophy of the reformers, would take on the role of small farmers as in presocialist times.

This attempt to place the past in the present and even in the future through a reversion of history, and simultaneously revitalize the mythical figure of the traditional Bulgarian peasant in postsocialism, has proven to be highly problematic, just as in other countries. It should be mentioned that the total lack of land registers in many of the Dobrudzha villages and the poor organization of the land registry offices in other parts of Bulgaria made it extremely difficult to define the borders of the land parcels as they had been in 1946. In several cases the local land commissions thought that asking the older members of the community to reconstruct the size and location of the individually owned land parcels would suffice. However, since human memory tends to be selective, as Maurice Halbwachs has shown, it is not surprising that the method chosen by state institutions, especially in the context of mistrust that the Bulgarian society typifies, was considered arbitrary and dubious. The upshot was an astonishing number of protests, court proceedings, pleas and disputes, not only between the state and the people involved, but also between former or new individual landowners. Contentious cases were handed over to the courts, but these were understaffed, did not enforce the new and constantly changing terms of the land reform laws, and were therefore unable to solve the cases quickly. The land commissions were soon blamed of siding with different parties and of dishonesty (if not corruption), and for many citizens the bad repute of the state's courts was once again confirmed. The perception of the permanent and widespread judicial uncertainty increased, especially among rural inhabitants of the Bulgarian Dobrudzha, as they already felt a deep mistrust of the official powers, in particular the courts.

Another serious problem with the land reform was the fact that redistributing the land according to the state of affairs in 1946 resulted in an extremely fragmented landscape, as we have pointed out. This was also true in the Bulgarian Dobrudzha where fragmentation had been a reality since 1878, when the Turks, retreating from the war, abandoned their land. In 1891, the Bulgarian minister of finances reported to the National Assembly (*sabranie*) that there were 26,315 vacant plots in the country, many of them in the Dobrudzha and most of them under two hectares in size (Teneva 1979, 1). Until 1878, when it was granted autonomy *de facto*, putting an end to Ottoman domination, Bulgaria applied Ottoman legislation – especially the law of 1865 regulating land inheritance. However, this regulation concerned only common and not private land, which is understandable because before 1840 Bulgarians did not own private land; it was only with the Tanzimat reforms beginning in 1839 that Muslim and non-Muslim subjects of the Ottoman Empire were able to enjoy legal equality and that Bulgarians were able to buy land themselves (Tanir 2005, 8).

In 1877 and the following years a transfer of land ownership took place, and only a decade later three quarters of the arable land was owned by Bulgarians. After 1878, during the so-called period of 'Europeanization', foreign law policies and practices from the western part of the Old Continent were imported. The process of creating independent state laws affected not only public administration and state and government structures, but also private ownership relationships. The new inheritance and land law from 1889 stated that the land was to be divided equally among all heirs, a circumstance which led to the progressive fragmentation of land parcels. To decrease the fragmentation of land ownership, the law was modified in 1896 (article 240), allowing men to buy out the land inherited by women. The law was changed once more in 1906, according to which men inherited twice more land than women if the inherited land was less than 50 hectares. The alarming trend of fragmentation, which paved the way for some serious socioeconomic consequences (Bell 1977, 13), was also clearly recognized by the then prime minister, Alexander Stamboliyski. Before his assassination in 1923, he drafted reforms for the consolidation of the class of small landowners. The land fragmentation reached its peak in 1946 when 92 per cent of all Bulgarian farms were smaller than 10 hectares, about 7 per cent of the land parcels were smaller than 20 hectares, and only 1 per cent of the landowners had more than 20 hectares (Minkov and Lazov 1979, 12). The objective of the 1991 land reform to return to the state of affairs in 1946 meant reintroducing the small-scale production of the past and worsening the fragmentation – many of the original owners of the small land parcels had died and their heirs had to divide the land even further between themselves.

The third fundamental problem with the return of land ownership to its 1946 state of affairs was that the land reform's beneficiaries were people who had little or no experience or knowledge when it came to agricultural work. The socialist industrialization of the late 1940s caused massive migration from villages to cities, producing the greatest population reduction in the agricultural sector within all East European satellite states (Eberhardt 1993, 35) including Bulgaria's socialist neighbours. This immense drive towards urbanization produced not only radical changes in employment, but also in social position, value system and lifestyle. Thus, migrants from the countryside gradually went to make up the new socialist urban middle class with its own values, living standards and ambitions in life. Members of this new social stratum with its distinct attitudes and social practices could hardly imagine a life as a peasant or a return to the countryside. According to our own observations, even the managers, technicians and often the workers of the agricultural farms in the Dobrudzha were now living in an urban social environment. They commuted daily between their town residence and the rural workplace as if they were industry employees. This was an entirely different daily routine from that of the classic peasant, whose schedule was determined mainly by the seasons and the weather. In these unpopulated regions, characterized by a high level of mechanized wheat production as well as intensive stockbreeding, the land was almost entirely deserted. In the villages one could meet only old people and a few qualified agrarian workers.

Unexpected Consequences and Awkward Agents: The Role of the *Arendatori* in the Postsocialist Agricultural Sector in the Dobrudzha

For the reasons mentioned above, the expected resurgence of the family-run farms based on small land parcels never took place. Both the people directly involved in agriculture (managers, technical workers and employees of the former collectivized production farms) and the new landowners, most of who lived in an urban environment, thought that the land law reform was absurd. Almost without exception the people involved described the new land law not so much as unjust, but rather as a folly thought up by incompetent political elites in the capital. Some critical voices from the Bulgarian Dobrudzha declared that politicians in Sofia were detached from the actual realities and consequently were unable to grasp the problems of the region's agricultural sector, not to mention solve them. First and foremost, turning large farms into thousands of small autonomous land parcels seemed irrational and heralded socioeconomic disaster, given Dobrudzha's geographical location and agricultural significance. One must add that today this stance is shared even by those who endorsed the land law over twenty years ago. Nowadays the reform is unanimously regarded as a complete fiasco that has had catastrophic consequences for the development of agriculture in the Dobrudzha region. This is essential, keeping in mind that the Dobrudzha is a largely agricultural region; the region grows the best quality cereal crops, it is known as the breadbasket (*zhitnitsa*) of the country, and it is of essential importance for food production in Bulgaria.

While there were obviously significant causes for dissatisfaction, several actors who were already present in the agricultural sector under socialism took initiatives that later proved to be economically sound and financially successful for them and their co-workers. Loopholes in the agricultural reform laws allowed them already in the early 1990s to develop economic strategies that they have maintained to this day. The main players in this new scenario, which the lawmakers did not foresee in the Bulgarian Dobrudzha as well as in the other fertile regions of Bulgaria, are the so-called *arendatori*. These are entrepreneurs in the agricultural sector that rent land from the new owners whose land was returned through the reform laws. The latter are unable or unwilling to farm it and rarely want to sell it. Most of them are urban dwellers barely familiar with a market-oriented agriculture. Several *arendatori* were members of the local political or agricultural elite during the socialist period. They were well-trained professional farmers who began their careers as functionaries in the socialist TKZS farms (Labour Cooperative Agrarian Farms). Although these old agricultural unions were dissolved and all the employees of these huge institutions were laid off in the first half of the 1990s, the land reform did not manage to take their leaders' power away. The goal of eliminating all traces of the communist past in the country's agricultural and industrial branches was not achieved because the local *nomenklatura* realized that they could seize and appropriate the best machines and equipment during the confusion that reigned in the wake of the fall of communism. At the same time they were able to mobilize their network of relationships from the past in order to rent the best land parcels from the new owners – that is, the ones who got it back during the agricultural reform. The *arendatori* also turned astonishingly quickly into remarkably capable capitalists. In the Bulgarian Dobrudzha, where the first *arendatori* appeared, some were able to get hold of more than 10,000 hectares. The data reveal that in 2003, for example, only 0.8 per cent of all agricultural farms in the country managed more than 50 hectares, but they farmed a stunning 78 per cent of the cultivated land (Republic of Bulgaria 2009, 15).

In addition, the *arendatori* recruited people from the agricultural collectives who belonged to their close circle of acquaintances and hired them as employees in their postsocialist companies. At first the *arendatori* engaged in highly speculative privatization ventures in the agricultural sector. They focused on intensive corn production with the use of pesticides, both neglecting the necessary improvement of the farmland and ignoring the ecological balance. Their strategies at those times were similar to the ones Max Weber described as 'pre-rational capitalism' (1956, 834), of which the short-term rent contracts (one to five years) are an example. Our data reveal that 91.6 per cent of all contracts of the interviewed *arendatori* were indeed for four years. Being economically active, the *arendatori* were aiming at establishing close social relationships with their employees and the actual landowners, while at the same time executing their strong economic power. The landowners had to agree to the conditions set by the *arendatori* concerning the amount of money or goods they received per rented hectare per year, as only through the economic activity of the *arendatori* could they gain income from their own land. The strategy of the owners was to only sell the land in exceptional cases, while expecting both an increase in land value and protection from high inflation.

Having the economic control and the necessary resources, the *arendatori* succeeded in gaining a high level of capital accumulation. However, the capitalist competition was severe and after a splendid start, several *arendatori* went bankrupt quickly. Yet in the Bulgarian Dobrudzha some have consolidated their success and they have become the leading figures in the agricultural sector to this date.

In the following case study, we will portray and analyse the career trajectory of one such individual who is representative for this category of *arendatori* and is considered to be a nearly ideal role model by the people of the Dobrudzha. We interviewed this person regularly between January 1992 and November 2009 in order to systematically reconstruct his social and economic trajectory (Giordano and Kostova 2002, 127). In January 1992 we were introduced to him by an employee of the regional section of the agricultural trade union in Dobrich, the capital of the Bulgarian Dobrudzha region. This was shortly before the agricultural reform laws came into force. At that time the central-right coalition's plans for agrarian reform had caused great anxiety everywhere, but they had not come into effect yet. In these regions that were legendary for their 'red' traditions one could expect great resistance, if not an open rebellion against putting the government's reform project into practice. Public opinion feared that the socioeconomic structure of the Dobrudzha region was fundamentally endangered. In this general atmosphere of fierce discussions, in which there was no lack of slogans and catchphrases against the decollectivization and the land restitution, we had our first meeting with our informant, who was known to be a staunch advocate of the socialist agricultural collectives' system. We were in a village about fifteen kilometres from Dobrich where the collective's main office was located. Here everything was still under our informant's control since this collective had not been dissolved yet. In our first long conversation he gave details about his socialist management policy. He was positive that the collective's economic success was due to his personal experience as an agronomist and his loyalty to the old party directives. Next, he noted the advantages of collectivization for a region such as Dobrudzha and pointed out that the policy of privatization and restitution were a fatal mistake. At the end of the interview he said in the presence of his employees,

'The members of this collective will never accept the decollectivization of agriculture. We will continue to do what we have been doing until now.'

About six months after the revised land reform law was put into effect, we met him again. In the meantime he had been dismissed, and his collective, through judicial intervention, had been placed under the power of a liquidation council which consisted of a small group of people who were very close to the new centre-right government. The second conversation with our informant took place in a small, cold room of the once-proud headquarters of the agricultural union in the town of Dobrich. This meeting missed all of the collectivist pride that had been central to our first discussion; it was a shorter and more dramatic conversation. He explained with unease and not without bitter irony that he was now just an unemployed person looking for a job in agriculture. He had various plans, as he stated, but none of them were carefully thought through yet. We learned that after the new land law came into effect the situation in the entire Bulgarian Dobrudzha was so unclear that he could only live from one day to the next, which made any kind of long-term planning impossible. When we pressed on to learn more about the immediate consequences of decollectivization in the Dobrudzha, he broke down, shook his head and explained in between sobs, 'What a catastrophe… All is lost… They [the politicians in Sofia and the members of the liquidation committees] have destroyed everything we accomplished in years and years of hard work.' At the end of the conversation, visibly defeated and unconvinced, he uttered, 'Probably the only prospect is the market economy, which will take years and years of work.'

Several years later, in May 1996, he surprised us by arranging our regular meeting in his old and by now closed-down collective building. He greeted us in his old office and it was immediately obvious that he was in much better spirits than the last time we met. He was very lively and seemed more confident than ever. Immediately after we entered his office he started to boast about his success. He left the impression that he had finally reconquered his old collective. He told us that he had started renting land parcels from the new owners, who lived in the cities and barely had an interest in agriculture, and that this way he had managed to gather enough land to create a profitable agricultural enterprise. He explained, 'In the Dobrudzha agriculture can only work on the basis of large plots of land, but those in Sofia don't understand that. So, we have to do things our way.' As in the past, he complained about the 'new politicians in the capital'. What could one expect from people who 'have never seen the countryside'? According to him this incompetent behaviour of the national political elite also explained why financial resources were so difficult to obtain, such as affordable bank loans to buy seed and machinery and to pay wages. Despite those difficulties he had managed to buy equipment that used to belong to the old collective, as the newly founded co-op in his village did not have the resources to buy it. He had also managed to recruit the best qualified and unskilled workers that used to work in the collective while he was still running it. At the end of the interview he insisted on inviting us to lunch at the privately operated inn that had recently opened in the village. There the owner and regular customers greeted him with respect and deference. From this observation we concluded that he had brought us to this little restaurant to show that he had won back the prestige he had enjoyed at our first meeting. Here he could demonstrate to us how central his role and his strategic position had become in the framework of his relationship network.

In 1998 we met him again. He was several hours late for our meeting so we had enough time to look around his establishment. From the much higher number of employees we concluded that his enterprise was developing successfully. When he finally arrived he announced he was currently farming 3,500 hectares. The business was running quite well, but he had to be on the lookout for corn speculators (*akuli* or 'sharks' as he called them) from the big cities, mainly Sofia, who tried to keep the buying prices low. He explained his plans to build additional silos to control market prices. We asked whether he wanted to buy the rented land sometime in the future. He responded with a cunning smile, 'The situation is still too uncertain; but this is a future goal indeed.' Then he suggested we take a look at his new storage facilities in order to relieve the pressure from the *akuli*. He proudly took us over to the granary of the closed-down collective, which he had renovated and equipped with brand new metal silos. We congratulated him, to which he responded, 'One needs good storage capacity in order to not feel the pressure from the speculators, as some of the *arendatori* and especially the new co-ops are.' In the end he requested an invitation to Switzerland (he insisted of course that he would pay for himself) because from what he knew he could learn there how to improve efficiency in the agricultural sector. At this point it was clear to us that from being a member of the old local socialist *nomenklatura* he had turned into a postsocialist capitalist.

We had further long conversations with him between September 2006 and November 2009, welcoming us to a brand-new three-story building in downtown Dobrich. He told us that he had left the old collective's run-down office to move to the much more pleasant premises of his current enterprise. The interviews took place in his personal office, where on a small but clearly visible shelf next to an icon of Jesus stood a carefully arranged display of trophies (cups and diplomas) that he had received in recognition of his outstanding (and for the time being nationally renowned) career as an 'agro-businessman'– that is, an independent agricultural entrepreneur. With some pride he announced that he was already cultivating 10,000 hectares, which according to him was the ideal size of a profitable enterprise in the Bulgarian Dobrudzha. He added that the land market was becoming a bit more flexible, as the owners were ready to sell because of the land's higher prices. He also noted that buying such extremely small land parcels was not always easy, since among the many heirs who had received the land back following the land reform there were often conflicting opinions and expectations, which frequently caused lengthy conflicts and disputes. Despite these difficulties and the long negotiations, he had managed to buy 5,000 hectares to date. Given the current situation in the Dobrudzha region, he viewed this as sufficient. The future would tell if additional land was needed.

After the conversation in September 2006, he suggested taking us to his country house on his estate. Along the way he showed us a great number of new silos under construction and again explained the key role of storage. After a short ride along the rather flat landscape, we saw his country house: a pseudotraditional, neorustic building which according to him had a true rural feel. A fence over two metres high surrounded the house. From above the walls one could make out a large, well-tended garden as well as a chapel, which he insisted we visit. He was especially proud of the small fresco on the altar, which in the tradition of Orthodox iconography depicted the twelve apostles rather realistically. In the garden he had installed a huge granite water basin, which he had bought and brought to Bulgaria from Romania and which had belonged to the Rotary Club in Dobrudzha before World War II. Finally, we visited the house and spent most of our time in a large hall that he had set up as a meeting place for his co-workers, containing a conspicuous portrait of Che Guevara. We also saw a small but significant display of official photographs from the communist era depicting the activities of the old agricultural collective, which had been dissolved more than eighteen years before. One could recognize the 'festive' opening ceremony and the subsequent 'festive' process of collectivization as well as the 'glorious' phase of mechanization. This unexpected exhibition of socialist memorabilia also included a reproduction of the founding act of the co-op from 1943, signed by his father. This proved what we had already surmised – that is, that our collocutor's father shortly after the advent of communism was among the most important and influential leaders of the 'red' collective movement in the Dobrudzha region. From this last visit to his agricultural empire's core we were able to conclude that his present profile represents a kind of dialectic bricolage, combining socialist nostalgia, neo-orthodox reinvention of the past and capitalistic orientation for the future. He is definitely not the kind of capitalistic entrepreneur of the Western model, giving credibility to Shmuel Eisenstadt's notion of multiple modernities (2002).

No Wealth without Personalized Trust Networks

Our informant should not be viewed solely as an example of the new rich and wealth-producing agricultural entrepreneur in the Dobrudzha region. He is at the same time a much admired, envied and probably also hated protagonist of the postsocialist era. Therefore, not only local *arendatori* but also those elsewhere in Bulgaria view him as a paradigm or model to be emulated. Almost without exception they perceive him as the touchstone of their own economic achievements. Our informant's achievements are a recurring topic in conversations with other *arendatori* in the Dobrudzha region. These people are always left wondering whether they will be able to reach his level of success and social prestige. From a sociological and anthropological point of view, how should we interpret the brilliant career of this agricultural entrepreneur?

Shortly after the fall of socialism, in general, but especially among the new political elites in Bulgaria's capital, the *arendatori* were actually viewed as negative social figures. They were perceived as staunch accomplices of the old system and as hostile and dangerous remnants of the local communist *nomenklatura* who needed to be curbed if not annihilated socially and politically. Nowadays this negative attitude towards the *arendatori* has changed. Although some political circles still find them objectionable, in general the *arendatori* are accepted because they have proven to be useful and even indispensable actors in the agricultural sector, able to create workplaces and produce and accumulate social wealth. A good indication are the changes in legal regulations by which the land's *arendator* has a right of first refusal if the landowner wishes to sell his property. Thus land can only be sold to another person provided that the *arendator* has refused it in writing.

Bearing in mind the difficulties when the new system was introduced, one could assume in line with rational choice theory or the reductionist *homo economicus* model that the success of some *arendatori* is simply the outcome of purely individual qualities and acquired capabilities held to be universal, such as willpower and persistence, rational planning, ability to make economic calculations, a good education, organizational skills, etc. Yet, notwithstanding the importance of these qualities, we also want to stress the significance of personal networks created in part during socialist times. Only those *arendatori* who had carefully maintained such relationships and were at the centre of these networks were able to survive during the first postsocialist years and achieve economic and social success.

To illustrate this point we will once again refer to our previous paradigmatic example. His entire enterprise is based on a close-knit network of highly personalized relationships between him and his closest family at the core. He acts as the person in charge, together with his wife and daughters who manage administrative and financial matters, as well as his sons-in-law who as agronomists and engineers direct the agricultural workforce and the construction workers. They make up the network's core. Without this structure of relatives, mobilized daily, running the business would have been impossible. For work in the fields the *arendator* relies on a trusted team of workers and tractor drivers who used to work for him at the old socialist agricultural collective. Already at that time they had developed a high-trust relationship with him, since he was their director. Of course some of the old employees had retired in the meantime, but their jobs were given to their children or other close relatives.

Moreover, a successful *arendator* has relationships of a personal nature with politicians and high-level administrators in the capital. These are absolutely indispensable when it comes to acquiring state or EU subsidies (such as the SAPARD fund and regional and agricultural funds). In return for these important benefits, the *arendatori* (as our informant and several of his colleagues have confirmed) had to siphon off 10 to 20 per cent of the received funds for the brokers. For politicians the *arendator* acts as a client who can secure votes for them through their network. The reciprocal exchange of corrupt monetary transactions or classic patronage services is typical of these personal relationships. In addition, the network of relations is reinforced in clubs such as Rotary, which provide the essential trustworthy and organizational environment for meetings aimed at winning over key contracts. An *arendator's* extended network also includes personal relationships with the individual owners of the land parcels he rents. As our informant emphasizes, maintaining such relationships guarantees the cultivated land's unity through the future continuation of the lease. Only this way could one make significant long-term plans for profitable agricultural activities.

The personal relationship network, which according to our observations is crucial to the *arendator's* success and the prosperity of the members of his network, may be represented as concentric areas with different levels of intimacy (Boissevain, 1974, 47). The following diagram illustrates the correlation that exists between the level of intimacy and the proximity to the network's core, which is cross-cut by the *arendator's* network. This is an ideal-typical representation of the four zones of intimacy plus an external zone. The first zone (A) comprises the *arendator's* family members who work for the company; the second one (B) includes agrarian workers who in the past worked in the socialist cooperatives and/or their relatives; the third one (C) contains local politicians as well as national bureaucrats who act as mediators between the *arendator* and the capital city's political establishment thanks to their personal contacts; while the fourth one (D) consists of the new landowners who rent their parcels to the enterprise. Finally, influential politicians who control the allocation of public resources (national and of the EU), with whom the *arendator* has no direct personalized relationship, are in the external zone (EXT). This is, from the point of view of the *arendator*, the space of social or public mistrust. It is important to add that those who, for various reasons, have no access to these networks are doomed to impoverishment, as the case of Romania also shows (Verdery 2003). These processes of marginalization affect the Roma in particular (Stewart 1997).

Scheme 1. Personalized network structure

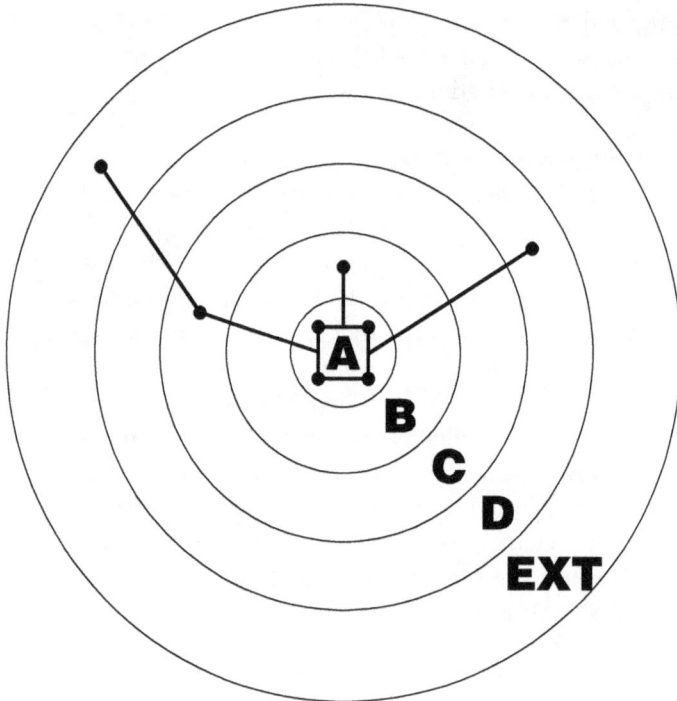

A	Intimacy zone 1: The family core
B	Intimacy zone 2: The co-workers
C	Intimacy zone 3: The politicians and the bureaucrats
D	Intimacy zone 4: The landowners
EXT	External zone: The social space for the public mistrust

Linking City and Countryside

Up to the end of World War II, Bulgaria as a predominantly agrarian country was weighed down by three major socioeconomic problems: the excessive fragmentation of land property, rural overpopulation (which could not be absorbed by an industrial sector still at the planning stage) and the consequent high rates of underemployment and unemployment in the countryside

(Duijzings this volume). As mentioned above, in the years after World War II socialism tried to remedy these thorny problems by launching a forced industrialization, modernization and urbanization process that included the agricultural sector (Duijzings this volume). Agro-industrialization mainly affected the country's more fertile and flat areas and led to a significant decrease in the rural population in regions like the Dobrudzha. After 1989, such regions were left with the legacies of the socialist economic system following its sudden, unexpected and ruinous collapse.

Clearly, those entrepreneurs who embarked on capitalist activities in the so-called transitional agricultural economy, such as the *arendatori*, have had to reckon with these structural, social and demographic specificities inherited from the previous system. Therefore, one of the most important aspects of their work has been to link city and countryside. In the Dobrudzha, as our exemplary case illustrates, practically all market transactions involve city and countryside and they will nearly inevitably go through section A of the ideal-typical network represented in the above diagram. For any dealings between people in section B and those in sections C, D or EXT, applying to the *arendator* himself or someone within his closer family proves useful if not indeed necessary. In fact, the diagram shows that there are practically no links between section B, which mainly consists of the *arendator*'s rural associates, and sections C, D and EXT, whose actors are prevalently urban. Accordingly, capitalist economic relations between city and countryside are virtually impossible without the role of the *arendator* assisted by some of his family's members. The *arendator* cannot avoid acting as broker between city and countryside if he wants his economic activities to thrive. Therefore, taking on this role, which also contributes to his prestige and power, is definitely in his best interests. We can reasonably assume that an *arendator* who lacks the ability to act as a liaison between city and countryside will fail and soon become bankrupt.

Our example indicates that the *arendatori* are somehow 'urbanites' whose economic interests are to a large extent dependent on the agricultural sector – that is, in the countryside. As our data show, in a globalized context the differences between city and countryside, just as those between 'rural' and 'urban', can no longer be conceived of in rigid dichotomous or binary terms (see also Kaneff this volume). However, to ensure continuity and expansion of their activities the *arendatori* must be accomplished and patient negotiators with city dwellers. One of the most important strategies calls for the ability to convince landowners to agree to long-term leases on their mostly microscopic land parcels, which are often located rather far apart from each other. The *arendatori* will be able to obtain an undivided stretch of farmland only through these often nerve-wracking negotiations, which become particularly difficult when there is more than one heir to a single land parcel. In this case, which is rather common, each person entitled to a part of the property needs to be won over. If an owner, out of spite or whatever other reason, should decide not to rent his plot to the *arendator*, the latter would have to cope with the outsiders owning land right in the middle of his farmland, with all the previously mentioned negative consequences in terms of the efficiency of his agricultural activities. Since these difficulties are notoriously common, *vox populi* has it that most *arendatori* resort to rather brusque methods – Mafia-style so to speak – to reach a solution in their own favour. Finally, the other 'urbanites' with which the *arendatori* must negotiate are those in control of the allocation of agricultural subsidies, especially in the capital. Without a skilled *arendator* (or cooperative president acting like an *arendator*) these funds administrated in the city would never reach the countryside. The *arendator*'s success depends on his activity as middleman between urban and rural cohorts and as negotiator between these two segments of society, playing highly flexible and hybrid roles and being perfectly at ease with moving between city and countryside.

Conclusions

Our chapter shows that the agricultural reforms after the fall of socialism could not attain the goals that the laws were aiming for, at least in the Dobrudzha region. New roles and practices developed which comprise sophisticated adaptations to the postsocialist situation, but which are also mutations of similar roles and practices developed under socialism. Alongside the unavoidable discontinuities related to switching to a new property and socioeconomic system, one can discern a number of important continuities in terms of practices, relations and symbols, too. In socialism, as in the postsocialist period, Bulgarians, especially individual agents operating in the economic sector, did not passively accept or blindly follow the system and its official directives. Often they kept the system at bay, if not weakened it, through active adaptation strategies such as personalized networks, which thanks to their adaptability turned out to be extremely useful in postsocialist times as well.

The *arendatori* have undeniably shown to be future oriented, playing a highly innovative role in the agricultural sector, effectively adjusting and reusing their personalized networks in the so-called transition. Paradoxically, the success and resulting wealth of these unique capitalist entrepreneurs and their entourage would have been impossible without the forms of social knowledge and capital acquired in socialist times. Returning to Fukuyama, this proves once again that theories based on the universality of Western models and their global applicability and exportability have an extremely limited explanatory potential. In Europe, the modalities of socioeconomic and political change proved to be far more complex and contradictory. They can be more suitably analysed through a much less dichotomous and more dialectic or relational view, such as that which we employed in this article (Tocqueville 1856; Simmel 1983; Balandier 1971; Bourdieu and Wacquant 1992). Our perspective provides an opportunity to consider the interplay between particular social facts that reductionist and essentialist approaches usually conceptualize as opposite and incompatible. As a result we achieve a more accurate grasp of both the relation between change and continuity as well as between city and countryside.

References

Abrahams, Ray, ed. 1996. *After Socialism: Land Reform and Social Change in Eastern Europe.* Providence: Berghahn.
Balandier, Georges. 1971. *Sens et puissance: Les dynamiques sociales.* Paris: Presses Universitaires de France.
Bell, John D. 1977. *Peasants in Power: Alexandar Stamboliski and the Bulgarian Agrarian National Union, 1899–1923.* Princeton: Princeton University Press.
Boissevain, Jeremy. 1974. *Friends of Friends: Networks, Manipulators and Coalitions.* Oxford: Basil Blackwell.
Bourdieu, Pierre and Loïc J. D. Wacquant. 1992. *An Invitation to a Reflexive Anthropology.* Chicago: University of Chicago Press.
Bulgaria: 20th Century. 1999. Sofia: Trud.
Creed, Gerald. 1998. *Domesticating Revolution: From Socialist Reform to an Ambivalent Transition in a Bulgarian Village.* University Park: Pennsylvania State University Press.
Eberhardt, Pjotr. 1993. 'Depopulation Processes in Rural Areas of East-Central Europe'. *Eastern European Countryside* 0: 31–40.
Eisenstadt, Shmuel N., ed. 2002. *Multiple Modernities.* New Brunswick: Transaction Publishers.
Fukuyama, Francis. 1994. 'Reflections on "The End of History" Five Years Later'. In *After History: Francis Fukuyama and His Critics,* edited by Timothy Burns, 237–58. Lanham, MD: Rowman and Littlefield.
Fukuyama, Francis. 1995. *Trust: The Social Virtues and the Creation of Prosperity.* New York: Free Press Paperbacks.
Giordano, Christian and Dobrinka Kostova. 2002. 'Die soziale Produktion von Misstrauen'. In *Postsozialismus: Transformationsprozesse in Europa und Asien aus ethnologischer Perspektive,* edited by Christopher Hann, 117–41. Frankfurt: Campus Verlag.
Halbwachs, Maurice. 1992. *On Collective Memory.* Chicago: University of Chicago Press.
Minkov, Mihail and Ivan Lazov, eds. 1979. *Poyava i razvitie na kooperativnoto zemedelie v Bulgariya.* Sofia: Zemizdat.
Republic of Bulgaria. *Rural Development Programme 2007–2013 (2009).* Sofia: EARD.
Said, Edward. 1978. *Orientalism.* New York: Pantheon.
Simmel, Georg. 1983. *Soziologie.* Tübingen: J. C. B. Mohr, Paul Siebeck Verlag.
Stewart, Michael. 1998. '"We Should Build a Statue for Ceausescu Here": The Trauma of De-collectivisation in Two Romanian Villages'. In *Surviving Post-socialism: Local Strategies*

and Regional Responses in Eastern Europe and the Former Soviet Union, edited by Frances Pine and Susan Bridger, 66–79. London: Routledge.

Tanır, Engin Deniz. 2005. 'The Mid-nineteenth Century Ottoman Bulgaria from the Viewpoints of the French Travellers'. MA dissertation, Graduate School of Social Sciences of Middle East Technical University, Ankara. Online: http://etd.lib.metu.edu.tr/upload/12606837/index.pdf (accessed 4 October 2012).

Teneva, Zlatina. 1979. *Narodno sabranie 1879–1944: Archives*. Sofia: Sofia University Publishing House.

Todorova, Maria. 1997. *Imagining the Balkans*. Oxford: Oxford University Press.

Tocqueville, Alexis de. 1856. *L'ancien régime*. Paris: Gallimard.

Verdery, Katherine. 2003. *The Vanishing Hectare: Property and Value in Postsocialist Transylvania*. Ithaca: Cornell University Press.

Weber, Max. 1956. *Wirtschaft und Gesellschaft*, vol. 2. Tübingen: J. C. B. Mohr und Paul Siebeck Verlag.

Chapter 7

INHERITANCE AFTER RESTITUTION: MODERN LEGISLATIVE NORMS AND CUSTOMARY PRACTICES IN RURAL BULGARIA

Petko Hristov

During the 1990s, Bulgarian villages experienced another major attempt at social engineering after the collectivization of agriculture under socialism: the process of privatization and land restitution, inspired by a combination of 'traditionalist' and neoliberal ideological principles championed by urban and global economic elites. However, the ways these policies were put into practice has raised important questions about their appropriateness, first of all because the local understanding of 'property' in the postsocialist context was far removed from what neoliberal architects of privatization had in mind, going beyond their understanding of it in terms of rights and obligations assumed by individual property owners. Because of this, a number of researchers have urged for the kind of 'property analysis that invokes the total system of social, cultural, and political relations and inquires into, rather than assumes, the nature of property conceptions' (Verdery 1999, 54; see also Hann 1993).

This chapter will deal with social practices in Bulgarian villages during the restitution of agricultural land, dominated by various cultural norms and values inherited both from the presocialist times and from the decades of collective farming. It deals with the ideological aspect and significance of privatization, seen as the 'centrepiece of the transition' in Bulgaria and other postsocialist states (Verdery 1999, 54). The restitution of land, which began during the early 1990s and was supported by Western financial organizations and advisors, brought to the surface discrepancies between the legal norms set by the restitution laws of the postsocialist years and the traditional inheritance practices. As these laws have emerged in a global context of neoliberal 'transition', these discrepancies can be seen as an example of Tsing's 'friction' (2005; see Duijzings this volume).

In this chapter, I would like to propose a different understanding of the concept of 'property' in the social practice of postsocialist Bulgaria, which is a concept 'only messily related to the Western blueprint' (Verdery 1999, 76). In a situation similar to the mountainous parts of northern Albania (De Waal 2004, 32), decollectivization led to claims made not by separate individuals but by entire family and/or kin groups, which had joined the socialist collective farms during the 1950s without dividing their land. The postrestitution relations amidst these groups reproduced – in many ways – traditional cultural norms of the past. My second, more general point pertains to the practical improbability of the neoliberal project to restore land ownership in its former 'real boundaries'. I insist on the impossibility of 'reversing' history; the idea to 'carry' the 1940s forward into the 1990s was an ideal rather than a realistic objective. But without embracing the idea that decollectivization was 'equivalent to de-modernisation' (Kozhucharova and Rangelova 2001, 38; see also Kaneff this volume), I nevertheless would like to point out that in a number of regions in Bulgaria, land restitution brought back some of the traditional disagreements and forgotten conflicts from the presocialist era.

The process of restitution facilitated the return of plots of land within the former 'real boundaries' of 1946, aiming to restore the agricultural sector which was considered to have been crippled by the massive land collectivization during socialist times.[1] In Bulgaria, which was a predominantly rural and agrarian country until the 1950s, this process of collectivization had been by far the most consequential aspect of socialist economic restructuring and modernization for the vast majority of the population (Wolf 2000, 8). My chapter is based on fieldwork in a number of regions (predominantly in the semimountainous midwestern part of the country), and it analyses the roots of these recent conflicts, which date back to the social realities of the 1930s and 1940s. Then, in many villages, daughters were 'willingly' excluded from the list of heirs when family real estate was divided, despite the fact that modern state legislation had upheld gender equality ever since the Turnovo Constitution of 1879. My contribution focuses on the ways in which customary inheritance practices and property relationships resurfaced after 1990, in the wake of the restitution process of the 1990s.[2]

This research has both theoretical and practical dimensions – not only does it draw our attention to the right of inheritance as a key regulator in family/kin relationships and a litmus test of women's social status in a given culture or society (Benovska-Subkova 2001, 8), but it also addresses the issue of land restitution being one of the main aspects of transition in Bulgaria.

This process has been characterized as an attempt at 'retraditionalisation' (Dobreva 1997, 99) or 'archaisation' of the agrarian sector, or as an attempt at reversing the course of history (see for instance Giordano and Kostova 2000, 167). Was this 'return to the future' – to use Christian Giordano's phrase – indeed a politically motivated attempt to revive presocialist society 'as if it were possible to ignore the epoch of socialism and return to an ideal point in history from where to start over at the present'? (Wolf 2000, 7) Or did the introduction of European legal norms as well as the establishment of a market economy show that the population's sense of justice has as little to do with the system of abstract legal clauses as the weekly market or annual fair has with the market economy (Sundhaussen 1997, 13)? Is it really because of the fast (and often forced) modernization of villages during socialism that the idea of reversing history in the agrarian sector turned into a paradoxical postsocialist 'reprivatisation without peasants' (Giordano and Kostova 1997, 135–49)? May we draw the conclusion, as the Croatian rural sociologist Stipe Šuvar (2004, 173) has argued, that former socialist countries (Bulgaria in particular) no longer have an 'agrarian' character, but have neither become fully 'non-agrarian'? None of these questions has a simple answer.

Anthropological research from the 1990s onwards shows that there has been a wide range of social and cultural responses to land restitution in Bulgaria, which is related to the variety of customary and legislative norms regulating family inheritance in villages. In my contribution I hope to shed light on the issue whether a 'return to the future' is possible at all. The discrepancies between modern, state-imposed institutional frameworks and everyday social practices – which are related to the traditional (folk) understandings of 'justice' and 'order' – are not new; the issue has been debated in different ways and on different occasions throughout the modern era, in the decades following Bulgaria's independence. The history and development of the Bulgarian countryside during the last 125 years has been marked by a perpetual and unceasing series of 'transitions': from so-called traditional conditions (often equated with obsolescence and conservatism) to modernity, from capitalism to socialist modernization, and during the last two decades from socialism to capitalism, EU membership, democracy and freedom (see Duijzings this volume). During all these decades of dynamic change, both Bulgarian and foreign scholars and policymakers have constantly attempted to observe, analyse and 'manage' this changing landscape of the Bulgarian countryside in an effort to understand and control these processes. Being biased either in favour of long-standing Bulgarian traditions or 'progressive' norms, many of them – being part of the governing elite of the country – have written with emotional zeal about the mismatch between customary practices and the modern 'European' and 'democratic' norms.

One of the most serious and distressing legal problems after Bulgaria's liberation from Ottoman rule was the extreme discrepancy between the constitutionally established laws and the behaviours and social practices of ordinary Bulgarians that these laws were trying to address. During the 1920s, the renowned Bulgarian legal specialist Venelin Ganev concluded his observations from the villages Boyana and Dragalevtsi (near Sofia) with a critique of what he called the Bulgarians' nihilistic attitude towards laws that directly concerned them (such as the criminal law, and even the civil law that regulated family relations). As Ganev wrote, 'Only because of the state authority's coercion does the Bulgarian abide by these alien, imposed laws, which are not a product of his own material and mental life and are not related to his national and cultural progress' (1921, 99). Regarding the norms that regulate family and marital relations concerning inheritance, the contrast between the customary and the official 'written' law was the most problematic because of the differences in the principles that govern these two types of regulation (Tsekova 2011, 254–5). Similarly to traditional Kanun rules followed in Albania which justify the expression 'There is no state, there is no law!' (De Waal 2004, 31), in semimountainous midwestern Bulgaria (the so-called Shopluk area) the notion that 'The law is like a door in a field – only fools go through it' was instilled as early as the initial stages of modernization.

All experts dealing with legal norms and customary practices concerning inheritance at the end of the nineteenth or the first half of the twentieth century (such as Petar Odzhakov, Stefan Bobchev, Ivan Evstatiev Geshov and Dimitar Marinov; for more details, see Kassabova-Dincheva 2002, 39–51) agreed that neither the initial legislative regulations (which gave equal rights to the two sexes, according to the Law of Inheritance of 1890)[3] nor the subsequent amendments to the law (which gave sons the right to inherit a share twice as large than that of daughters)[4] had the desired impact. Yet none of these authors came up with proposals for more satisfactory regulations that would correspond to social reality. Described as 'taking social traditions into consideration', the legal compromises turned out to be only a partial and unsatisfactory solution, equally unacceptable for the villages in western Bulgaria, which had family and kinship structures based on patrilineal principles, as for the ones in central and eastern Bulgaria, where these traditional kinship patterns were not dominant anymore (Hristov 1999, 56–76). In the first case, the decision was considered unjust towards the sons, through whose children the genealogy continued to exist, and in the second case towards the daughters who were seen to have contributed to their fathers' wealth and possessions through their labour (Tsekova 2011, 261).[5]

Some of the leading ethnographers and legal specialists at the time actively studied the norms of Bulgarian customary law. There is indeed no doubt that complex family and kinship patterns and the practice of excluding female heirs from the process of inheritance existed in western Bulgaria throughout the first half of the twentieth century, which was proven by a number of High Court decisions confirming and sanctioning traditional norms in court practice (see Ignatiev 1926, 7–10). As Christian Giordano and Dobrinka Kostova conclude later, regarding the postsocialist social landscape, 'In the countryside a gulf between the legal frame and the social practices is becoming increasingly deep.' According to them, this rift is a clear social indicator of a conflict between state 'legality' and cultural 'legitimacy', which is probably affecting the whole country (2000, 173). Looking at the postsocialist transition, this analysis still seems to be valid, although more research is needed to clarify the situation.

Let us look at postsocialist Bulgarian villages at the end of the last century. The social realities of the 1990s were dominated by the process of restitution and reprivatization of agricultural land, producing an especially confusing picture that should be understood as neither explicitly upholding nor rejecting the legislative norm restoring equal inheritance to the two sexes. In order to assess to what extent history was indeed being reversed in the postsocialist period, we may briefly consider the situation of family relations and inheritance in midwestern Bulgaria during the 1930s and 1940s. In some of the villages where I carried out fieldwork and interviews, the legally defined right of daughters to acquire a share (*miraz*) of the father's real estate, though this share was much smaller than that of sons, began to slowly make its way into social practices after World War I.[6] A relatively common practice in villages during the 1930s was to give a moderate dowry (*zestra*) to the daughter at her wedding – a certain amount of money or (more rarely) a small field or meadow, with the father publicly declaring that the dowry was given 'so that the bride would not lay claim to a share when her father's property [*bashtiniya*] was later divided among her brothers' (Moskova 1980, 52).[7] This type of wedding gift can actually be considered as a 'hidden' *miraz*. Its size varied, reaching up to one third of a brother's share, but it was always smaller than what was specified by law.[8] In the rare cases when brothers gave a small garden or meadow to a sister when dividing their father's estate, this was largely considered a symbolic gift, so that she can have a share of her father's household too. The lack of regulation and customary norms of giving dowry in some of the villages led to conflicts between relatives: during the 1930s in the village of Berende the sisters from one particular family were given dowry (in private) in the form of money at their wedding; however, when the heritage was divided, one of the sisters took legal action against her brothers and received a *miraz* as well.

Even though she had a legal right to claim her share, she was excluded from further contact with the family.[9]

This was not the only such case. There was also a lack of customary norms regarding the division of the mother's *miraz* at her death (brought into the household at marriage); this was resolved through a variety of practices. The mother could choose to give it to the son with whom she spent her final years, or she could divide it among all her children,[10] while other villages followed the traditional rule of dividing the mother's *miraz* only among the daughters, again as *miraz*.[11] The introduction of dowry in addition to the traditional wedding trousseau (*cheiz*), the changes in wedding gift exchange and inheritance in the studied regions during the 1930s and the 1940s, and the lack of customary regulations for the practices described, are all indicative of the demographic and social transformations that were changing family and kinship patterns in the villages in question (see Hristov 1999, 71; Benovska-Subkova 2001, 9).[12] Seen in comparison, the social practices in midwestern Bulgaria were similar if not almost identical to those in the Vranje region in southeastern Serbia, where there was a similar discrepancy between traditional norms and state legislature (Djordjević 2003, 76–87). Yet in the case of Serbia this situation continued to exist into the decades after World War II, under the specific conditions of Yugoslav socialism where land collectivization was not carried out. Providing a daughter with a *zestra* as a 'hidden' *miraz* differed from the traditional practice of 'compensating' for any physical or other imperfections of the bride (Hristov 1999, 56–76) – for instance if she was lame, deaf or blind ('s kusur' – 'with flaws') or if it was known that she was not a virgin. Her family had then to compensate for these defaults with money or land in order for her marriage to be made possible at all.[13]

In the decade before World War II, dowry became a condition for the bride's successful marriage, turning her into a desired partner for suitable local young men, especially if the latter belonged to the administrative elite: 'Men in government occupation were rare and they sought women with a large dowry for marriage', as one of my respondents explained.[14] This change in customary practice made evident the emergence of individual family households in the social structure of the village, with a tendency of neolocality after the marriage. It is not a coincidence that the rare joint or extended family households that were preserved during the 1940s (such as the Ketserovi family in Kalotina) refused to accept brides with land dowries since this would disrupt the traditional social order and the equality among the sisters-in-law (*eturva*).[15] This, however, was becoming an exception. In short, the *miraz* became an 'inevitable evil' in Bulgarian villages in the decades before collectivization (similarly to villages in eastern Serbia – cf. Benovska-Subkova 2001, 12).

Until now, we have traced in detail the social practices of family relations and inheritance in the decades preceding socialism, in order to understand the traditionally negative attitude towards the *mirazchiyka* (the sister that took *miraz*) in the village community (Luleva 1999, 91; Benovska-Subkova 2001, 8) – that is, towards the sister who demanded a share of her father's inheritance and took advantage of legislative norms which were considered unjust. The traditional belief was that the sister claiming her share was harming her brothers and that she had a moral obligation to give up her legal right because it would bring bad luck ('hair nema da vidat' – 'they won't do well' – see Moskova 1980, 53) or lead to a permanent 'break up' with her brothers (Pesheva 1993, 272).[16] This belief was still prominent in villages in midwestern Bulgaria even until the large-scale socialist land collectivization during the 1950s.[17] Most often in these villages patrilineal families or kin groups entered the socialist collective farms (the so-called Trudovo Kolektivno Zemedelsko Stopanstvo or TKZS)[18] without dividing their property. If division did occur, however, sisters usually gave up their shares of the father's heritage in favour of their brothers'.[19] Literature on the topic provides descriptions of sisters from different regions who more or less 'willingly' gave up their heritage rights during the 1940s and the 1950s (Kassabova-Dincheva 2002, 40); Ulf Brunnbauer writes about similar practices among Bulgarian Muslims in the Rhodope Mountains (Brunnbauer 1999, 57). Katherine Verdery's comment regarding villages in postsocialist Romania that 'property is more than just rights and obligations [...]; it entails complex meanings, often revolving around ideas about labour, persons, community, and kinship' (1999, 65) holds true for the Bulgarian rural context as well.

The restitution of agricultural land in Bulgaria during the early 1990s reproduced some of the inherited social and cultural stereotypes in family relations by reawakening some already fading (and almost forgotten) conflicts among relatives. Social practices in postsocialist villages were extremely varied and in many ways dominated by the specific realities of deserted villages in the semimountainous regions of midwestern Bulgaria. It would be an oversimplification to conclude that the process of land restitution restored the old customary rules of inheritance, or revived the conflicts between the modern legislative norms that gave equal rights to men and women and the varied traditional practices of inheritance that resulted in inequality between sons and daughters. After the socialist decades of extensive and forced industrialization and urbanization, agriculture had changed drastically, and the former village landowners had migrated to the big cities. In this light, Giordano and Kostova's observation that the postsocialist process of restitution was a process of 'reprivatisation without peasants' is spot-on (2000, 168). Conflicts between relatives nevertheless occurred, and it would be interesting to trace their development and the ways they were overcome. During the 1990s one could hear villagers say, 'Why did they return that land for us to break our kinship!' ('Kude ya vurnaha taya zemya, ta da si razvalim rodninstvoto!' – Grebenarova 2001, 80). Whereas in postsocialist Romania or Albania Verdery's concept of 'fuzzy property' seems appropriate (1999, 54; see also De Waal 2004, 43), in Bulgaria of the 1990s the contradictory coexistence of past customary practices and modern legislative norms continued.

The discrepancy between traditional social practices and the norms of legal equality between sons and daughters did indeed play out in the context of agricultural land restitution. The expectation was that sons should receive the land in line with the traditional practices and this made some of them reluctant to accept their sisters' rights over land acquired after restitution. Considering that in most cases in midwestern Bulgaria the direct heirs were adults of both sexes, the strategies to achieve this were varied: anything from brothers publicly declaring their unwillingness to discuss their inheritance rights with their sisters and brothers-in-law (who wanted to profit from their wife's land inheritance rights)[20] to the 'accidental' exclusion of sisters from claims submitted by heirs from 1992 onwards.[21] The new law caused conflicts even among the women who represented different generations in the family of a long-deceased legator – Deema Kaneff, for instance, describes a land restitution conflict in the village of Talpa in midnorthern Bulgaria, between the 60-year-old Maria supported by her daughter, and her 78-year-old mother who was defending her sons' interests (1998, 22).

In most cases such conflicts were judged in terms of the traditional social norms of the 1930s and the 1940s, and channelled accordingly. On frequent occasions elderly female heirs declared to be willing to give up their right of inheritance over the restituted and undivided land of their fathers.[22] Often the restituted land was transferred undivided into the newly formed cooperative (private) farms, with the acquired revenues from agricultural production (in the form of flour, corn, etc.) divided equally among all heirs, including the sisters. Equality among heirs was often expressed through the annual submission of a share of the natural 'land rent' by brothers, who took part in the local cooperatives, to their sisters, who lived in the city, during a family visit. As many of these cooperatives did not function properly and brought no profit to landowners, the restituted land was also often given to individual fellow villagers to work, with part of the harvest (most often half of it – *na izpolitsa*) handed over to relatives living away from the village. In this case, there was no significant difference in the relations between relatives who had the right of inheritance and new leaseholders who took on leases of contiguous agricultural land (see also Giordano and Kostova's chapter in this volume, who describe relations between owners and so-called 'new leaseholders' in the Dobrudzha).

The comparative research I carried out between proximate rural regions on the two sides of the border, in Bulgaria (the Kyustendil region) and Serbia (the Vranje region), shows that in postsocialist Bulgarian villages the new legal norms guaranteeing equal inheritance rights between men and women are considered 'normal', while the entire process of restitution is treated as 'something new' (in comparison with practices during the socialist period); whereas in Serbia traditional norms still predominate – here sisters still very rarely inherit land. The motivation given is adherence to social norms – the sister does not wish to break up the social ties with her brothers by taking a share of the father's heritage: 'Why would I need land when I'd have no family?' Yet if she agrees to acquire a small field or meadow, this is commonly justified by emotional rather than social reasons – particularly the wish to 'keep a memory of her father' (Djordjević 2005, 183). Still, sisters most often give up their share of the inheritance in favour of their brothers, while the brothers' ceremonial 'taking the sister out to dinner' as a sign of gratitude has become the norm in this part of Serbia during the last decades of the twentieth century (Djordjević 2003, 84). As in Bulgaria, though, land in southeastern Serbia has had not only an economical role but has also been important in shaping family/kin relations. In both cases we see restituted land function as 'symbolic capital' in the relations between brothers and sisters, rather than as a capital resource capable of turning the owners into 'entrepreneurial farmers' (cf. Hann 1993, 313 for Hungary).

In conclusion, it is clear that the idea of the 'reversibility of history' and the return to a Bulgaria of 'small peasants' is impossible to accomplish (Giordano and Kostova 2000, 172); during the 1990s, the sad reality of large areas of abandoned land in a number of regions in Bulgaria has provided the most inarguable proof against this traditional 'agrarian' dream of right-wing Bulgarian politicians. In the postsocialist reality of midwestern Bulgaria, the social attitudes and behavioural stereotypes of circumventing ('getting around') the law – attitudes inherited from the period before the mass collectivization of land in the villages and dictated by the traditional social practice of excluding female heirs from the process of inheritance – have determined the behaviour of only part of the adult men and women who were socialized in this environment.

The predominant part of the generations that grew up during socialism did not inherit these traditional understandings, and are now adhering to modern social norms and practices that are based on a shared understanding of equality of the sexes during inheritance, which was always the main principle in contemporary legislature. These generations, with the help of modern norms, have largely overcome the discrepancies with traditional social attitudes and the disagreement among themselves in the search for effective social strategies for family survival in the conditions of economic crisis in postsocialist Bulgaria. At the start of the new century, the presocialist customary practices are slowly superseded by contemporary legal norms promoting equality between men and women. It is clear that decades of socialist modernization and urbanization (despite the fact that they were imposed forcefully 'from above') have transformed social relations in terms of gender equality. This is followed by additional changes in the social and cultural realities of Bulgarian villages, where Bulgaria's EU membership has turned some of these deserted villages into attractive sites for foreign investment, especially for elderly Europeans (mostly Britons) and Japanese who come to spend their old age in the 'exotic' and 'unspoilt' Balkans. They bring along a different attitude to property and to the rural landscape in general (see Kaneff this volume). These new uses of land and attitudes towards the rural in Bulgaria, however, require separate research.

Notes

1 The collectivization process was carried out between 1948 and 1958, in two main stages (Migev 1995; Giordano and Kostova 1997, 135–7).

2 This process started in 1991 with the Law on Land Ownership and Land Cultivation, followed by amendments to the law from 1992 onwards (Giordano and Kostova 2000, 166).

3 Petar Odzhakov described cases in northeastern Bulgaria of brothers who went bankrupt as they were forced not only to give money as dowry on their sister's wedding (as traditional compensation for the cancelled inheritance rights), but also a land share (*miraz*) when dividing up the father's patrimony according to the new laws (Odzhakov 1885, 152). Similarly, Dimitar Marinov described the resistance of some villages in northwestern Bulgaria against the new legal norms that gave equal *miraz* to both sons and daughters (Marinov 1894, 98).

4 The change of 1896 gave the right to brothers to buy the shares of land from their married sisters, while the change of Article 21 of the Law of Inheritance in 1906 gave sons the right to acquire a share twice as large as that of daughters in land and moveable property that was considered part of the farm (Bulgarian *State Gazette* no. 29, 7 February 1906). In the Bulgarian juridical literature of the time, these changes were considered as a concession to customary practice, however without fully sanctioning the traditional norms (Tsekova 2011, 253, 280).

5 A dominant principle in patrilineal kin systems in Europe which determined the traditional norms of inheritance was the exclusion of women (daughters in particular) from the inheritance of important landed property (Kaser 2008, 65). This was also reflected in the loss of the father's family name (or maiden name) after marriage.

6 Such practices developed in the villages around Sofia (see for instance Pesheva 1993, 272). For semimountainous villages in northwestern Bulgaria (the regions of Vidin, Vratsa, and Montana), see Donchev (1996, 67).

7 This is the case of a woman born in 1920 in the village of Tuden. Such practices also existed in the Pirin region; Detelina Moskova provides the example of a father who

announced at the wedding: 'Look what trousseau [*cheiz*] I'm giving to her – that's her share of my property, she shouldn't later ask for more' (Moskova 1980, 52).

8 As one of my respondents said, 'If *miraz* is given, the father determines how much – he's the one that gives it!' (a woman born 1924 in the village of Shuma).

9 This information was provided by a female respondent born in 1920 in the village of Berende.

10 A male respondent (born in 1920 in the village of Komshtitsa) told me, 'The *miraz* goes with the mother. She decides whom to give it to. She may divide it among all her children, or she may give it to the son that takes care of her.'

11 This information was provided by a female respondent born in 1922. Cf. the notes by Detelina Moskova about the same practice in the Pirin region (1980, 53).

12 The *zestra* (in the form of a sum of money, i.e., capital) or *miraz* (consisting of fields, vines or meadows) are given to the bride at her wedding and considered her (not her husband's) property (*peculium*). The *miraz* given as part of the father's heritage, and the daughter's participation in the division of the father's patrimony after his death, are late phenomena in the social practices of Bulgarian villages (Baldzhiev 1892, 145–6; Vladigerov 1942, 31–4; Georgiev 1979, 56). The traditional gifts (*cheiz, prikya, spap, veno, ruba*) that the bride took to the groom's home after the wedding do not – from a legal point of view – correspond to the dowry according to Roman-Byzantine law (Tsekova 2011, 267).

13 In the village of Tuden, a grandmother gave her gold coin necklace to the virgin bride as an additional gift so that she would not be sent back (a female respondent born 1920 in Tuden). See Pesheva (1993, 272) for an example of a special dowry given in the form of a piece of land in the region of Sofia by the brothers of a crippled sister. This land was afterwards transferred to the groom by her family as a donation (Hristov 1999, 58). For both sides it was clear that this land was given as compensation. Though conforming to the law, this transfer was motivated by traditional norms (Tsekova 2011, 268).

14 It concerns here a female respondent born in 1922, in the village of Kalotina.

15 Of the five daughters-in-law in the Ketserovi family only one tried to have a meadow as dowry at her wedding: 'After the wedding they sold the meadow and gave the money to her so there wouldn't be any quarrels among the sisters-in-law' (a male respondent born in 1919 in the village of Kalotina). In the entire region men were convinced that the 'quarrels' among sisters-in-law were the reason for the division and break-up of complex family households (a male respondent born in 1920 in Komshtitsa).

16 A woman born in 1940 in the village of Gubesh told me how her father refused her mother to acquire *miraz* in her home village Gintsi: 'How could I go take some of the brother-in-law's land in Gintsi?' ('Kak che idem yaz da zemem ot imoto na shureite u Gintsi?').

17 In the Tran region older women used to say: 'A sister that takes from her brothers' land won't do well!' ('Koya si uzne ot bratyata imot, ona nema da prokopshe!') (a female respondent born in 1914 in Rani Lug). In northwestern Bulgaria it has been noted that brothers may curse a sister who demands her share from the father's land with 'See no good from that land!' (Donchev 1996, 67).

18 This was the Bulgarian version of the collective farms of Soviet type; in translation: Labour Collective Agricultural Farm.

19 I came across a touching story of a woman born in 1904 in Prekruste (married into another village) which illustrates this: when her father's property was divided in the

1940s, her two brothers gave a certain amount of money to their two sisters as a compensation for the shares they had given up. She did not wish to take away the land from 'the orphans' (her brother was a widower) but they convinced her to accept the compensation: 'That's not right, you were also born in this house and have worked in it.' She is still grateful for her brothers' decision, which was a notable exception in these villages.

20 The ethnologist Slavka Grebenarova provides examples from the Rhodope region. Even before they acquired the notarial act for the land in question, the brothers declared to their sisters, 'You have no business here!' (Grebenarova 2001, 80). In 1993, I witnessed three brothers in the village of Nasalevtsi, Tran region, publicly cursing a brother-in-law from another village who 'came to seek *miraz* at old age!'

21 A female municipal worker in the 'Studentska' municipality in Sofia was called repeatedly to the police station to act as a witness regarding the intentional or unintentional 'forgetting' of sisters when brothers submitted agricultural land inheritance declarations in the former villages of Darvenitsa and Malinova Dolina (between 1994 and 1997).

22 About similar practices in northwestern Bulgaria during the restoration of ownership over agricultural land, see also Benovska-Subkova (2001, 16).

References

Baldzhiev, Vasil. 1982. 'Studiya varhu nasheto personalno sapruzhesko pravo'. *Sbornik za narodni umotvoreniya* 7: 111–59.

Benovska-Subkova, Milena. 2001. 'Statusni roli, vlast i tsennosti v semeystvoto'. *Bulgarska etnologiya* 2: 7–25.

Brunnbauer, Ulf. 1999. 'Musulmanski i hristiyanski domakinstva v Rodopite ot vtorata polovina na XIX do parvata polovina na XX vek'. *Bulgarska etnologiya* 1–2: 44–69.

De Waal, Clarissa. 2004. 'Post-socialist Property Rights and Wrongs in Albania: An Ethnography of Agrarian Change'. *Conservation and Society* 1–2: 19–50.

Djordjević, Jadranka. 2003. 'Ravnopravieto na polovete pri nasledjavane: Realnost i ilyuziya'. In *Sotsializmat: Realnost i ilyuzii: Etnologichni aspekti na vsekidnevnata kultura*, edited by Radost Ivanova, Rachko Popov and Ana Luleva, 76–87. Sofia: Etnografski Institut s Muzey.

_____. 2005. 'Nasledjivanje u postsocijalističkom periodu u Bugarskoj i Srbiji'. In *Vsekidnevnata kultura na bulgarite i surbite v postsotsialisticheskiya period*, edited by Radost Ivanova, 175–85. Sofia: Etnografski Institut s Muzey.

Dobreva, Doroteja. 1997. 'Arbeiten im Kollektiv: Offizielle Norm und tatsächliches Verhalten in einem bulgarischen Gebirgsdorf in den 1950er Jahren'. In *Das Dorf in Südosteuropa zwischen Tradition und Umbruch*, edited by Frank-Dieter Grimm and Klaus Roth, 196–223. Munich: Südosteuropa-Gesellschaft und Institut für Länderkunde.

Donchev, Kamen. 1996. 'Obichayno nasledstveno pravo na bulgarskoto selo sled osvobozhdenieto do 40-te godini na XX vek'. *Bulgarska etnologiya* 2: 65–77.

Ganev, Venelin. 1921. 'Nasheto obichayno pravo i negovoto otbelyazvane'. In *Jubileen sbornik v chest na S. S. Bobchev*, 99–109. Sofia.

Georgiev, Georgi. 1979. *Osvobozhdenieto i etnokulturnoto razvitie na bulgarskiya narod: 1877–1900*. Sofia: Bulgarska Akademiya na Naukite.

Grebenarova, Slavka. 2001. 'Semeyniyat i rodninski konflikt v malkiya grad i rolyata na zhenata v postsotsialisticheskoto obshtestvo'. *Bulgarska etnologiya* 2: 79–100.

Giordano, Christian and Dobrinka Kostova. 1997. 'Bulgarian Land Reprivatisation without Peasants'. *Ethnologia Balkanica* 1: 135–49.

_____. 2000. 'Understanding Contemporary Problems in Bulgarian Agricultural Transformation'. In *Bulgaria: Social and Cultural Landscapes*, edited by Christian Giordano, Dobrinka Kostova and Evelyne Lohmann-Minka, 159–75. Fribourg: University Press of Fribourg.

Hann, Chris M. 1993. 'From Production to Property: Decollectivization and the Family–Land Relationship in Contemporary Hungary'. *Man* 28 (2): 299–320.

Hristov, Petko 1999. 'Durkinata niva i svatbeniyat daroobmen'. *Bulgarska etnologiya* 3–4: 56–76.

Ignatiev, Stefan. 1926. *Yurisprudenciyata na VKS*. Sofia.

Kaser, Karl. 2008. *Patriarchy after Patriarchy*. Berlin: LIT Verlag.

Kaneff, Deema. 1998. 'When "Land" Becomes "Territory": Land Privatization and Ethnicity in Rural Bulgaria'. In *Surviving Post-socialism: Local Strategies and Regional Responses in Eastern Europe and the Former Soviet Union*, edited by Sue Bridger and Frances Pine, 16–32. London: Routledge.

Kassabova-Dincheva, Anelia. 2002. 'Ot obichay kam zakon?' *Bulgarska etnologiya* 2: 39–55.

Kozhucharova, Veska and Rossitsa Rangelova. 2001. 'Rurality and Late Modernity in Transition Countries: The Case of Bulgaria'. In *Food, Nature and Society: Rural Life in Late Modernity*, edited by Hilary Tovey and Michel Blanc, 19–43. Aldershot: Ashgate.

Luleva, Ana. 1999. 'Izmereniya na rodstvoto vuv vsekidnevnata kultura na edno zapadnobulgarsko planinsko selo'. *Bulgarska etnologiya* 1–2: 85–101.

Marinov, Dimitar. 1894. 'Narodnoto obichayno pravo'. *Zhiva Starina* IV. Ruse.

Migev, Vladimir. 1995. *Kolektivizatsiyata v bulgarskoto selo (1948–1959)*. Sofia: Stopanstvo.

Moskova, Detelina. 1980. 'Obichayno pravo'. In *Pirinski kray*, 47–66. Sofia: Etnografski Institut s Muzey.

Odzhakov, Petar. 1885. *Obichayno nasledstveno pravo*. Ruse.

Pesheva, Rayna. 1993. 'Tradicionni formi na socialna organizatsiya'. In *Sofiyski kray*, 268–80. Sofia: Etnografski Institut s Muzey.

Sundhaussen, Holm. 1997. 'Vom Vor- zum Frühkapitalismus: Die Transformation des Dorfes und der Landwirtschaft im Balkanraum vom 19. Jh. bis zum zweiten Weltkrieg'. In *Das Dorf in Südosteuropa zwischen Tradition und Umbruch*, edited by Frank-Dieter Grimm and Klaus Roth, 29–48. Munich: Südosteuropa-Gesellschaft und Institut für Länderkunde.

Tsekova, Snezhana. 2011. 'Vliyanieto na obichaynopravnite koncepcii pri urezhdaneto na semeyno-brachnite i nasledstvenite otnosheniya v Bulgaria sled Osvobozhdenieto'. In *100 godini ot rozhdenieto na prof. Mihail Andreev*, edited by Malina Novkirishka-Stoyanova and Dimitar Tokushev, 250–71. Sofia: Universitetsko Izdatelstvo 'Sv. Kliment Ohridski'.

Šuvar, Stipe. 2004. 'Selo u tranziciji (nekoliko opaski o globalnom procesu deruralizacije)'. *Teme* 3: 167–75.

Tsing, Anna. 2005. *Friction: An Ethnography of Global Connection*. Princeton: Princeton University Press.

Verdery, Katherine. 1999. 'Fuzzy Property: Rights, Power, and Identity in Transylvania's Decollectivization'. In *Uncertain Transition: Ethnography of Change in the Postsocialist World*, edited by Michael Burawoy and Katherine Verdery, 53–81. Lanham, MD: Rowman and Littlefield.

Vladigerov, Todor. 1942. 'Agrarni otnosheniya v Bulgaria: Etnografski svedeniya'. *Godishnik na VTU 'Dimitar A. Tsenov'* 5: 1–102.

Wolf, Gabriele. 2000. 'Proektat "Raduil": Etnolozhko izsledvane na seloto mezhdu "mikroistoriya", "prezhivyana istoriya" i "sobstven zhivot"'. *Bulgarska etnologiya* 4: 5–16.

———. 1997. 'Der gebaute sozialistische Raum: Die räumlich-funktionale Umgestaltung eines bulgarischen Dorfes seit den 1950er Jahren'. In *Das Dorf in Südosteuropa zwischen Tradition und Umbruch*, edited by Frank-Dieter Grimm and Klaus Roth, 165–95. Munich: Südosteuropa-Gesellschaft und Institut für Länderkunde.

Chapter 8

RURAL, URBAN AND RURBAN: EVERYDAY PERCEPTIONS AND PRACTICES

Daniela Koleva

In this chapter, I will address the main question of the volume – how rurality is being remade under globalization – applying to social imaginaries a conceptual tool that has already been introduced in the initial chapters. Following Kaneff, I will engage with the concept of 'positionality' (position in relational space/ time within the global economy) suggested by geographer Eric Sheppard to capture 'the shifting, asymmetric, and path-dependent ways in which the futures of places depend on their interdependencies with other places' (2002, 308). The advantages of this concept are that it is relational and thus captures the aspects of connectivity, that it involves power relations and thus can account for inequalities, and that it is dialectic and thus helps to understand the agency that both reproduces and changes its earlier configurations. While Sheppard has developed the idea of positionality in the context of economic geography, he has noted its applicability to the 'space of discourse' as well (321–2) and it is this relevance that I would like to explore further. I expect that the interdependence (albeit asymmetric) and optionality implied in the idea of positionality might also be fruitful for our understanding of the 'micro' level of everyday experiences and social imaginaries.

As Duijzings has argued in the introduction, postsocialist transitions have led to the exposure of the countryside to global flows and hence to the blurring and partial collapse of spatial categories such as 'centre–periphery' and 'urban–rural'. While the relevance of the traditional urban–rural binary can be questioned (see Kaneff this volume), it seems that postsocialism has triggered new cultural and ideological engagements with the notions of 'urban' and 'rural' in public discourse. Therefore, while the boundaries between them may have become less clear in geographical terms, 'in cultural and ideological terms [...] people clearly differentiate the two, contextualizing each category within their own lives' (Duijzings this volume). Cultural production – both professional and vernacular – has been critical to the ways in which this differentiation occurs. This chapter will explore a case of cultural production of the 'urban' and 'rural', and the ways in which these representations are used to construct narratives of self and other, form notions of locality and authenticity, and establish ideologies of *Gemeinschaft*, etc.

Throughout the twentieth century, the opposition between town and countryside has been as pervasive – although perhaps not always as politically salient – as national, ethnic and religious divisions. Like the latter, the urban–rural opposition has sometimes been used to articulate ideological causes and support political arguments, whereby 'the rural' and 'the village' is normally associated with conservative values defending the nation, tradition and ethnic purity. In spite of the homogenizing efforts of the communist regime, the urban–rural division has remained an important aspect of everyday life in Bulgaria, as it continues to inform people's life choices and self-perceptions.

Stressing the experiential significance of the urban–rural divide, Gerald Creed and Barbara Ching (1997) emphasize the social construction of place, which is based on power relations and cultural hierarchies similar to those underlying orientalism (cf. Said 1978). Therefore, 'the rural' is systematically marginalized and chronically devalued (Creed and Ching 1997, 17). The term they use – 'rusticity' (unlike 'rurality' which is more neutral) – suggests that rural places are laden with immanent characteristics, of which lack of sophistication is probably the most important. Because of this it is difficult to identify and construct a positive sense of belonging to the rural as a place that is culturally valuable in itself. I do accept Creed and Ching's idea of the urban gaze having constitutive power, but I also intend to question the dichotomy between the urban and rural by looking at perceptions and experiences of their actual positionalities in the case of present-day Bulgaria. In doing so, I will follow Creed's argument (this volume) for a broader notion of positionality, articulating the ideas of 'urban' and 'rural' with other cultural categories, such as 'global' and 'local', 'modern' and 'authentic', *Gesellschaft* and *Gemeinschaft*. I will consider the urban–rural divide firstly in terms of how it is imagined, drawing my data from a nationwide opinion poll, and secondly, how it is experienced, drawing on fieldwork in the mountain village of Gorna Bela Rechka in the northwestern part of Bulgaria. My aim is to identify a variety of nuances and local meanings of the opposition between the 'urban' and 'rural', as well as look at people's flexible and ambiguous self-positionings within this dichotomy. On the basis of my analysis I will be challenging the idea of the urban–rural divide as a static ideological opposition.

Perceiving the 'Urban' and 'Rural'

To get some idea of the perceptions Bulgarians hold about the countryside and its residents, I will now turn to a nationwide opinion poll conducted in 2003 for the UNDP as part of the Human Development Report dedicated to the rural regions of Bulgaria (Mihailov et al. 2004).[1] I will consider only questions that probe stereotypes about the countryside, even though they were far from central to the poll, as such. Starting from the assumption that the 'urban' is usually associated with being modern and civilized, and the 'rural' with being backward and traditional, a couple of questions were formulated to test the salience of these associations at the level of contemporary everyday mentality. The respondents were given a list of lifestyle characteristics compiled from popular culture and media discourses (hence inevitably biased towards the 'urban') and they were asked to pick the ones they considered attributable to the 'modern person'.[2]

Rural residents agreed with urbanites that a 'modern person' uses new information and communication technologies. Unlike urbanites however, they more often imagined a modern person as someone who has a university education, reads books and newspapers, lives in a large city, watches Slavi Trifonov's TV show and listens to new pop-folk music.[3] Rural residents were more inclined to give 'socially desirable' responses and thus let themselves be 'manipulated' by the suggested options more easily. As a rule, they picked a greater number of the suggested lifestyle characteristics as typical of the 'modern person'. Therefore the percentages of positive endorsements for each trait were generally above the national average in the rural areas and considerably higher than the percentages in Sofia. The few exceptions are telling: for rural residents, active engagement with sports, medical prophylactics and, most notably, cohabitation were less recognizable as part of a 'modern' lifestyle than they were for urbanites.

A modern person:	Rural	National	Sofia
Works on a computer	87.6%	88.1%	92.8%
Buys a new mobile phone whenever s/he can afford	70.1%	66.5%	69.9%
Reads newspapers	73.2 %	67.6%	57.1%
Has a university education	73.0 %	62.5 %	40.9%
Reads books	67.7%	61.2%	44.4%
Lives in a large city	60.9%	51.3%	46.8%
Watches Slavi Trifonov's show	51.1 %	40.6 %	25.3%
Listens to new pop-folk music	39.4 %	28.7 %	11.7%
Is engaged with sports in his/her leisure time	63.9%	67.9%	65.6%
Takes care about medical prophylactics	64.7%	65.1%	68.8%
Lives with a partner without being married	49.0%	54.0%	68.6%

Source: UNDP/ASA (2003).

The phrasing of the question 'How is a modern person recognized?' makes it difficult to differentiate whether the selected traits reflect the respondents' observations of the actual state of affairs (an 'empirical' notion), or whether it captures their opinion of the desired one – that is, the ideal 'modern person' as they see it (a 'normative' notion). Most likely, the normative notion bleeds into the empirical one. In any case, given that the rural population is on the average older, poorer and less educated, it tends to construct the 'modern' outside of itself, in spatial terms (the 'modern person' is likely to abide in cities), in terms of knowledge and skills (the 'modern person' is a university graduate and a user of new technologies), and in terms of lifestyle (the 'modern person' indulges in reading and in conspicuous consumption).[4] It can be assumed that such constructions probably rely more on normative ideas than on personal experience. This hypothesis is supported by the fact that forms of popular culture most easily accessible for rural residents – TV shows, pop-folk music and folklore – do not feature high on the scale of 'modern-ness'. Constructing the 'modern' as outside or even opposed to the 'rural' is also evident from the fact that only about one quarter of the rural residents (24.5 per cent) respond that they would like to be a modern person (as opposed to the national average of 31.6 per cent), while 45 per cent respond squarely negative (28.7 per cent national, 14.5 per cent Sofia). Again, it is not entirely clear whether these responses indicate an opposition to the 'modern' lifestyle as described in the previous question. They may rather suggest that respondents from rural regions have developed what Bourdieu terms a 'taste for necessity' (1979, 435–48); that is, they do not see a chance for themselves to be modern and hence – based on what is considered 'normal' for them – just accept the inevitable.

The survey data demonstrate that the old division between 'rural as traditional' and 'urban as modern' seems to persist. However, the 'rural' and 'traditional' is not necessarily perceived negatively: in the poll, the statement that 'the village is a symbol of Bulgarian backwardness' is neither refuted nor corroborated (receiving a score of 3.05 on a 1–5 scale where 1 means 'strongly disagree' and 5 'strongly agree'), while statements such as 'the village is a symbol of Bulgarian roots', and 'the peasant is hard-working', 'hospitable' and 'maintains traditions', command the highest levels of support (national averages 4.10, 4.16, 4.11 and 4.09 respectively). Thus, the 'rural-as-traditional' seems to carry positive connotations and is relatively highly valued. A closer look at the responses of different groups leads to interesting insights: while rural residents see themselves first and foremost as hard workers (4.36, the highest score), Sofia residents tend to be less convinced (3.80); while the former consider rural life hard (4.26, second highest score), the latter consider it to be healthy (3.95). These attitudes seem to reflect a romanticized image of the village as a stronghold of traditions, traditional virtues and life close to nature – an image constructed primarily from the outside as well as cultivated by classic Bulgarian ethnography and literature.

Do you agree that:	Rural	National	Sofia
The peasant is a hard worker	4.36	4.16	3.80
The peasant is hospitable	4.25	4.11	3.85
The peasant maintains traditions	4.14	4.09	4.05
The village is a symbol of Bulgarian roots	4.19	4.10	3.85
The village is a symbol of Bulgarian backwardness	3.15	3.05	2.82
Rural life is hard	4.26	4.01	3.61
Rural life is healthy	3.74	3.77	3.95
There is envy and petty-mindedness in the village	3.20	3.03	2.61
The peasant is gullible	2.79	2.75	2.26
The peasant is stingy	2.63	2.65	2.53
The peasant is conservative	3.10	3.21	2.96

Source: UNDP/ASA (2003).

Thus, the survey data present what seems to be a complex ideological and axiological positionality. On the one hand, they testify to the reproduction of the dichotomy of 'urban' as modern and sophisticated versus 'rural' as traditional and simple. On the other, perhaps surprisingly, negative stereotypes about the 'village' and 'peasant' are actually not as strong as might be inferred from Creed and Ching's argument about the cultural hierarchies between the sophisticated 'urban' and the uncivilized 'rustic'. What the poll seems to point out is that 'rurality' rather than 'rusticity' is the dominant notion, even to the extent that Sofia residents see 'peasants' in a more favourable light than the latter see themselves. Does this undermine Creed and Ching's thesis? To my mind, that would be too hasty a conclusion. These positive attitudes towards peasants reveal a certain idealization of the 'rural' that might represent a form of critique of (post)modern urban culture rather than genuine knowledge of the countryside. Rural backwardness is reconceptualized as rural idyll, as a 'moral image to inspire or discipline urban behaviour' (1997, 20), not as a real alternative to urbanity. This axiological reversal of the urban–rural hierarchy does not really challenge the positional superiority of urbanity: the 'rural' is again constructed from the outside by the urban gaze – a kind of 'orientalist' attitude conditioned by symbolic and political demands. Or, as Creed and

Ching write, the cultural value of the 'rural' is only established by urban authorization, be it activist environmentalist rhetoric or nostalgic evocation of a simple life close to nature.

Living the Urban–Rural Division

The second part of my argument will reverse the perspective to see how the changing positionality of one particular rural place is perceived, practiced and negotiated by its inhabitants. It is based on fieldwork I carried out in Gorna Bela Rechka, a small village in the western part of the Stara Planina (the Balkan mountain range) near the small town of Varshets, once well known in the region as a spa resort. The village comprises some sixty households, a good share of them consisting of one person only. With the exception of two younger families (one of which keeps the local pub and the other the local shop), all residents are retired or facing retirement. Thus, Bela Rechka can be seen as representative of the numerous 'dying' villages in Bulgaria, a consequence of sustained depopulation during the past few decades.[5] Yet Bela Rechka is perhaps not a typical case. It can be singled out because of its residents' heightened awareness of the urban–rural distinction and their conscious attempts at self-positioning within or across it, which is triggered by two factors: past rural–urban migration and the present opening up of the village to the world via the annual Goatmilk Memories Festival. As for the first, none of the villagers I met had spent their entire lives in the village. During their working lives, many of them had migrated to urban areas (mostly the regional centre Vratsa and the capital Sofia) to take up predominantly blue-collar jobs. Those who had stayed in the village spent years in the collective farm before moving or commuting to the nearby town of Varshets working in low-qualified jobs in the service sector. After retirement they returned to stay in Bela Rechka permanently or for the spring and summer, commonly engaging in subsistence farming. Past migration and present seasonal mobility between city and village make attempts to define the residents of Bela Rechka as 'ruralites' or 'urbanites' rather pointless, which has interesting implications for their self-identification.

The second factor that has enhanced the positionality of Bela Rechka relative to nearby localities, and contributed to the villagers' heightened awareness of it, is the Goatmilk Festival, organized annually since 2004 at the end of May by the Nova Kultura (New Culture) Foundation from Sofia. The festival was initiated by journalist Diana Ivanova and has evolved into an important event for the village, organized from the outside but aided by the local authorities and included in the cultural calendar of the municipality. It gathers participants from different countries and a variety of creative fields – journalists, actors, photographers, musicians, alternative artists, architects, etc. – to discuss the topics of memory and identity and their artistic articulations. The topics range from memories of socialism, family history and oral history, through new regimes of memory, to ideas for the future of the region, which is the poorest and the most underdeveloped in Bulgaria. Discussions run parallel with workshops on ethnic music and dance, experimental theatre and jazz performances, photo exhibitions and screenings of documentaries and multimedia projects, while participants also explore local food, music and crafts.[6] With its focus on intellectual debate, artistic activities, engagement with local issues and strong reliance on volunteering, the festival has hitherto avoided developing into a site of mass tourism or a 'metro-rural idyll', as is the case with other villages which increasingly provide a stage for the performance of mythical rurality.[7]

The culmination of the festival each year is the visit of the Varshets brass band, resulting in *horo* dances in the village square. This is the moment when the village community and festival community interact most intensely. Not being paraded as rural protagonists in a culture-managerial consumerist fantasy, villagers are free to join all the activities, which they sometimes do. Some of them offer accommodation for the participants and, most importantly, they all enjoy the atmosphere of the event for three or four days and talk about it for the rest of the year. On my first visit, I was struck by how often villagers referred to the festival as a distinctive feature of the place.[8] In the next section, I will present local perceptions of the urban–rural dichotomies, derived from fifteen recorded biographical interviews (Koleva 2007) and about twenty informal interviews (including two group interviews) which were conducted with villagers in the summer of 2006 and during the festivals of 2007, 2009 and 2011.[9] The structure of this section highlights the ways in which the notion of rurality implicates other categories, demonstrating its relational character.

Urban–rural as global–local

Saying 'hello' in Bela Rechka always takes a while as the greeting naturally evolves into a conversation about where I am from and what brings me here. As soon as I start explaining, 'I live in Sofia, but I was born in...', I am immediately interrupted with them saying, 'Okay, fine, so you are from Bulgaria.' That the topic is so quickly exhausted should not come as a surprise: for the past couple of years, villagers have welcomed guests from Europe and beyond, from countries such as Poland, the Czech Republic, Slovakia, Turkey, Austria, Germany, Belgium, Britain, Switzerland and Norway – all of whom participate in the festival. The villagers have also told me about their children and grandchildren living in different places such as Macedonia, Spain, the US and even Korea. As a result of the global spread of visitors and relatives, the inhabitants are aware of their village being situated in a geographical and virtual space which they could have hardly imagined a decade ago. Due to such 'shortcuts' (Duijzings this volume), their world has widened, reaching far beyond the nearby towns, which used to set the spatial limits of their experience in the past. Now their networks often bypass these towns to extend across national borders. What used to be 'far away' (Bauman 1998, 13), a place about which one knows little and does not feel obliged to care, has become 'near' – familiar and obvious. In this context, many interviewees tend to present their return to the village as 'freedom of movement' in the above Baumanian sense – that is, a matter of choice rather than need. A former army officer tells me, for instance, that he preferred to come back to where he was born, and a recently retired clerk claims that no one could make her 'back out' of the village. 'As long as I breathe and my eyes are open, I will stay in the village and I am certain that one day we will bring tourism back here', the former mayor declares; she has spent years as a restaurant manager in the regional centre before returning to the village to take care of her old parents. (She did not comment on the fact that her return coincided with the privatization of the restaurant and her redundancy.) Yet since moving to the countryside is a common way of coping with impoverishment after retirement (Asenova and McKinnon 2007, 393–4), it is difficult to say whether such self-presentations reflect a free choice or indeed a choice out of necessity (Bourdieu 1979, 435–48).[10] In some cases, living in the village allows elderly people to remain relatively independent from their adult children; their satisfaction with rural life may be interpreted as a satisfaction with their own physical condition allowing them to make such a choice.

Urban–rural as modern–authentic

Of the basic countryside resources – food, landscape, clean water and air – Bela Rechka cannot boast plenty of the first, but awareness of the others seems to be developing. Very much like the respondents of the poll, the inhabitants of the village stress the tough physical work and hardships of rural life. As one elderly man ironically says, he 'can't recommend it'. At the same time, on some occasions, they praise rural life as healthy and close to nature. Some of my interviewees claim that they feel 'imprisoned' in the apartments in town and look forward to coming back in the summer.

They wax lyrical about the fresh air, the clean mountains, the pure water and the little pleasures of rural life: 'I cultivate a vineyard and make my own wine and 50 litres of rakia from the marc. And I like very much the spigot to go "kriits" and I like to sit down to a steak. I like it very much but work is needed – not praying but a hoe', one of them explains evoking a popular saying. On numerous occasions, villagers tend to praise homemade products. One mentioned to me, for instance, the hemp chemises[11] which she used to weave and sew at home in her youth: at first she complained that there was nothing else to wear, but later she told how young women who came for the festival the year before dressed up in those chemises and did a photo shoot. Thereafter, she stored away her chemises lest they be stolen: 'There are so many memories attached to them', she explained. No doubt the Goatmilk Festival has contributed to the villagers' awareness of the performative and marketing potential of the landscape, their traditional technologies and homemade products. They sometimes sell goat cheese to participants, though they do not specifically produce it for sale. The optimistic scenario for the future of the village, mentioned by some inhabitants, includes the development of rural tourism and the selling of village houses to affluent urbanites from Bulgaria and abroad; in fact, since the start of the festival, two houses have indeed been sold, so this scenario does not seem entirely unrealistic. Thus the village is imagined by its inhabitants in an 'urban' aestheticized way as a form of heritage – a 'museum' of nature and tradition, and a counterpoint to civilization; not a real alternative but rather a temporary sanctuary from it (see Koleva 2004). At the same time, this romantic imaginary tends to be exploited in a pragmatic business-like manner in emerging plans to manage that heritage in line with new environmental and recreational interests, commoditizing and 'selling' the village as a rural refuge for urbanites and as a site of ecotourism. The structural weakness and the lack of resources have so far prevented initiatives that might potentially lead to 'Disneyfication' of the village.

Urban–rural as consumption–work

In spite of their nostalgia for the earlier years of the collective, when the place was full of people, the villagers never forget to mention that payment was poor and that that was the main reason why most of the inhabitants migrated to urban centres. They explain that, in their youth, they did not see any prospects for themselves in the village in terms of jobs: 'All young people ran away. There is no way of life here.' Another motive seems to have been the living standard – the villagers like to enumerate the acquisitions they or their adult children have accumulated in town: apartments, cars, central heating. Urban residence seems to be associated not only with more comfortable jobs but with a rise in social status and higher levels of consumption. Nevertheless, urban migrants have continued to resort to forms of production characteristic of the rural economy, obviously because they represent ready-made and predictable patterns that are easy to implement, and provide certainty in a period of adaptation to new living conditions (Matić 2005, 147). For decades, they used to come back on weekends to do agricultural work. A considerable part of their food was thus home grown and conserved in jars. Thus different generations of the same family lived (and some still do) in what Julian Konstantinov has termed 'rural–urban households' (Konstantinov 2001), with continued dependency of urban residents on their retired rural relatives. Most villagers in turn rely on their towns kin for services and assistance, such as medical treatment in case of health problems and supplies of consumer items that are not available in the village. When talking about these practices, they seem to associate rurality with work, which they understand to be hard agricultural labour, and urbanity with a more comfortable life and a better living standard. Although their occupations are always mentioned, urbanites feature in the villagers' conversations mostly as consumers (buying cars, taking food from the village, etc.). Even when they speak of their own earlier life in town, informants tend to stress acquisitions rather than work. In some sense, this is an idealization of urban life reciprocating the romanticized image of the countryside above.

The festival has not changed these associations; the artistic activities that participants engage in – though welcomed by villagers, as 'they make us merry' (*veseliat ni*) – confirm the idea that what urbanites do is not 'real work'. On the other hand, villagers feel they work by providing accommodation and food for the visitors (for modest payment) in much the same way as they do for their visiting relatives from the town. In their subsequent endless conversations about the festival, they refer to their lodgers affectionately as 'the children' or 'my girls'. There is clearly a generational aspect to this: most informants belong to the postwar generation who have inherited the work culture and modest consumption patterns of their predecessors. The next generation – that is, that of their children – has been socialized in a very different economic and sociocultural situation and therefore holds quite different views of work and consumption, more closely related to what the villagers imagine as the urban lifestyle.

Urban–rural as Gesellschaft–Gemeinschaft

One of the consequences of rapid social and cultural change in the village is a growing sense of insecurity and isolation, even where, as in Bela Rechka, relatively strong social ties exist and one can hardly speak of socially disintegrated households or neighbourhoods. Against this backdrop, the villagers indulge in memories of past collectivism and mutuality. Haymaking is a frequent topic; it used to be the most important joint campaign, where everybody – men and women – would be mobilized. The men would line up to cut the hay and the women would follow behind stacking it. Meanwhile, a lamb would be slaughtered and cooked in a cauldron over the open fire, and after work, everybody would eat and drink and sing together. Working together and feasting together went hand in hand. Another interviewee stresses that life used to be merrier before, because villagers would gather in the evenings, sit together or dance *horo*.

Leaving for town is considered an individualistic life strategy which has ultimately led to the dissolution of the rural community. However, none of my informants ever blames or criticizes those who left for the city. On the contrary, many stress that in a way the village continues to exist, as solidarity between villagers has been preserved in town. Informal networks have been instrumental in helping newcomers settle and in providing them with jobs and housing. A few interviewees mention that migrants from Bela Rechka used to work in a heating plant in Sofia and lived in blocks of flats near the plant, 'like a village': they were in constant contact and used to help each other, keeping an eye on each other's children and taking them to school when parents were working in shifts.

No doubt, the present situation of the elderly villagers contributes to their views on rural life as collective and egalitarian. As everyone is now retired, the differences in social status that have undoubtedly existed in the past (even in the classless socialist society) do not seem to be so important any longer. Former inequalities can now be easily ignored, as the villagers' situations are now similar: they all receive very small pensions, all have problems of deteriorating health and all place their hopes on their grandchildren. Furthermore, they all face newly emerging inequalities that make them feel like losers. Finally, they all adopt the same traditional strategies and technologies of self-subsistence which they have learned from their predecessors. Thus their solidarity is rooted not in a political ideology, but in shared experience and routine daily activities necessitating collaboration (such as taking turns to graze the goats). These practices are not contradicted by the fact that in the end every individual prioritizes his or her own interests and his or her own property. Nor did village solidarity prevent them from making 'individualistic' decisions such as moving to town earlier in their lives.

Conclusion: Redefining Rurality

This chapter has attempted a broadening of the notion of positionality onto the 'space of discourse', to capture the ways in which 'the rural' has been imagined, defined and experienced in everyday life. Focusing on a particular case, it sought to understand how these imaginaries and definitions intersect with, reflect or affect the lives of rural people. In some respects, the case of Bela Rechka seems to confirm Creed and Ching's notion of the hegemonic urban gaze constructing 'rusticity' and conferring value on it. The Goatmilk Festival can be seen as just that: young urban intellectuals own the cultural capital to valorize rural practices and products, discovering and engaging artistically with them. Thus they transform these practices and products into 'culture' – equally in their own eyes as in the eyes of the rural inhabitants. Highlighting the superiority of urbanity, the rusticity thesis, however, somehow fails to capture the complex dynamics of urban–rural interactions and fundamentally ignores and misses the ruralites' point of view. By implying their passive givenness as the objects of urban construction, the analysis risks reproducing, on another level, the essentialism of these notions of rurality and rusticity that it sets out to criticize. That is why it seems important to examine how the dynamics of urban–rural encounters in the case of Bela Rechka lead to various repositionings, and to do it from the perspective of the 'rural' and the 'ruralites' as well.

The villagers of Bela Rechka started their careers as peasants for whom agriculture was a way of life. With the introduction of monthly salaries in the socialist collective, and then with the subsequent transformation of the collectives into state-owned 'agrarian-industrial complexes', peasants grew into agricultural workers for whom agriculture became a salaried occupation (Jääts 2004; see also Creed 1999). Symbolically at least, they were more favourably positioned in the social landscape of the village. Most of them changed occupation in the course of their working lives, as a result of which they spent years living in town practising 'urban' occupations. Thus they experienced privileged positionality due to their spatial mobility, which in this case meant upward social mobility and accumulation of social capital (connections both in the village and in town). This relational identity, co-dependent on occupation and residence, has kept surfacing in the ways in which villagers position themselves in all four dimensions of the urban–rural distinction discussed above: they have been urbanites for a good part of their lives, and now they are again ruralites, but living in a privileged village; they identify with valued traits of rurality but easily dissociate from derided ones based on their urban experience; and they play global relational 'shortcuts' against the 'urban gaze'. Albeit situated low in the cultural hierarchy, they do not passively absorb traits imposed on them from the outside but employ and adapt them selectively, thereby actively engaging in a process of self-identification. This is also visible in the way the local identity of Bela Rechka is constructed. Having neither sufficient agricultural potential, nor acknowledged historical, cultural or artistic heritage, villagers evoke a vague and somewhat ambivalent notion of rurality, embracing both elements in a pragmatic response to outside (that is, urban) interests. While nostalgic about

the rural agricultural past, when the village was full of life, they now have begun
to see other dimensions of rurality, not necessarily linked with agriculture. These
evolving attitudes can be interpreted, following Ivaylo Ditchev, as a sign of the
end of postcommunist transition, a sign of stabilization that brings folklore and
nature into the spotlight (Ditchev 2005, 8).

The case of Bela Rechka is an example of the changing vision of rurality,
which is shifting towards a wider, nonagrarian perception of the countryside
as a result of the diminishing economic and cultural importance of agriculture
on the one hand, and the growth of cultural and environmental interests on
the other. Therefore, a wider array of possible positions and relations has
become available, overriding the bipolar model; the 'rural' does not seem to
be opposed any more to the 'urban' as was agriculture to industry, but it is
now rather perceived as socially, economically and culturally integrated with
urban life. Of course, as Creed (this volume) has pointed out, such a neoliberal
integration is fraught with further rural devaluation.

Even this limited and cursory look into the perceptions and local
meanings of the 'rural' and 'urban', mediated by people's experiences, shows
that maintaining a strict opposition between the two leads to a hegemonic
essentialization of the 'rural' and the 'urban' and their conceptualization
as static entities. The reproduction of the dichotomy obscures the complex
dynamics and interconnections resulting from the experience and renegotiation
of the 'rural' and the 'urban' in everyday life and at the sites of the (vernacular)
cultural production of rurality, urbanity and a hybrid 'rurbanity'. So we end
up deterritorializing rurality and urbanity, seeing rurality rather as a 'created
field' (Tisenkopfs 1999) – a field that is constantly under construction through
the discourses and practices of various social actors, and through their creative
capacities and interests. New actors have emerged that weave new connections
between urban areas and the countryside, leading to further changes in their
positional dynamics. As a result, instead of a spatial division based on social
and geographical distance, the urban–rural distinction seems on its way to
becoming much more of a cultural and ideological division, a pair of 'ideal
types' to think with, to engage with and relate to.

Notes

1 The poll was carried out by the Agency for Social Analyses (ASA) over a two-month
period (February–March 2003), using a nationally representative two-stage random
sample boosted in the villages. It included a total of 1,432 face-to-face interviews of
which 629 were carried out in villages. An extensive questionnaire elicited opinions
on the quality of life in the countryside, including employment, social services and
health care, education, etc., as well as evaluations of newly implemented programmes
to support agriculture and the development of rural regions.

2 It is worth keeping in mind that the Bulgarian word for 'modern', *moderen*, also means 'fashionable'.

3 Slavi Trifonov is the host of a popular evening show on one of the national TV channels, combining interviews with guests, political satire and music (mainly parodies of popular hits). First broadcast in 2000, it is one of the longest running ongoing TV shows in Bulgaria. Pop-folk or *chalga* (known as *manele* in Romania, *chalgija* in Macedonia or *turbofolk* in Serbia) is a popular music genre which can best be described as ethnopop. It emerged in the 1990s and combines elements of local folklore with Turkish, Greek and Roma music, using rhythmic and repetitive melodies. The neutral term 'pop-folk' was used in the questionnaire to avoid any of the negative connotations attached to *chalga*.

4 The average age for the rural cohort was 53 years, the national average age 47 years, while the average age in Sofia was 43 years. As for the level of education of the respondents: 59.9 per cent of the rural population had lower or primary education, while 3.7 per cent had university education; nationally these figures were 30.4 per cent elementary or primary education and 17.6 per cent university education; for Sofia 5.8 per cent elementary or primary education and 45.8 per cent university education. Monthly income per household in Bulgarian lev: rural 234.89; national 335.99; and Sofia 520.32.

5 Édouard Conte and Christian Giordano have noticed that Bulgaria (alongside the former Czechoslovakia and the Baltic countries) was most affected by the collectivization of agricultural land under socialism, producing a drastic fall in the share of the rural population by 42 per cent (1998, 28). Forced collectivization campaigns in 1948, 1950–51 and 1957–58 produced a rural exodus. The restitution of agricultural land in the 1990s did little to reverse this process; on the contrary, the economic hardships of the postcommunist transition in fact exacerbated the rural exodus. However, not all regions are equally affected: villages in developed agricultural regions, satellite villages of urban or tourist centres, as well as villages predominantly inhabited by minorities have often retained most of their populations.

6 Information on this festival can be found online: http://novakultura.org/goat-milk/en/ (accessed 15 February 2013).

7 For instance, the 2008 festival included and amalgamated with a two-year project to restore the stolen church bell: the activities included the collection of stories about the bell and its theft, an essay contest, a campaign to raise funds for the construction of a bell tower and the casting of a new bell, a sound installation, and finally a book describing and reflecting on the whole experience (Ivanova 2009). In 2011, the highlight was the abandoned houses: a discussion was held with mayors from the region about their future, and one such house was the stage for a poetry evening.

8 According to a 2007 study, the festival has brought certain economic, social and ecological benefits, but it has first and foremost changed the way the inhabitants of the village perceive themselves; it has boosted their self-confidence and self-respect (Vulkovski 2007).

9 The fieldwork was carried out as part of the project *Remembering Communism: Memory 'From Below'* (2006–2007) of the Institute for the Study of the Recent Past, funded through the MATRA-KAP Programme of the Dutch Embassy in Sofia (Daniela Koleva, ed. *Varhu hrastite ne padat malnii: Komunizmat – zhiteiski sadbi* [Lightning does not strike bushes: Communism – life stories]. Sofia: Institute for the Study of the Recent Past, 2007). I have also used interviews carried out by other members of the fieldwork team: Vanya Elenkova, Slavka Karakusheva and Alexandra Petrova.

10 Many villagers combine two coping strategies identified by these authors: moving to the countryside in spring and summer and living with their children's families in multigenerational households during winter. The festival offers opportunities for some of them to adopt a third strategy – earning some extra income in order to complement their pensions – but these opportunities are very limited as the festival mostly depends on volunteer work.

11 An item of traditional clothing usually made of cotton and worn under a woollen sleeveless dress or jacket. The visible parts around the neck, the sleeves and the lower rim of women's chemises were often decorated with fine embroidery.

References

Asenova, Darinka and Roddy McKinnon. 2007. 'The Bulgarian Pension Reform: Post-accession Issues and Challenges'. *Journal of European Social Policy* 17 (4): 389–96.

Bauman, Zygmunt. 1998. *Globalization: The Human Consequences*. Oxford: Polity.

Bourdieu, Pierre. 1979. *La distinction: Critique sociale du jugement*. Paris: Minuit.

Conte, Édouard and Christian Giordano. 1997. 'Sentiers de la ruralité perdue; reflexions sur le post-socialisme'. In 'Paysans au-delà du mur', special issue of *Études rurales*, 138–40: 11–33.

Creed, Gerald. 1999. 'Deconstructing Socialism in Bulgaria'. In *Uncertain Transition: Ethnographies of Change in the Postsocialist World*, edited by Michael Burawoy and Katherine Verdery, 223–43. Boston and Oxford: Rowman and Littlefield.

Creed, Gerald and Barbara Ching. 1997. 'Recognizing Rusticity: Identity and the Power of Place'. In *Knowing Your Place: Rural Identity and Cultural Hierarchy*, edited by Barbara Ching and Gerald Creed, 1–38. New York: Routledge.

Ditchev, Ivaylo. 2005. *Prostranstva na zhelanieto / zhelania za prostranstvo: Etyudi po gradska antropologiya*. Sofia: Iztok-Zapad.

Ivanova, Diana, ed. 2009. *Kak se pravi kambana*. Sofia: Zhanet 45.

Jääts, Indrek. 2004. 'Working in a Kolkhoz: The Case of the Oisu Area, Central Estonia (1948–1964)'. In *Arbeit im Sozialismus: Arbeit im Postsozialismus: Erkundungen zum Arbeitsleben im östlichen Europa*, edited by Klaus Roth, 91–108. Münster: LIT Verlag.

Koleva, Daniela. 2004 (2000). 'Narrating Nature: Perceptions of the Environment and Attitudes Toward It in Life Stories'. In *The Roots of a New Political Agenda: Environmental Consciousness*, edited by Paul Thompson and Stephen Hussey, 63–75. New Brunswick: Transaction.

———, ed. 2007. *Varhu hrastite ne padat malnii: Komunizmat – zhiteiski sadbi*. Sofia: Institut za Izsledvane na Blizkoto Minalo (Institute for the Study of the Recent Past).

Konstantinov, Julian. 2001. 'Nahrung vom Dorf, Beziehungen durch die Stadt: Über den gegenwärtigen Charakter des bulgarischen Land-Stadt-Haushalts'. In *Vom Nutzen der Verwandten: Soziale Netzwerke in Bulgarien (19. und 20. Jahrhundert)*, edited by Ulf Brunnbauer and Karl Kaser, 43–67. Vienna: Böhlau Verlag.

Matić, Miloš. 2005. 'Urban Economics in a Rural Manner: Family Economising in Socialist Serbian Cities'. *Ethnologia Balkanica* 9: 131–49.

Mihailov, Docho, Antoaneta Simova, Daniela Koleva, Diana Kopeva, Zhelyu Vladimirov, Lyubomir Dimitrov and Yanka Kazakova. 2004. *Rural Regions: Overcoming Development Disparities, National Human Development Report: Bulgaria 2003*. Sofia: United Nations Development Programme.

Said, Edward. 1978. *Orientalism*. New York: Pantheon Books.

Sheppard, Eric. 2002. 'The Spaces and Times of Globalization: Place, Scale, Networks, and Positionality'. *Economic Geography* 78 (3): 307–30.

Tisenkopfs, Talis. 1999. 'Rurality as a Created Field: Towards an Integrated Rural Development in Latvia?'. *Sociologia Ruralis* 39 (3): 411–30.

Vulkovski, Yuriy. 2007. 'Vliyanie na festivala varhu mestnata obshtnost'. In *Goat Milk: Tetradki ot Bela Rechka*, edited by Diana Ivanova, 113–59. Sofia: Fondatsiya za Nova Kultura.

Chapter 9

THE KOPRIVSHTITSA FESTIVAL: FROM NATIONAL ICON TO GLOBALIZED VILLAGE EVENT

Liz Mellish

Anthropologists have shown that festivals tend to constantly evolve, acquiring different characteristics and roles depending on changing political contexts and circumstances. In 1992, one of the leading scholars in the field, Jeremy Boissevain, commented that since the 1970s, the number of festivals in Europe had been steadily increasing (1992, 2) and this trend has continued in the subsequent years, albeit on a global scale. There has been a long history of anthropological interest in festive behaviour, and studies have been undertaken that cover a wide spectrum of topics including the links between festivals and tourism, ritual, commemoration, identity and political formations.[1] Conclusions from these studies have revealed that the term 'festival' can be used to refer to a broad range of forms of cultural events with a wide variety of purposes and audiences. Festivals can have ancient roots, they may be established by a regime to serve its own political purposes, or created as a commercial event. Festivals have often changed their meanings over time, adapting to modern circumstances in attempts to protect their future existence.

When defining festivals I draw from Stoeltje, who observes that festivals are 'collective phenomena' which take place 'at calendrically regulated intervals and are public in nature, participatory in ethos, complex in structure and multiple in voice, scene and purpose' (2002, 271). In other words, festivals need a location and an occasion in which to take place, sufficient participants (performers and audience), public or private funding, and in many cases a 'message' or intention that serves the 'commercial, ideological, or political purposes of self-interested authorities or entrepreneurs' (262). Stoeltje also observes that events carrying the name 'festival' in their titles are 'generally contemporary modern constructions' (261) – a view reinforced by Anca

Giurchescu, who comments that in Eastern Europe the term 'festival' was not in linguistic usage before the communist period, hence any event that has 'festival' in its title is either a creation by the political regime prior to 1989 or has its origins in the postcommunist period.[2]

David Guss, when studying festivals in Venezuela, observed how festivals that began as local or national events can enlarge their semantic fields over time so that they are 'no longer limited to the interpretation of a single community', but shift to become commercial enterprises that engage in a 'national and even global discourse' (2000, 174). My contribution to this volume will look at one such festival, the National Festival of Bulgarian Folklore (Natsionalen Sabor Koprivshtitsa),[3] that has taken place in the museum village of Koprivshtitsa, in the Sredna Gora Mountains of central Bulgaria approximately every five years since 1965. In this chapter I reflect on how, as a result of this festival, a small rural town in Bulgaria has, over a period of over forty years, become the focal centre for members of a global network of Bulgarian folk music and dance enthusiasts, and has consequently shifted its 'positionality' (Sheppard 2002, 318; also see Kaneff this volume) from an icon of the Bulgarian nation to holding a place in a global touristic frame of reference.

The Koprivshtitsa Festival is an occasion where multiple presentations of Bulgarian music, song and dance take place. Following Singer (1955, 27) I would refer to these presentations as cultural performances.[4] Guss outlines four key elements of such cultural performances which can be applied to the Koprivshtitsa Festival. He sees these as 'clearly framed events' set apart from everyday life, and 'important dramatizations that enable participants to understand, criticize and even change the worlds in which they live' (2000, 7–9). He acknowledges that such performances are 'sites of social action where identities and relations are continually being reconfigured' and that they can be subject to multiple interpretations, especially when such 'local forms become entangled within national and global debates' (10–12). When interpreting the performances during events such as the Koprivshtitsa Festival, consideration has to be taken of the contemporary sociopolitical and economic contexts in which they take place (Silverman 1985, 103), and of how these change over time, both in the local microcosm of the festival and in the global world in which it is embedded. Giddens sees globalization 'as the intensification of worldwide social relations which link distant localities in such a way that local happenings are shaped by events occurring many miles away and vice versa' (1990, 64). Over the history of the Koprivshtitsa Festival the internal social relations that at the outset linked this small rural town to Sofia, the national centre, have been replaced by linkages to groups of people who participate in Bulgarian folk music and dance in all continents of the world. Thus, as Appadurai observes regarding the process of globalization, this has resulted in Bulgarian culture becoming 'an arena for conscious choice' that is linked to 'multiple and spatially dislocated audiences' (1996, 44).

This chapter will look at how the Koprivshtitsa Festival has changed from a primarily national Bulgarian state-funded event into a commercialized global event over a period of several decades in which the social, political and economic contexts have fundamentally changed. In doing this, I will distinguish three partly overlapping groups of people. The first is the 'local participants', by which I mean the Bulgarian villagers or members of groups performing 'authentic' folklore that live in Bulgarian towns. The second group consists of 'Bulgarian urbanites' (including members of the Bulgarian diaspora), some of whom are, or previously were, members of urban-based professional and amateur folk ensembles or *horo* clubs.[5] The third group is the non-Bulgarian visitors to the festival who are part of a global cultural cohort of Bulgarian folk music and dance enthusiasts, whom I will refer to as 'folk tourists'.[6] After introducing the reader to the Koprivshtitsa Festival in which local performers have always played a key role, I will then consider the folk tourists who first came to the festival during the socialist period and who have come in ever greater numbers since the end of socialism. I will describe how their interest in Bulgarian folk music, dance and song inspires them to make the journey to the Koprivshtitsa Festival. This will then be followed by an analysis of the postcommunist festival, which has seen an increased interest among Bulgarian urbanites. I look at the performances, including the impromptu gatherings and spontaneous performances by folk tourists and the ways in which the festival has taken on the trappings of an international fair, responding to changes that have taken place since 1989 both within Bulgaria and on a global scale. I finally conclude by suggesting that these adaptations have enabled the Koprivshtitsa Festival to continue to take place under these changing conditions.

This chapter is written from the viewpoint of an 'outsider' – a non-Bulgarian folk dance enthusiast who is an insider in the global world of Bulgarian folk music and dance. The research is based on the author's visits as a 'folk tourist' to the six editions of the Koprivshtitsa Festival held between 1986 and 2010. I have been able to participate and carry out observations over a period of 25 years, and as such my longitudinal study benefits from the depth of time which Guss considers to be often lacking in studies of festive traditions, which are commonly based on a single viewing (2000, 3). I have supplemented my personal observations and reflections with an analysis of discussions regarding the last four editions of the festival on the East European Folklife Centre (EEFC) mailing list,[7] whose members share an interest in Southeast European folklore, and information gathered through short interviews, email exchanges and discussions with other folk tourists and Bulgarian urbanites who have attended the Koprivshtitsa Festival.

Setting, Festival History and Performers

The small town of Koprivshtitsa lies nestled in the Sredna Gora Mountains and is located around one hundred kilometres east of Sofia. It was a flourishing crafts and trade centre in the nineteenth century and it is principally known for its involvement in the April 1876 uprising against the Ottomans (see Duijzings this volume). After the uprising the trading opportunities with the Ottoman Empire dwindled, and the consequent loss of commerce resulted in the town falling into economic decline and the vibrant life in the town ending. This resulted in the outstanding architecture of the National Revival period in Koprivshtitsa being preserved. Due to this architectural heritage and its role in the 1876 uprising, Koprivshtitsa has retained an important place in the national mythology and was designated a museum town in 1952, one of many Bulgarian towns and villages that were granted this status during the communist period (Ditchev 2004, 3).

To the outsider it looks more like a large village than a town. On nonfestival days it is a sleepy place that lives primarily from farming and tourism, then suddenly around every five years it becomes a vibrant and busy centre, besieged by thousands of Bulgarians and non-Bulgarians who climb up the hill behind the town to the Voivodenets meadows where the festival takes place over three days in early August. For the urbanite, and especially the non-Bulgarian urbanite, Koprivshtitsa has all the trappings of a rural idyll: old houses, attractive scenery, a peaceful ambiance, a river running through the centre, cobbled streets and horse-drawn carts passing through the town during the day. Since around 2000 many of the traditional (nineteenth-century) houses have been bought by upper-class Bulgarian urbanites from Sofia who use them as weekend retreats from their busy lives in the city and some have converted them into modern guest houses with private facilities and Wi-Fi connections in all the rooms.

The Koprivshtitsa Festival is called a *sabor* (fair) and was established in the communist period as the major national event in Bulgaria for amateur performances of 'authentic' village folklore.[8] The term *sabor* was previously used for religious (saint's day) fairs held in town and villages, and under socialism it was also adopted as a designation for state-funded competitions of folk music and dance (Buchanan 2006, 171).[9] The Koprivshtitsa Festival formed the culmination of many local, district and regional competitions held throughout Bulgaria prior to the main festival. Thus this festival fits into the genre of national festivals established in the second half of the twentieth century and funded by national and socialist states with the intention of solidifying national pride.[10] Under socialism, these events were frequently used to reinforce centralized cultural politics in locations where traditional ways of life were fast disappearing (Cash 2002, 1) – the intention being that by bringing 'tradition to the stage' the reproduction of these cultural forms was allowed to continue, but only under close state supervision (Kligman 1988, 258).[11]

The groups that are eligible to perform at the Koprivshtitsa Festival are known as *izvorni*.[12] These are mixed-age and ability village *kolektivi* (collectives) who perform what is termed as 'authentic village folklore'. The subject of the political influence on the material performed by these *kolektivi* in the communist period has been covered extensively elsewhere.[13] Suffice to say here that their performances were overseen by folklore specialists (Singer 1955, 29) who prior to 1990 ensured that individual creativity did not step outside the official guidelines (Buchanan 2006, 169). Groups tailored their performance to what they thought would be acceptable by the judges in order to win the necessary local and regional rounds, hence the opportunity to perform in Koprivshtitsa. Until 1991 state control over cultural politics meant that the performances had to conform to the 'unified mono-ethnic image of the nation-state' (Silverman 1989, 147), so texts of traditional songs were subtly changed, performers had to wear complete folk costume (147),[14] only traditional instruments were allowed (57) and any elements that were deemed to be non-Bulgarian were banned – for example, the *zurna* (a reed instrument) played by Roma musicians, and the wide trousers (*shalvari*) worn under aprons by Muslim Pomak women.

Despite all these interdictions the individuals who have participated in these groups viewed and still view the opportunity to perform at Koprivshtitsa as their ultimate competitive goal. The competition between performers is twofold: firstly, there is informal competition between groups who try to outdo the performances by similar groups; and secondly, all the groups perform in front of a panel of judges who have the authority to 'judge the authenticity of their performances and to compare their aesthetic impact' (Panova-Tekath 2011, 183). The performers take immense pride in the medals that they win and they wear them conspicuously at subsequent festivals. Buchanan comments that in communist times these medals provided a 'means of achieving distinction in an economy holding few financial incentives for the average person' (2006, 168) and I would hold that this still applies in postcommunist times, when most individuals are faced with economic difficulties. Until the 1986 festival the state funded travel to the festival for eligible folklore groups and many 'hangers-on' from all over Bulgaria. Some came only for the day that they were competing, others stayed and camped outside the village on a large campsite – nicknamed 'tent city' by the folk tourists – with the intention of having a big party. The number of performers increased steadily from festival to festival with 4,000 participants recorded in 1965 to in excess of 12,000 in 1986.[15]

The 'Folk Tourists' at the Koprivshtitsa Festival

Bulgarian folklore began to attract foreign interest in the mid-1950s, when folk musicians were attracted by the 'wild music' from this Balkan country with unusual musical rhythms, dancers by the variety of dances and intricate footwork, and singers by the unique open-throated style of singing.[16] According to Mirjana Laušević, who traced the history of the US Balkan scene in her book *Balkan Fascination*, the majority of the participants date the origins of this interest to the 1960s and 1970s (2007, 205). In the UK, a Bulgarian dance group and band were set up by individuals who had travelled to Bulgaria in the 1950s.[17] By the mid-1960s a handful of Western folklorists, folk musicians and folk dance teachers started to travel to Bulgaria, visiting villages to collect material.[18] Due to travel restrictions to the Eastern Bloc at this time, these trips were arranged through official channels, thus the contacts foreign researchers made were with approved artists, although this did not preclude the formation of life-long friendships between the Western visitors and Bulgarian musicians, singers and choreographers.

There was a small foreign presence at the first Koprivshtitsa Festival. Ethel Raim from New York, who developed an interest in Bulgarian singing after having heard a recording of the Philip Koutev Ensemble, made her first trip to Bulgaria in 1965, during which she attended the first Koprivshtitsa Festival (Laušević 2007, 210). Djidjev comments on the role of the first festival in promulgating the interest in Bulgarian music song and dance among foreign experts, who later returned to the festival bringing groups of folk tourists (2005, 146). By 1971 organized groups of folk tourists from the US were present at the Koprivshtitsa Festival, although at this time only the most dedicated would make the decision to cross the Iron Curtain. Those that ventured to the early festivals were mainly teachers and researchers of Bulgarian music, song and dance who were eager to expand their repertoire by collecting material from the 'source' (Silverman in Laušević 2007, 220). During the 1970s the foreign interest in Bulgarian folk music, song and dance also took off in countries such as the Netherlands, Germany and the Far East. By the 1980s the number of organized tours had begun to increase. In 1986, around 2,500 foreign tourists attended the festival, and this generated discussion on how their attitudes to Bulgarian folklore differed from that of the Bulgarians, with Buchanan commenting that some Bulgarians considered that the Japanese visitors treated the staged performances as more valuable than did their Bulgarian colleagues (2006, 393).

As each group went back home and spread the word, the number of folk tourists increased steadily every five years, widening the participation to group members who did not consider themselves to be teachers or researchers. These trips, as Laušević comments, enabled many folk dancers to develop 'a better understanding of the connection between music and dance' (2007, 207). After 1991, when global travel became easier and cheaper and the travel restrictions to the former East European communist countries were relaxed, the number of folk tourists increased dramatically, with trips being arranged by many Bulgarian dance teachers, musicians and singers in collaboration with tourist agencies. Organizers from the US advertised the Koprivshtitsa Festival as 'an event so amazing that Bulgaria usually takes five years to recover from it'.[19] Messages posted on the EEFC website emphasize the unique character of the event: 'We will stay in the village of Koprivshtitsa for the festival, as this gives us the opportunity to attend all the events, all night long, if necessary… so as not to miss a single moment of the festival.'[20]

So what do these 'folk tourists' expect to see? Their first introduction to the festival may have been a snippet of video or a few pictures during a cultural session at a dance course. Intrigued by this introduction, enchanted by the exoticness, encouraged by their friends, they then decide to make a trip to see 'the real thing': three days of saturation in Bulgarian folklore in one location, and in the majority of cases with all arrangements taken care of by a tour operator. The expectations of the folk tourists are bounded by their experience of Bulgarian folk dance and music from 'outside' Bulgaria in a situation where cultural elements are appropriated and in the process acquire new meanings and forms. This 'outsider' audience also has contradictory views on what they expect to see, and their own value system as to what they consider 'authentic'. They may wish to see folklore presented as 'in the village' and not adapted for the stage, but as Laušević comments, 'Many Balkan music and dance enthusiasts to the present day are not aware of the differences between the regional village styles and the state representations of the same', and also 'do not understand that the various Balkan countries had their own representation of their "folk"' (2007, 221). They are often drawn to events such as the Koprivshtitsa Festival by a desire to have an 'authentic experience' – wanting to share in the 'real life' of the places visited (MacCannell 1973, 594). But does a stage performance in an idyllic village on a stage in the hills above a 'real' (museum) village give them an 'authentic' experience? Are they sharing in the 'real life' of Bulgarians who perform at this festival? Does the enactment of a virtual village on a stage in the hills above a 'real village' not form a 'heterotopia' (Foucault and Miskowiec 1986, 24) for the folk tourists?[21] It can be argued that the performances on the hills above Koprivshtitsa may have a staged, superficial, liminal or heterotopic quality which has little to do with the daily life of their participants (MacCannell 1973, 595).

The format of the performances at the Koprivshtitsa Festival has not fundamentally changed over the festival's history. The performances take place on six or seven acoustically separate stages, each region being allotted a half-day slot, with the winners from each region then performing on the central stage, from where the performances are broadcasted on Bulgarian television. Since 1981 an additional stage has been set up in the Koprivshtitsa school grounds, where children's groups perform for a separate class of medals. Since 1995 there has also been a stage in the central square of the town which is used during the daytime for Bulgarian groups and in the evenings for visiting foreign groups.

The official programme in 1991 described the events as a rare opportunity for thousands to sample 'the centuries-old traditional art of Bulgaria in its *pristine condition* amidst appropriate surroundings' (emphasis added). However, in order to portray 'village life' on a stage far from the village, choreography is essential. National festivals are made up of a composite of multiple local festive forms which are taken from their local roots to a specified location, where they are performed at a specified time. The agents in this transfer are the local cultural specialists, who are responsible for selecting 'the most attractive samples' of their local customs or music, song or dance tradition (Panova-Tekath 2011, 183) and combining these into a choreographed short performance for a formal staged setting with a seated audience. Performances have to be contained in a much shortened time frame, hence only selected fragments of traditions can be presented. As Djidjev has commented, in order to produce these a good knowledge of the folklore is essential, and in order to retain audience interest the performance material must include 'diversity, contrast, culmination, and contemporary sensitiveness' (2009, 91, 105; quoted in Vlaeva 2011, 130).

The performances often take the form of a short play or 'mini-spectacle' (Cash 2002, 1) based around an excerpt of a traditionally much longer ritual or custom. Kaneff, who attended the Koprivshtitsa Festival in 1986, comments that it is possible to see 'an entire range of folkloric customs, taken from their cyclic contexts and from locations all over Bulgaria [...] performed together totally detached from their traditional contexts' (2004, 151). The folk tourists, the majority of whom are not fluent in Bulgarian, sometimes comment that they find these mini-spectacles a little tedious, as they are unable to appreciate the subtleties of local meaning imbued in such local performances without the necessary contextual insider knowledge (see Guss 2000, 13). In addition to the mini-spectacles, the performances include traditional songs by individuals and choirs, or instrumental solos and performances by small children who are barely tall enough to be seen by the audience. During the communist period it was rare to see a group performing dance suites, and some folk tourists expressed surprise at the small part played by Bulgarian folk dance in the festival. A number of more unusual talent show items are also included, such as the re-enactment of an argument between a husband and wife, or a man imitating animal noises. The mix of items is remarkably similar to the current genre of popular TV talent shows, such as 'Britain's Got Talent', especially as a panel of judges decides which items will go on appear on national TV.

Over the postcommunist years the increasing touristic and commercial orientation of the festival has led to a shift in emphasis of performances, although this has resulted in tensions between performances tailored for the judges and those tailored for the audience. By 1995 more village dance groups had appeared, replacing the individual performers who became a minority, and this trend has continued. In 2005 there was also an increase in the number of short enactments of 'spectacular' rituals, with a corresponding decrease in the mini-spectacles where the emphasis is on dialogue. However, in 2010, when the number of groups that were allowed to go through from the regional rounds was limited due to financial constraints, there appeared to be a slight reversal in this trend.

Bulgarian Urbanites at Koprivshtitsa

When the Bulgarian communist regime fell in 1989, rumours abounded outside Bulgaria as to whether the Koprivshtitsa Festival would continue. The expectation was that unless private or foreign sponsorship was found, large national festivals such as Koprivshtitsa might disappear (Buchanan 2006, 315). This situation existed throughout Eastern Europe and the festivals that continued had to seek new audiences and new sources of funding, as was the case with the International Festival of Mountain Folklore (Miedzynarodowy Festival Folkloru Ziem Gorskich) in Zakopane, Poland (Cooley 2005, 129–30). Despite these difficulties the Koprivshtitsa Festival continued to take place, primarily attracting Bulgarians. In 1991 one attendee noted that the foreign visitors seemed to be in a distinct minority;[22] in 1995 many Bulgarian urbanites who had previously seen the festival on television came to see it for themselves. The 2000 festival coincided with a temporary dip in enthusiasm for 'authentic' folklore among Bulgarians and so their numbers fell while folk tourist numbers increased. From 2005 (and especially by 2010) there had been a resurgence of interest in Bulgarian dancing among urbanites who were seeking their own 'local identity' to fulfil their 'longing for continuity in a fragmented world' (Boym 2001, xiv) and to provide them with a defence mechanism against the processes of cultural homogenization as a result of globalization. Over this period many Bulgarian members of the urban-based *horo* clubs made the journey to the festival; the leaders viewing the performances as a source of new material needed to satisfy the growing number of participants (Panova-Tekath 2011, 186–7). There was also a change in attitude to the Koprivshtitsa Festival among this segment of the population. Discussions I had with professional and amateur urban-based Bulgarian dancers in the 1990s had revealed that they viewed the performances at Koprivshtitsa as unsophisticated rural or 'rustic' folklore, inferior to that performed by themselves on stage, and they had no interest in attending the festival. However, from around 2005 attitudes altered and many of these urban-based dancers made the journey to the village and spent time both watching the performances and joining in the impromptu social dancing in the evening.

Impromptu Performances: International *Communitas*

One of the highlights of the Koprivshtitsa Festival for many Bulgarians and foreign tourists are the impromptu performances that take place on the festival site beside the official stages, as well as in the town centre and all night in 'tent city'. Kaneff refers to the complex and symbiotic dynamics between the official and unofficial performances, as the same individuals participate in both the official folklore onstage and the unchoreographed folklore offstage (2004, 153n; for the communist period, see also Silverman 1989). These impromptu performances are the sites where the real spontaneous *communitas* is created (Turner 1969, 177). Prior to 1991 participation in this *communitas* was limited to Bulgarians and a few selected foreign visitors who negotiated the boundaries between the 'front and back regions' through local friends, as in the case of one of my informants who wrote that in 1981 guards prevented foreign tourists from entering 'tent city', where all-night parties were taking place, although it was possible to gain entry by joining onto a group of Bulgarian friends. After 1991 the situation was relaxed and the folk tourists were able to join in dancing and playing music, freely mixing with the locals.

There are many occasions where spontaneous performances take place. One or more musicians may start playing at a cafe on the festival site or in the town, and soon a group of dancers will appear. This may be a group of folk tourists, joined by one or two elderly Bulgarians in folk costume, or a group of Bulgarian urbanites who are members of an urban folk ensemble or a *horo* club, who come to the festival primarily for the all-night parties in 'tent city', where they can mix with talented folk musicians and dancers from all over Bulgaria. Impromptu performances can also be commissioned by folk tourists. One evening in 2000 I joined a line of dancers in the town centre who were following a musician playing the *zurna*. When the musicians passed through a wooden gateway into a hotel courtyard it was made clear to me that this performance had been 'arranged' by the organizer of a US-led tour. As I was not part of this group I was only allowed to participate as long as the musicians remained in the public space. However, by 2010 visiting urbanite

Bulgarian dancers managed to infiltrate similar private events with relatively little resistance, taking over leading the dancing and also negotiating entry for their non-Bulgarian friends.

Folk Tourists as Performers

In 1995 the Koprivshtitsa committee made the decision to invite groups from abroad – both Bulgarians living abroad and foreigners who perform Bulgarian folklore – to take part in the festival by performing on the stages in the centre of Koprivshtitsa in the evenings.[23] This decision, being counter to the previous ethos of the event, opened up new possibilities for folk tourists; instead of just being passive consumers they could now become active participants.[24] In each subsequent festival the number of participating foreign groups has increased.[25] For some of the folk tourists a performance at the Koprivshtitsa Festival is their ultimate dream, and these performances are usually warmly received by 'the thousands of Bulgarians in the audience'.[26] This new development raises interesting questions: to what extent can these performances of Bulgarian folk dance and song by non-Bulgarians be considered 'authentic', as was initially the *raison d'être* of the festival? While they enjoy dancing Bulgarian dances and playing Bulgarian music, can these non-Bulgarian folk enthusiasts dance or play 'as a Bulgarian'?[27] This reversal of the performers' and audiences' roles also raises the issue of 'who is the other'. Is it the Bulgarian villager performing 'authentic' folklore, or is it the Japanese women who the Bulgarian participants and audiences view with delight as they perform 'their dances'? Although in 1995 some folk tourists commented that they did not consider these performances by non-Bulgarians to be 'the real thing', ten years later the same performances had become accepted as an established part of the festival with other members of this global 'cultural cohort' enjoying watching performances by friends whom they had made during previous folk tourism trips in Bulgaria and elsewhere, thus reflecting the increased globalization and 'networks of interconnectivity' (Woods 2007, 487) among those involved in the practice of Bulgarian folk music and dance during this period.

From National Festival to International Fair

The changes in funding after 1989 caused great uncertainty both for performers and audiences. Around 1991, a combination of a resurgence of interest in Bulgarian folk song and music following the expansion of the world music industry and the greater ease of travel meant that a trip to the Koprivshtitsa Festival was a 'must' for all potential folk tourists, but the question was 'would the festival take place?'[28] Although the festival did take place, many of the performers who had qualified in the local and regional rounds were forced to withdraw as they could not afford the costs of transport to Koprivshtitsa. This uncertainty continued during the next edition in 1995, as is highlighted in messages posted to the EEFC mailing list between late 1994 and spring 1995. It was reported that the Bulgarian Ministry of Culture was unable to provide funds and that sponsors were needed to cover costs of around 100,000 US dollars.[29] The decision to go ahead was finally made in March 1995, but even then the messages posted to the EEFC list reflect continuing uncertainty as to the exact dates of the festival. This made planning tours and booking flights in advance very difficult. The problems of funding and sponsorship continued into the 2000 and 2005 editions. Performances ended earlier, as without central government funding groups had to obtain local sponsorship to cover the costs of travel to the festival, which meant that often 'the performers were not certain that they would get to the festival until the last minute'.[30]

During socialist times the handful of stalls selling food and drinks had run out by the last day, and there were only one or two caravans on the festival site selling plastic toys, badges and Balkanton (the Bulgarian state-owned label) records. Then, after the end of socialism, commercialization kicked in when, in 1991, a seemingly unregulated and unplanned mass of traders invaded the festival site setting up stalls selling food, drinks and cheap plastic toys, similar to those that could be found at any local fair. They were joined by a few folk-specific traders selling bootleg cassettes of folk music from the backs of their cars and traditional instrument makers selling their wares, thus catering to the consumerist desires of the folk tourists. By 1995 the festival had taken on more of the trappings of a commercial fair, with numerous stalls offering folk crafts, instruments, cassettes and CDs, folk costumes and embroideries, which one EEFC member described to me as 'crass commercialism; one huge, unorganized rummage sale', while in the village the main street was lined with a similar selection of stalls, selling bric-a-brac, food and drink, and local produce. Since 2000 some forms of regulation appear to have been put in place, with sales pitches being marked out, and stalls being arranged in a more orderly fashion. In 2010 these pitches were visibly policed by members of the organization team, who checked that vendors were not overflowing their displays of goods for sale into adjacent pitches.

This commercialization brings out mixed views and emotions in the folk tourists when their expectation of having an 'authentic' experience clashes with their own or other people's shopping instincts. Some prefer to not 'see' the commercialism, reflected for instance in the photographs they take, which capture only the 'ethnographic' aspects of the festival. However, this does not prevent them from taking full advantage of the opportunity to buy treasured folk items that they had been unable to purchase 'at home'.[31] This 'shopping mania' can upset the less acquisitive, as one EEFC member commented: 'I had to turn away as I saw others "descending" upon a table or blanket laid with handcrafts',[32] although by 2010 this frenzy to purchase had diminished due to the availability of similar goods on the Internet through sites such as eBay and those set up by local vendors who were willing to ship items overseas.

The New Millennium: The Globalized Festival Experience

In 2005 Djidjev commented that Bulgarians should 'direct their efforts towards improving the conditions which are offered to the tourists' (2005, 148) at events such as the Koprivshtitsa Festival in order to expand their international tourist potential. By that time the expectations of the folk tourists had mellowed: their desires to meet 'the other' and experience the rural idyll merged with their demands for modern levels of communication and comfort. In other words, they now started to see the village as part of the globalized world, expecting higher standards of accommodation with appropriate private facilities. Certainly the experience of the Koprivshtitsa-bound folk tourists has changed in this direction over the years. Before 1990 the accommodation available for foreign visitors was either rooms in traditional private houses or camp beds in the local school, and this accommodation was at a premium, with groups often staying in small hotels in nearby towns and travelling to Koprivshtitsa by coach on the festival days. This situation did not change until around 1995, when some of the traditional houses were renovated for use as guest houses. A limited number of rooms with private facilities became available, and this change coincided with rising expectations among visitors. It was noted that in 2000 there was no mobile phone signal in Koprivshtitsa, but by 2005 both a mobile phone signal and ATMs had reached this 'rural idyll', and by 2010 the majority of the visitors stayed in rooms with private facilities and Wi-Fi, with such trappings of the globalized world being considered as the norm by the majority of visitors, including those that had experienced the rural idyll of the earlier festivals.

The availability of global communication technology also allowed visitors access to more insider information on the festival programming. In 2005 advance information about the festival was available for the first time on the Koprivshtitsa town website, and a detailed listing of the groups who had qualified at the regional competitions was published on this site in the weeks preceding the festival.[33] This was in contrast with the earlier festival, when locating a copy of the official colour programme presented a logistical challenge, as the number of copies available was limited and there was no obvious point of sale. Some folk enthusiasts found that 'it was very frustrating to be *in* Koprivshtitsa and there being no detailed program (indicating village, song, dance or custom name) for the stages'.[34]

By 2005, one American commented that a trip to Koprivshtitsa provided 'more of a western festival experience. [...] It felt a little slicker, like the organizers had learned from previous festivals', but 'it still felt like a reunion and like the competition that it was'. At least twenty nationalities of folk tourists were present at this festival with the result that, as one UK participant commented, 'you climb up to the top of the hill and bump into a friend from Boston who you last saw three years earlier at the US Balkan Folk camp'.[35] As the world outside has changed, so has the necessary planning for a trip to the festival. Travel plans and accommodation arrangements are now made on the Internet and meetings with friends are set up in advance by email with the Koprivshtitsa Festival providing a unique social networking site for Bulgarian folk enthusiasts from all over the world, whose paths have previously crossed elsewhere or on the Internet. Plans are still made up to a year before the next scheduled festival, as even in the twenty-first century a trip to Bulgaria involves considerable expense and planning for all except those based in Europe, so physical distance and economic constraints still form barriers despite the benefits of email and the increased ease of travel.

Conclusion

In this chapter I have explored the changes in the Koprivshtitsa Festival that have enabled it to enlarge its semantic field to encompass a global urbanized and touristic audience in the twenty-first century, assisted by communication through modern media and increasing ease of global travel (Guss 2000, 4). In cases where festivals such as Koprivshtitsa evolve over time, the resulting changes can alter the event to such an extent that the festival no longer fulfils its initial role and their audiences dwindle; often this results in their financial backing being withdrawn, or else the locals turn their backs on the now globalized event and create a new festival that can fulfil the original purpose in the local community.[36]

I would consider that the continuity of such festive events can be broken if there are substantial changes in any of the essential criteria that are necessary for a festival to be organized, and that these criteria have to either remain constant or evolve in an appropriate manner. In the case of the Koprivshtitsa Festival this can be seen in that the festival location and the broad usage of the arena regarding the placing of the festival stages have remained constant throughout the festival's history. The timing of the festival has continued at (approximately) five-year intervals, so the participants (performers and audience) 'know' when to expect the next edition to take place. Funding has been made available through one means or another, until 1990 from the state and subsequently a mixture of state and private funds, from sponsorship and commercial enterprises. The Bulgarian performers have included many of the same individuals or groups depending on their selection by the judges, whereas the make-up of audience and the addition of non-Bulgarian performers have changed over time in line with changes in the global situation.

Finally I would propose that for a festival to continue it cannot lose sight of the ethos that led to its foundation and that draws performers and audiences, so in the situation where a festival ceases to fulfil its initial role, financial backing may be withdrawn. In the case of the Koprivshtitsa Festival, although it is has evolved over time it has still retained its core function: to provide a showcase of Bulgarian 'authentic' or village folklore. Although other aspects have been added, such as the craft fair that provides foreign visitors the chance to buy folklore memorabilia and the opportunity to themselves become performers, they still play a secondary role to the main purpose of the festival.

The rural town of Koprivshtitsa fits into a Bulgarian frame of reference as a museum village, a tourist destination and weekend resort for wealthy Bulgarian urbanites. But it also sets itself apart from other museum villages in Bulgaria by the extent of its global connections, as every five years for a period of three to five days it becomes a meeting point for members of the global cultural cohort of Bulgarian music and dance enthusiasts. So I conclude that the Koprivshtitsa Festival, situated and embedded as it has been in the changing contexts of communist to postcommunist Bulgaria, is a composite 'cultural performance' with multiple symbolic meanings and a wide range of participants and visitors from Bulgaria and the rest of the world. It earned its prestigious place on the world festival stage in the communist period and has succeeded in holding on to this position into the twenty-first century, by inserting itself into the world calendar of 'must visit' festivals for a global audience of Balkan folk music and dance enthusiasts.

Notes

1 On the links between festivals and tourism, see Bendix (1989); on festivals and ritual, see Mach (1992); on festivals and commemoration, see Guss (2000); on festivals and identity, see Cooley (2005) and Davies (1997); and on festivals and political formations, see Cohen (1993).
2 Personal communication with Anca Giurchescu, 28 July 2012.
3 I will hereafter use the shortened form 'Koprivshtitsa Festival'.
4 Singer defines a cultural performance as having 'a definitely limited time span – at least a beginning and an end, an organized program of activity, a set of performers, an audience, and a place and occasion of performance' (1955, 27).
5 *Horo* clubs are urban-based clubs where urbanites learn Bulgarian dances, thus borrowing the idea of recreational Bulgarian dancing from the non-Bulgarian enthusiasts.

6 Turino defines a cultural cohort as a 'cultural / identity unit based on a restricted number of shared habits and parts of the self' (Turino 2008, 235).

7 The archives for this list can be found online: http://www.eefc.org/ or searched more directly through http://archive.iecc.com/search.phtml/eefc (accessed on 4 October 2012).

8 Vlaeva comments that the first organized folk festivals took place in Bulgaria in 1960 as part of the government's efforts to centralize cultural politics. Following this, two major festivals were organized in 1965: the Koprivshtitsa Festival for authentic Bulgarian music and dance, and the International Folk Festival in Bourgas, which presents folk traditions from across the globe (Vlaeva 2011, 130).

9 Smaller regional *sabori* were also held in intervening years.

10 In Romania the Cântarea României festival was established in 1974. Also, traditional fairs in Romania known as *nedeia*, typically held on rural hilltop locations, were appropriated by the regime and changed into state-organized regional festivals. In Albania, the first National Folklore Festival (Festivali Folkloristik Kombëtar) was held in Gjirokastra in 1968 (Ahmedaja 2011, 5).

11 In the case of post-1990 Bulgaria, the title 'National Folklore Festival' is also used by a number of other smaller festivals.

12 *Izvoren* literally means 'source' (as an attributive adjective) or 'from the source'. These groups are also referred to as 'groups for authentic folklore'.

13 See, for example, Buchanan (2006) and Rice (1994, 2004). Bulgarian government statistics listed 22,760 collectives with over half a million participants in 1987. The majority of these were female folk choirs (Buchanan 2006, 168).

14 One Bulgarian informant told me that in the communist period the participants were instructed to wear their heavy folk costumes all day long, and in 1986 (when I visited the festival for the first time) this still appeared to be the case. Since 1991 the majority of participants only wear their full costumes while performing.

15 Although these figures come from official sources they have to be treated with caution.

16 These reasons were commented on by Steve Murillo in *Balkan Dancing*, an educational film he made in Los Angeles in 1968. See: http://www.youtube.com/watch?v=Tyhcm99lwDI (accessed 4 October 2012).

17 The Bulgarian dance group was established in the late 1950s, and the band Dunav in 1964.

18 Ethnomusicologist Tim Rice first visited Bulgaria in 1969, and Bulgarian dance teachers Yves Moreau and Jaap Leegwater were there in 1966 and 1969 respectively. See their webpages: http://www.bourque-moreau.com/ and http://www.jaapleegwater.com/ (accessed 4 October 2012).

19 EEFC archives, October 1994.

20 EEFC archives, October 1994, March 2000.

21 Foucault uses the term heterotopia to refer to sites where 'a kind of effectively enacted utopia in which all the other real sites that can be found within the culture, are simultaneously represented, contested, and inverted'.

22 EEFC archives, October 1994.

23 Pressing financial needs and the aging of Bulgaria's dancing population were given as the reasons for this.

24 I would still regard these individuals as 'folk tourists' as their participation in the festival was limited to one brief performance as part of their tour to the festival.

25 In 2005, the non-Bulgarian performers included groups from the Netherlands, US, China, Japan and Hong Kong.

26 EEFC archives, 23 August 1995, concerning the performance of a US-based Bulgarian choir.

27 See Rice (2008) for a fuller discussion on how a non-Bulgarian can learn to play Bulgarian music in a way that is accepted by insiders as being 'like a Bulgarian'.

28 It is not possible to ascertain the number of foreign tourists since 1989, as the requirement for foreigners to travel through Balkantourist or register with the police has been dropped. From personal knowledge the numbers attending from the UK increased from around 25 to nearly 100 in 1991.

29 EEFC archives, Martha Forsyth, 9 August 1994.

30 EEFC archives, 3 May 2005.

31 Laušević quotes one of her interviewees who compares folk dancers to stamp collectors, who want 'all the paraphernalia that goes along with the dance' (2007, 237).

32 EEFC archive, Robin LaPasha, 25 August 1995.

33 http://www.sabor-koprivshtica.mct.government.bg/ (accessed on 4 October 2012).

34 EEFC archives, Larry Weiner, 15 September 2005.

35 The 2005 festival included folk tourists from the UK, the US, Germany, Netherlands, Belgium, France, Norway, Sweden, Denmark, Israel, Australia, New Zealand, Japan, Hong Kong China, Russia, Canada, Austria, Israel and Australia.

36 Guss presents such a situation in his case study of the festival of San Juan in Venezuela, where the festival became dominated by commercial enterprises to such an extent that the locals set up a new festival in order to take back ownership and restore the festival to its original (religious) purpose (Guss 2000, 45). Also, recent news reports indicate that this may also happen in connection with the Guča brass band festival in Serbia, where *trubaci* from southern Serbia are discussing having their own event, as they are dissatisfied with the Guča festival (EEFC archives, 17 August 2012, referring to a news article by Vojkan Ristić, 'Umesto Guče "Truba fest" u Surdulici', published in *Danas*. Online: http://www.danas.rs/danasrs/srbija/hronika/umesto_guce_truba_fest_u_surdulici.73.html?news_id=246045. [accessed on 4 October 2012]).

References

Ahmedaja, Ardian. 2011. 'The Role of the Researchers and Artists in Public Presentations of Local Music and Dance in Albania'. In *Proceedings of the Second Symposium of the International Council for Traditional Music Study Group on Music and Dance in Southeastern Europe*, edited by Elsie Ivancich Dunin and Mehmet Öcal Özbilgin, 3–14. İzmir: Ege University State Turkish Music Conservatory.

Appadurai, Arjun. 1996. *Modernity at Large: Cultural Dimensions of Globalization*. Minneapolis: University of Minnesota Press.

Bendix, Regina. 1989. 'Tourism and Cultural Displays: Inventing Traditions for Whom?' *Journal of American Folklore* 102: 131–46.

Boissevain, Jeremy. 1992. *Revitalizing European Rituals*. London: Routledge.

Boym, Svetlana. 2001. *The Future of Nostalgia*. New York: Basic Books.

Buchanan, Donna A. 2006. *Performing Democracy: Bulgarian Music and Musicians in Transition*. Chicago: University of Chicago Press.

Cash, Jennifer. 2002. 'After the Folkloric Movement: Traditional Life in Post-socialist Moldova'. *Anthropology of East Europe Review* 20: 61–76.

Cohen, Abner. 1993. *Masquerade Politics: Explorations in the Structure of Urban Cultural Movements*. Oxford: Berg.

Cooley, Timothy J. 2005. *Making Music in the Polish Tatras: Tourists, Ethnographers and Mountain Musicians.* Bloomington: Indiana University Press.

Davies, Charlotte Aull. 1997. '"A oes heddwch?". Contesting Meanings and Identities in the Welsh National Eisteddfod'. In *Ritual, Performance, Media*, edited by Felicia Hughes-Freeland, 141–59. ASA Monographs. London/New York: Routledge.

Ditchev, Ivaylo. 2004. 'Monoculturalism as Prevailing Culture'. *Eurozine* 1 (8). Online: http://www.eurozine.com/articles/2004-02-05-ditchev-en.html (accessed 4 October 2012).

Djidjev, Todor. 2005. *Bulgarian Folk Music.* Sofia: Chriker.

Foucault, Michel and Jay Miskowiec. 1986. 'Of Other Spaces'. *Diacritics* 16: 22–7.

Giddens, Anthony. 1990. *The Consequences of Modernity.* Stanford: Stanford University Press.

Guss, David M. 2000. *The Festive State: Race, Ethnicity, and Nationalism as Cultural Performance.* California: University of California Press.

Kaneff, Deema. 2004. *Who Owns the Past? The Politics of Time in a 'Model' Bulgarian Village.* New York: Berghahn.

Kligman, Gail. 1988. *The Wedding of the Dead,* Berkeley: University of California Press.

Lauševic, Mirjana. 2007. *Balkan Fascination: Creating an Alternative Music Culture in America.* New York: Oxford University Press.

MacCannell, Dean. 1973. 'Staged Authenticity: Arrangements of Social Space in Tourist Settings'. *American Journal of Sociology* 79: 589–603.

Mach, Zdzislaw. 1992. 'Continuity and Change in Political Ritual: May Day in Poland'. In *Revitalizing European Rituals*, edited by Jeremy Boissevain, 43–61. London: Routledge.

Panova-Tekath, Gergana. 2011. 'Teaching Bulgarian Folk Dances to Amateur and Professional Dancers from Bulgaria and Germany'. In *Proceedings of the Second Symposium of the International Council for Traditional Music Study Group on Music and Dance in Southeastern Europe*, edited by Elsie Ivancich Dunin and Mehmet Öcal Özbilgin, 182–92. İzmir: Ege University State Turkish Music Conservatory.

Rice, Timothy. 1994. *May It Fill Your Soul: Experiencing Bulgarian Music.* Chicago: University of Chicago Press.

_____. 2004. *Music in Bulgaria.* Oxford: Oxford University Press.

_____. 2008. 'Towards a Mediation of Field Methods and Field Experience in Ethnomusicology'. In *Shadows in the Field: New Perspectives for Fieldwork in Ethnomusicology*, edited by Gregory Barz and Timothy J. Cooley, 42–61. Oxford: Oxford University Press.

Sheppard, Eric. 2002. 'The Spaces and Times of Globalization: Place, Scale, Networks, and Positionality'. *Economic Geography* 78: 307–30.

Silverman, Carol. 1983. 'The Politics of Folklore in Bulgaria'. *Anthropological Quarterly* 56: 55–61.

_____. 1989. 'Reconstructing Folklore: Media and Cultural Policy in Eastern Europe'. *Communication* 11 (2): 141–60.

Silverman, Sydel. 1985. 'Towards a Political Economy of Italian Competitive Festivals'. *Ethnologia Europaea* 15: 95–103.

Singer, Milton. 1955. 'The Cultural Pattern of Indian Civilization: A Preliminary Report of a Methodological Field Study'. *Far Eastern Quarterly* 15: 23–36.

Stoeltje, Beverly J. 2002. 'Festival'. In *Folklore, Cultural Performances, and Popular Entertainments: A Communications-Centered Handbook*, edited by Richard Bauman, 261–71. New York: Oxford University Press.

Turino, Thomas. 2008. *Music as Social Life: The Politics of Participation.* Chicago: University of Chicago Press.

Turner, Victor. 1969. *The Ritual Process: Structure and Anti-structure.* New York: Aldine de Gruyter.

Vlaeva, Ivanka. 2011. 'Strategy of the International Folk Festivals in Bulgaria in the Last Two Decades'. In *Proceedings of the Second Symposium of the International Council for Traditional Music Study Group on Music and Dance in Southeastern Europe,* edited by Elsie Ivancich Dunin and Mehmet Öcal Özbilgin, 129–36. İzmir: Ege University State Turkish Music Conservatory.

Woods, Michael. 2007. 'Engaging the Global Countryside: Globalization, Hybridity and the Reconstitution of Rural Place'. *Progress in Human Geography* 31: 485–507.

Chapter 10

FASHIONING MARKETS: BRAND GEOGRAPHIES IN BULGARIA

Ulrich Ermann

ATINA (moderator):	So you think that people in the countryside have a different approach to clothing?
TSETSKA:	Yes, brands are definitely more meaningful there – fashion, you know, the way people are wearing it. A person may like to dress like a folk singer, or imitate someone else, but you definitely cannot wear one item there from one year to the next. The wardrobe is replaced annually. You cannot wear the same shoes for one year.
ATINA:	But you said there is countryside and countryside, people and people…
TSETSKA:	Yes, I am talking about smaller towns like Plovdiv and Sandanski…
RAYA interrupts:	In Plovdiv they are so vain…
TSETSKA:	I am indeed not talking about villages…
ATINA:	And why is it so?
TSETSKA:	It's normal. You drink coffee outside there. You stroll on the main street, the local place to watch and be seen. The whole town passes by and watches you, and if you go one day like this, the next day you will have to go like that. You have to look different. I myself have noticed recently that people don't go shopping where they live. It's important for them to come to Sofia to do their shopping, so that they can be different.[1]

This excerpt from a group discussion with five middle-aged women about fashion in Bulgaria illustrates not only the importance of clothing for people's identity, but also the relevance of spatial categories and dichotomies (such as between town and countryside) in practices of social distinction and stratification. In this exemplary group discussion, surprisingly one participant argues that brands play a much greater role in smaller towns than in the Bulgarian capital; the smaller the town, the greater the concern to distinguish oneself by wearing clothes different than those others wear, or those one was wearing the day before. This extract is only one of many group interviews carried out in different locations in Bulgaria, and even though it may not be fully representative of the opinions and actual practices concerning clothing and fashion in Bulgaria, it is a good example of how urban–rural dichotomies are reproduced through discourses on shopping and consumption (see also Duijzings this volume; Koleva this volume). When people talk about fashion (how it is bought, used and perceived) spatial and temporal dichotomies and 'positionalities' always come into play, such as between centre and periphery, old and new, tradition and modernity, backwardness and progressiveness, and so on (see Kaneff this volume; Creed this volume).

Fashion brands are a key element in such narratives. They function as markers of identity both on the individual and group level, and are instrumental in creating social distinctions. They are a dominant feature of post-Fordist modes of production – that is, the new 'consumer capitalism' and 'economy of signs' that has emerged from the 1990s onwards (see Lash and Urry 1994). The fundamental shift that has occurred is that economic valuations rely increasingly on sign values and the symbolic aspects of goods and commodities; business models of both manufacturers and marketers are now primarily focused on the anticipation of consumer habits and lifestyles (Ermann 2007). In Bulgaria, however, the historical road to this new 'consumer capitalism' has been very different than in the West. Whereas in Western Europe it evolved from the preceding stage of production-oriented capitalism, in Eastern Europe it was introduced almost overnight after four decades of socialism. In addition, the chronic scarcity of consumer goods in the state-led socialist economies of Central and Eastern Europe had prompted a great yearning for Western products and a much greater appreciation of their symbolic power. In the East, Western brands and consumer goods stood for freedom and a 'good and normal life', even though – or precisely because – the socialist authorities recognized them as the symbols of an ('evil') imperialist and capitalist system. Because of the previous symbolic significance of Western goods, consumerism became one of the defining features of socialist society (Pine 2001).

Many of the attributes of contemporary consumer capitalism are not specific to the socialist context. They can be found across the world as a consequence of the global shift to a sign- and consumer-oriented economy. What I will argue in this chapter is that the global spread of this sign economy also produces certain 'brand geographies' in which the relations between different parts of the world are configured in terms of centres and peripheries. We can observe 'brand geographies' at work at different points along various global value chains, a phenomenon which comprises all stages from the production and distribution to the consumption of clothes and fashion. The sites where fashion products are typically manufactured – that is, where their value is ultimately created – are usually different from those where brands are made.

Both products and brands depend on the value perceptions of buyers and consumers in various locations in the world, which is predominantly an outcome of marketing. Marketing provides the communicative connection between producers and consumers. Kotler et al. define it as 'the process by which companies create value for customers and build strong customer relationships in order to capture value from customers in return' (2007, 7). Thus marketing is about synchronizing producer and consumer objectives; it strongly engages in the creation and fashioning of markets through what I would like to call 'performativity' – that is, through performative utterances and business practices (Austin 1973). I use this concept of performativity here in two ways (see Berndt and Boeckler 2007). Firstly, in the sense of 'performance' as a commercialized form of *self-presentation* (Goffman 1959) and the creation of value through the theatrical representation of brands as lifestyle markers (Neckel 2006). And secondly, in Michel Callon's sense of 'performativity' or 'performation' (1998; Callon et al. 2002), meaning a process of economic *self-realization* carried out on the basis of practical models and theories of 'doing business' in a market economy.

Fashion and the restructuring of the apparel and fashion industries in Bulgaria is used here as an example to analyse the role of 'consumer capitalism' in in a socialist economy. I will illustrate the concepts of 'brand geographies' and 'performativity' through the example of Bulgaria's fashion markets. I will also show that the attempts by Bulgarian apparel producers to launch their own brands can be regarded as a strategy to break away from their subordinate role as mere manufacturers for West European core brands. At the same time, Bulgarian consumers use brands to act out modern lifestyles, which represents a similar strategy to undo their peripheral position – or improve their 'positionality' (Kaneff this volume) – in the symbolic geographies and cultural cartographies of Europe. I will start by describing consumer capitalism's main characteristics, followed by a brief discussion of Bulgaria's apparel industry. I will then look at Pirintex, an apparel manufacturer in rural Bulgaria which has been involved in the production of global brands, but also has made its first steps in the direction of developing its own brand. In the next example I turn to the company Rila Style, which is an illustration of both the mobilization of spatial images and performativity of spatial semantics for the configuration of international value chains and sites of production and consumption. In addition, excerpts from consumer interviews and group discussions will provide an idea of people's thinking about consumer habits as well as fashion and brands. On the basis of these examples, I will try to draw some conclusions by analysing how, in the context of the fashion industries, spatial dichotomies and valuations of production sites are performed and acted out on different national and global scales.

Consumer Capitalism and Brands

The term 'consumer capitalism' has been used by a variety of authors such as Naomi Klein (2000), Jeremy Rifkin (2000), Slavoj Žižek (2002) and Benjamin Barber (2007). They agree that this is a new mode of capitalism in which marketing and consumption play a central role. As Klein has indicated in her book *No Logo* (2000), 'Brands, not products!' is the key motto of this new capitalist paradigm which has brought about radical changes in the economy. She cites Phil Knight, the former chief executive officer of Nike: 'For years we thought of ourselves as a production-oriented company, meaning we put all our emphasis on designing and manufacturing the product. We've come around to saying that Nike is a marketing-oriented company, and the product is our most important marketing tool' (44).

The main function of brands is no longer to prevent imitation by designating origin, but to create and flag up identities and lifestyles. Brands reflect an economy of signs, in which consumption 'must not be understood as the consumption of use-values, as material utility, but primarily as the consumption of signs' (Featherstone 2007, 83; Slater 1987, 157). From the excerpts of the conversation given at the beginning of my contribution it is clear that this is even the case in rural areas.[2] Even though rural regions are primarily seen as sites for physical manufacturing (not for the performance of brands) it can be safely assumed that rural economies are now also predominantly sign and consumer oriented.

Nigel Thrift (2006, 302) has interpreted this shift as a change in the relation between production and consumption, in which consumers are adopting a more active role. The novelty, however, is not that economic values are symbolically mediated, it is that the symbolic value of products in the form of brands is now consciously accepted and applied as a principle of production. Sign values are no longer seen as an after-effect of production, but as the very objective of doing business. Joanne Entwistle has pointed out that this leads not only to an 'aestheticization' of everyday life, but also to an 'aesthetic economy' in which 'aesthetic values are generated as part of the calculation of economic markets' (2002, 321). As Daniel Miller points out, brands produce their own 'virtual consumers', and in this respect, 'models which are thought to be descriptive of economic relations have become so powerful that they become in and of themselves the forces that determine economic relations' (2000, 197).

Thus, brands can be analysed as a mechanism to create supply and demand (Callon et al. 2002). It is no longer an add-on, a mark to identify an origin that is fixed; it has become a tool to reconfigure production (Lury 2004, 27; see also Holt 2004; Arvidsson 2005; Moor 2003; and 2007). In socialist contexts, brands also function as performative vehicles of modernization, commonly understood as 'Westernization'. As in all modernization theory the destination is predetermined: Western Europe and North America hold the image of the East European future (Stark 1996, 994). Brands are the clearest symbols of the newly established market economies and consumer societies; they connect the identities and dreams of (potential) consumers with the business objectives of producers and retailers (see Humphrey 1995; Fehérváry 2002; Krăsteva-Blagoeva 2001; Patico and Caldwell 2002; Stitziel 2005).

Since brands are utilized for symbolic identification and the creation of lifestyles, they can obtain very different and contradictory meanings. On the one hand, they are the key vehicles for transporting and promoting a globalized economy, imposing a homogenized consumer culture. On the other, they may also be used to counter these trends, by creating countercultural or subcultural identities through 'alternative' brands or by appropriating well-established brands in an unconventional and even subversive manner. This 'friction' (Tsing 2005) or tension between neoliberal cultural hegemony and the forces that contest it is often cast in spatial and temporal terms; whereas common brands represent the West and the global, the antibrands represent the East and the local. The global brands stand for the present, whereas alternative or antibrands are linked to the precapitalist (often socialist) past or an anticipated or desired alternative future.[3]

Fashion Made in Bulgaria

Since 2007, the Bulgarian apparel and fashion industry has seen increasing labour costs as a result of economic growth and the introduction of EU regulations.[4] Rising costs have led to a reduction in offshore assembly production in Bulgaria and the displacement of production to other low-wage countries (Begg et al. 2003; Pickles et al. 2006). Some local manufacturers have attempted to sustain production and increase their share in the value chain through the creation of designs and brands, which has led to a rise in the number of so-called 'original brand manufacturers' in Bulgaria (Gereffi 1999).

Yet the share of production of local brands is still low compared to the manufacturing that is subcontracted from abroad. Typically, Bulgarian firms produce for global brands, and only produce for local brands in case orders are low or production capacity remains unused.

Another tendency is the adaptation of European standards regarding product quality and brand promotion. Brand building strategies are now dominated by attempts to 'Europeanize', 'Westernize' and 'globalize' local brands. Nevertheless, there are important impediments to this process. One problem is that it is difficult to enter global brand markets due to the limited access to 'performative resources' such as sponsoring Western celebrities (see Tokatli 2007). The upgrading strategies recommended by Western business consultants are not always feasible or appropriate, as most local apparel and fashion producers cannot afford large investments in design, branding and marketing. Apart from that, both the fact that domestic and export markets are able to absorb only a limited number of new brands does not help either. In spite of these obstacles, an increasing number of Bulgarian firms are trying to create their own brands in order to keep production going and to enhance market opportunities.

The value chain model – an analytical tool developed by Gereffi et al. (2005) – has now been adopted into the practical business models of local managers and entrepreneurs. Through the intermediate role of Western consultants, the concept of upgrading has thus moved from theory to practice in the case of Bulgaria. As the manager of a Bulgarian fashion house told me in an interview, 'In the socialist period we just produced fashionable clothes. In the last fifteen years we learned a lot. [...] Specialists from Europe helped us [...]. Now we produce ideas of how you can dress yourself and how to distinguish yourself from other people. [...] Without high quality you could not create value [...]. Only the symbolic value is important for the clients today.'[5] He exactly reiterates what consultants and marketing specialists have told him in order for a 'modern economy' to work: the credo is no longer to produce goods and user items, as under the centrally planned socialist economy, but ideas, images and lifestyles.

Pirintex

The company Pirintex was established in 1994 as a German–Bulgarian joint venture. It is based in Gotse Delchev, a small town in southern Bulgaria close to the Greek border. Before relocating to Bulgaria, the German director owned a firm for apparel production in Greece after closing his family business in Germany during the 1970s. The number of employees increased rapidly from 25 in 1994 to 2,700 in 2007. Today it is one of the largest apparel producers in Bulgaria and the most important employer in the region. The director does not regret the choice for a peripheral and rural location: 'I am glad that I have chosen this location, far removed from the big currents and centres. This is a rural area with people who are keen to work and willing to learn. I don't like big cities: I grew up in a small village myself, and I know that the big cities always form the social trouble spots. Justified or not, I am therefore rather anxious of cities.'[6] In combination with his personal preferences it is clear that he also benefits from the low wages in the countryside and appreciates his position as the only large company supplying jobs in the region.

Pirintex is the main manufacturer of Hugo Boss suits; the company also produces for Joop, Tommy Hilfiger, Cinque and other brands. While all manufactured goods are exported to Western Europe, Hugo Boss has nevertheless been running huge marketing drives in Bulgaria, such as billboard campaigns in Sofia during 2006 and 2007. According to one market researcher whom we interviewed, the rationale has been to do something about the low level of brand loyalty in Bulgaria. Currently, not many Bulgarians can afford buying Hugo Boss products, but it is important to introduce the brand for consumers who may become customers in the future. It is clear that the owner of this German brand, an Italian enterprise group, spends more money on brand promotion through advertising than on the actual production process. As part of this strategy, Hugo Boss runs partnerships with music, art and sports events and also produces appropriate testimonials.

Like other companies in a similar position, Pirintex has tried to become less vulnerable to the increasing labour costs and less dependent on the 'global' brands. One of its strategies has been to launch its own brand for the Bulgarian market, Rollmann, named after the director, who is also the president of the German–Bulgarian chamber of commerce. As the cost of a finished Rollmann product is 6 or 7 per cent of the retail price, the main part of the added value can now be realized within the company. As the owner told me, whereas for global brands it is not an option to let customers know where their products are manufactured, for his local brand it makes sense to make the origin known: 'The value at the point of sale may be at most 50 per cent of a high value brand, but the quality is the same. Without us producing the high value brands we cannot launch a local brand because no one would have confidence in its quality.'[7] Because customers are aware of this, he is able to sell his own brand. In other words, the experience and reputation acquired through the manufacturing of global brands is important for the ability to establish high quality local brands. He benefits from a free rider situation, where the symbolic value of global brands such as Hugo Boss percolates down to the local brand. Yet the entrepreneur would lose his customers if he would compete against these global brands on the same global markets.

As the market in globally branded fashion is hard to penetrate, 'locally branded' products cannot be sold on the same markets anyway.

Rila Style

The company Rila Style was established in 1972, and during the socialist period the company was part of Kombinat Rila, the largest cluster of apparel production sites in Bulgaria. After its privatization in the early 1990s, the company became a manufacturer and subcontractor for Western brands. A decade later the firm's management and its British owner decided to launch their own brand, Battibaleno, in order to retain a higher share of the added value. More effort went into design and marketing. As in the case of Pirintex and many other local firms, foreign businessmen and/or consultants have been the driving forces behind these 'upgrading' strategies. According to the sales manager, the Italian brand name was chosen because of the anticipated preferences of Bulgarian consumers for Italian fashion. She explained: 'The Bulgarians love Italian fashion and the Italian way of life [...]. Marketing specialists found that there is no other way to succeed on the Bulgarian market than to copy Western brands.'[8] Most young consumers whom I talked to during my research knew the brand, and indeed the majority was convinced that this was an Italian brand. As is the case with Western brands, the company tries to separate the Italian brand image from the actual production process, which has been largely relocated from central Sofia to the small town Vratsa and other rural sites in Bulgaria. To reinforce the favoured 'Western' image, the brand has been registered in the UK.

As the Battibaleno manager told me, it is hard for a local brand to compete with global brands: 'We buy the same materials as Max Mara, we produce almost the same models of a suit or a coat, which is sold by us in Bulgaria ten times cheaper than the Max Mara equivalent, and of course, our most loyal clients buy us, not Max Mara.'[9] Nevertheless, many potential customers prefer to buy products of the globally recognized brand Max Mara and they are ready to pay the higher price. In the long run only brands will be profitable, no longer the manufacturing of apparel, as is already the case in 'Europe' (that is, 'Western Europe'), she explained. To boost the brand, the company hired designers from France, Sweden and other West European countries, as well as from Bulgaria. The raw fabrics were primarily bought from factories in France, Italy and Spain, but also from a Bulgaria-based Italian textile producer. One reason to avoid Bulgarian fabrics is to prevent local competitors from imitating Battibaleno products after a new collection is launched.

Half of the production volume is sold on the Bulgarian market in Battibaleno brand stores and the other half abroad, in similar stores in the USA, Guadalupe, Greece, Switzerland, Azerbaijan and Russia (while in Germany, Austria and France franchises stores existed but were unsuccessful and closed down). Russia provides potentially the largest market, but the problem is that customers there prefer to buy fashion made in France, Italy, Spain or England and do not think highly of fashion 'made in Bulgaria'. Thus, the idea was born to relocate the finishing process (in particular the ironing) to France, in order to be able to sell Battibaleno products as 'made in France'. Although this plan has not yet materialized (due to problems with the French partners) it is still under consideration. Another idea for the future is to completely outsource the production process to countries like Turkey or Moldova. In that case, the company's position in the value chain can be upgraded, and the firm will be able to exclusively focus on design, marketing, branding, presentation and sale, subcontracting the production elsewhere.

This case illustrates that the concept of industrial upgrading and the attempt to become more independent from transnational brand names leads to a shift from the production of clothes to the production of signs and lifestyle symbols. The 'tag' or designation of the product's origin ('Made in…') is a crucial factor in the spatial organization of the value chain, having a decisive influence on the brand's reputation and on consumer demands. This leads to the incongruous situation in which Bulgarian producers put significant effort into creating 'real' French or Italian fashion through performative 'authentication' (Jackson 2002, 9). What can be called 'value chain management' requires the organizational and spatial dissociation of the physical manufacturing process from the production of symbolic meanings and signs.

Buying and Wearing Branded Clothes

Brands help to articulate the new social distinctions that have emerged in Bulgaria and in other parts of the socialist world. The nouveau riche, for instance, use brands to show that they can afford expensive and exclusive items. Young hedonists affirm, sometimes in an outright ironic fashion, the dominant images of a luxurious consumer taste, which is, for instance, the case in the popular *chalga* (Bulgarian pop-folk music) culture. Following these motifs, fashion advertisement campaigns in Bulgaria are often provocative, playing out a mix of images linking the neoliberal subject with Balkan stereotypes. One typical character is the burlesque of the successful businessman or businesswoman, whereby fashion models pose with an extroverted and often exhibitionist expression of ruthlessness and egoism, indicating that they will stop at nothing for individual gain. Other typical characters produced in *chalga* music video clips are sparingly dressed women displaying exaggerated sexual motifs. They are often presented in pornographic poses, while men are typically shown as violent 'mafia' types. The more intellectually inclined middle classes dissociate themselves from this *chalga* or nouveau riche culture, which they regard as uncivilized and uncultivated, representing an unfortunate mix of urban hedonism and rural primitivism.[10] They prefer to buy Western brands if they can afford them and avoid dressing flamboyantly or ostentatiously. Some try to resist the ubiquitous brand fetishism by not caring too much about brands, or in more extreme cases, by displaying an explicit antibrand attitude. The majority of consumers cannot afford branded clothes anyhow. Many of those wishing to wear branded clothes (particularly young people) often settle for one or two pieces or cheap imitations, which seems to be the case for people on low income in rural regions.[11]

Yet as the following excerpt from a group discussion shows, these phenomena are not entirely new. Already under socialism, brands played an important role in everyday life, mirroring cultural hierarchies between different spaces and political systems.

> RAYA: I was going to tell about Zhaki. It's really a funny story. We have a mutual friend [Zhaki], whose father is from Dupnitsa, but she grew up in Germany, in the GDR [the German Democratic Republic]. And she went back to Dupnitsa where her father told her that there's a major Adidas plant in Blagoevgrad: 'I'll buy you some tennis shoes' [he promised her]. Hence he buys her the tennis shoes with the three stripes, and she's so pleased, you know, because in Bulgaria everyone was wearing them; one got them from the flea market, someone else from the factory, the next from who knows where. She then goes back to Halle [at the time a town in the GDR], where she's from, and she goes to school and they stop her at the door. They say: 'What's this?! We don't allow this sort of thing here so you have to take the shoes off!' 'Take them off?' she said. 'They are from Bulgaria – everybody's wearing them there, they're made there.' And then they made her rip off the three stripes.[12]

The story shows that different 'brand spaces' existed even under socialism, with varying modes of valuation of consumer goods and brands, including or excluding people from certain collectives. Then in the socialist era, new 'brand spaces' emerged. In the sphere of production, Bulgarian companies started to work as subcontractors for internationally known fashion brands (especially in the south close to the Greek border) (Begg et al. 1999). In the sphere of consumption, branded clothes became an important vehicle for sociospatial differentiation. For instance, in a discussion with a group of women in their twenties, one of the participants, Zhenya, refers to the production of branded clothes in her hometown Petrich:

> ZHENYA: I am from Petrich. It is like heaven in Petrich, as in Ruse, you know, because of the *ishlemes* [subcontracted production firms]. It is like heaven because of all the workshops, of the Greeks, of... For example, I acquainted myself with one of the largest factories in Petrich, Bella Stil, which sews almost exclusively for Cerruti, only for the big brands, right?[13]

While Kalina talks about her own shopping habits in the provincial towns Blagoevgrad and Pazardzhik, in both of which she has been spending time:

> KALINA: In principle, while living in Blagoevgrad, I go shopping in Pazardzhik. But when in Pazardzhik, I get my clothes from Blagoevgrad. Basically, I have to be different, not wearing clothes bought from that place; I mean, in this way, I am different than others living in the city.[14]

Such stories reflect the importance of brand spaces and of spatial and temporal categories in articulating processes of economic and cultural advancement after socialism. People try to connect to certain places and disconnect from other places as well as the past, the present and the supposed future by wearing branded clothes, providing examples of the 'performativity' of fashion and brands.

Paradoxically, the deeply felt desire to catch up with Western consumption styles and avoid motifs of backwardness has often exactly the opposite result: it reproduces and confirms the aura of backwardness, of being not really 'European', 'Western' or 'modern'. Even though East European consumers are aware of brands and lifestyles, they are very often stereotyped (particularly in the 'West') as lacking experience and sophistication. The efforts to catch up with Western styles and master the art of the individual sign economy is seen to lead to cheap imitations and exaggerations, which are the outcome of low purchasing power in economies such as Bulgaria. Indeed exaggerations are usually linked to low economic status, whereas understatement is typically connected with a more 'mature' level of consumption and higher standard of living. In some cases, however, exaggerations or conspicuous imitations have a subversive quality, reflecting resistance against processes of cultural homogenization as well as expressing local, national or even 'Balkan' or 'East European' identities.

Some participants of our group discussions (all in their forties) shared their observations about 'rural' people in Sofia, confirming some of the points made above:

DARINA: In my opinion, to begin with, they come from a small community, where it is hard to get information. When they come to the big city, they want to stand out in every possible way, through their clothes, hairstyles, etc. Hence they completely change their appearance, in order for them to fit into the new community.

IVAYLO: Yes, and in the end, what have they seen? We know that in small towns, the choice of goods that can be bought is more limited. When they move to live in the big city, they look for trends to follow, so that they can fit into society. If they see that everyone at the table is dressed in a particular way, I am sure that they will try to do their best to catch up with the rest, because those little knit sweaters just won't cut it.

DARINA: I had a couple of colleagues from the countryside; one that I remember, she had perhaps four pieces, but for a long time she was trying hard to save money, so that she could buy herself something from this specific store, because its reputation was a little better. I personally am unable to say where a particular item of clothing is bought, for me this isn't very important, but for her it clearly had great significance. Actually, now that I think of it, I didn't pay much attention to this before.[15]

The ability of urban consumers to use brands and fashion in a more subtle and sophisticated manner is one of the most common themes in narratives about consumption, lifestyle and modern life. People from the provinces or rural parts of the country are commonly perceived to be less experienced with the sign economy and they also have fewer opportunities to insert themselves into consumerist dreams. On a global level, however, Bulgaria as a whole can be described as one large 'province' where consumers are less skilled in the 'proper' application of symbols of mass consumption compared to people in the 'West'. Apart from the general point I am making, this has other interesting implications; despite the low purchasing power of Bulgarians the marketing activities of particular brands is likely to be very effective because brand loyalty is low. Unlike consumers in the more 'mature markets', Bulgarian consumers are not yet committed to certain brands and they can be won over easily. Low brand loyalty therefore corresponds with high brand awareness, said to be typical for 'peripheral markets'. This is also the case for rural areas, as a quotation of one interviewee (20 years old, from Kazanlak) illustrates:

KRISTINA: In the countryside, the display of brands is noticeable because wealthy people are fewer in number, so it makes an impression. It's something different and special, whereas in the bigger cities it's much more common practice and no one looks at one another. It's nothing extraordinary, something totally normal and commonplace. And in the big cities incomes are higher, which suggests that more people will dress in branded clothes.[16]

Conclusions

This Bulgarian case study shows the existence of certain brand geographies which can be characterized as follows: exclusive 'global brands' are geographically anchored in the traditional centres of global fashion and they create insurmountable barriers for Bulgarian brands that wish to enter into their markets. The main obstacle is global media presence, which is difficult to achieve. Since brand spaces are predominantly created through the media, it is imperative for any global brand to invest in advertising and in sponsoring of celebrities and events. Therefore, the creation of value takes place in the global media and business centres within the framework of largely closed, monopolistic or oligopolistic markets.

In spite of these conditions, some Bulgarian manufacturers have managed to launch their own 'local brands', upgrading their position in the value chain and becoming less dependent on manufacturing for 'global brands'. They are successful in terms of creating their own niche markets, which are predominantly domestic even though some succeed in entering export markets, too. However, it remains difficult, if not impossible, for them to enter into serious competition with the 'global brands'.[17] Even the most successful new local brands are unable to realize comparable profit margins from the production of added symbolic value. If such a success were to be achieved, it would create opportunities to outsource and offshore physical production, relocating labour-intensive manufacturing processes to low-wage countries and retain sign-intensive processes (design, advertising and symbolic value creation) in Bulgaria or move them to other countries closer to the global centres.

Brand spaces are like global villages, where a limited number of globally recognizable brands are the primary and dominant markers of consumer capitalism across the world. Local brands occupy their own local niches, intertwining in their brand communication both imitative and alternative or subversive strategies. However, the values attached to 'the local', 'the regional' or 'the national' for local customers is still low in the Bulgarian fashion industry. Bulgarian consumers continue to prefer Italian, French or Spanish fashion, and hence producers and marketing specialists create brands and products which go on satisfying their customers' desire for such fashion items – by using, for example, Italian designers, choosing Italian labels as brands and mimicking Italian fashion styles.

The conversations of Bulgarians about brands and fashion reflect notions of modernity and modernization, and of progress and backwardness at different scales or levels. On the most general level, Bulgarian producers as well as consumers often describe themselves as backward in comparison to the West: producers are said to be not competitive in terms of generating symbolic values, while consumers are depicted as being in search of a 'modern life', following too readily the models that are provided by the media and cultural industries in Western Europe and North America. On the lower national or regional scales, similar centre–periphery relations can be observed, for instance, between urban and rural areas: cities are the places where brands and high brand values are created, while the countryside predominantly engages in forms of conspicuous consumption which may border on brand addiction, especially among young people. Seen from the centre (whether global or national) fashion consumers in the periphery are unable to properly value brands and styles, and as such they reveal themselves as 'peasants', 'Balkanites' or 'East Europeans'.

Economic restructuring in socialist Bulgaria has caused a tectonic shift from communism to consumerism, a process of straight transition from a planned socialist economy to consumer capitalism, with high importance attached to brands and other sign values. But this shift is fraught with contradictions. Despite the switch to a sign economy, local production is still focused on the physical and technical aspects of the production process and it is clear that many consumers still value product quality more than brand image. Their efforts to 'catch up' with Western consumer culture and break away from their rather 'peripheral' position seem to be somehow self-defeating, not dissimilar to the efforts by manufacturers and suppliers to upgrade their position in the global value chain. One explanation for these failures lies in the restricted performativity of brands from the 'new Europe' – that is, in the limited possibilities to create value through the generation of symbolic value in the media (Lee 2006). Performance is largely dependent on the values attached to the places and spaces of production, distribution and consumption. Local brands face the problem that the dominant and hegemonic discourses confirm their peripheral position and their economic and cultural backwardness. They are only to a limited degree included in the global village of fashion; even though brands and their symbolic value flow regardless of political and geographic boundaries, the places where these values are cashed are restricted to the global centres, ultimately strengthening asymmetric economic and power relations between different parts of the world.

Notes

1 This group discussion was organized by Christian Geiselmann and took place in Sofia on 10 March 2011. I would like to thank Yuliana Lazova and Diliana Daskalova for providing the transcripts and translations. All the group discussions and interviews referred to in this chapter were carried out as part of the project 'Marken(t)räume' ('Brands, dreams and spaces') at the Leibniz Institute for Regional Geography in Leipzig, Germany, funded by the Deutsche Forschungsgemeinschaft (DFG), Code ER 475/3-1.

2 This is evidenced by the fact that the physical production costs of the clothes manufactured in Bulgaria are in many cases less than 10 per cent of the sales revenue (including labour and material costs), while more than 90 per cent goes into the design, distribution and marketing (including branding and sponsoring).

3 See especially Smith and Rochovská (2007), who have formulated the notion of 'domesticating neo-liberalism' in socialist societies by analogy to Creed's (1998) concept of 'domesticating socialism' in the everyday life of rural (and urban) populations; see also Pickles's notion of the 'diverse economies of actually existing post-socialism' (2010, 133f.).

4 For the political dimensions of Bulgarian apparel production in the preaccession period, see Pickles (2002) and Smith et al. (2005).

5 Interview carried out in Ruse by the author (20 April 2008). In the following, all interviews were carried out by the author, unless otherwise indicated.

6 Interview carried out in Gotse Delchev (12 April 2007).

7 Interview carried out in Gotse Delchev (12 April 2007).

8 Interview carried out in Sofia (26 March 2008).

9 Interview carried out in Sofia (5 November 2010).

10 For a similar aversion against *chalga* music among Bulgarians living abroad (in Germany), see Krăsteva-Blagoeva (2010, 259).

11 As Deema Kaneff has pointed out, 'Rural inhabitants cannot compete in a society whose ideology now values material wealth, domination of the economy above all else, and whose symbols 'speak' to these values. In short, economically oriented symbols remain exclusively the property of a new class of prosperous and therefore powerful urban elite' (2002, 45f.).

12 Group discussion in Sofia (10 March 2011).

13 Group discussion in Sofia (18 March 2011).

14 Group discussion in Sofia (18 March 2011).

15 Interview carried out in Sofia by Kristian Bankov (4 August 2008).

16 Interview carried out in Sofia by Maria Kundzheva (23 May 2008).

17 There are only few examples of companies worldwide that have successfully entered the market of 'globally branded' clothes and fashion. Mavi Jeans from Turkey is one of them (see Tokatli and Kızılgün 2004).

References

Araujo, Luis, John Finch and Hans Kjellberg. 2010. 'Reconnecting Marketing to Markets: An Introduction'. In *Reconnecting Marketing to Markets*, edited by Luis Araujo, John Finch and Hans Kjellberg, 1–12. Oxford: Oxford University Press.

Arvidsson, Adam. 2005. 'Brands: A Critical Perspective'. *Journal of Consumer Culture* 5 (2): 235–58.

Austin, John. 1973 (1955). *How to Do Things with Words*. William James Lectures, 1955. New York: Oxford University Press.

Barber, Benjamin. 2007. *Consumed: How Markets Corrupt Children, Infantilize Adults, and Swallow Citizens Whole*. New York: W. W. Norton.

Begg, Robert, John Pickles and Poli Roukova. 1999. 'A New Participant in the Global Apparel Industry: The Case of Southern Bulgaria'. *Problemi na Geografiyama* 3 (4): 121–35.

Begg, Robert et al. 2003. 'Cutting It: European Integration, Trade Regimes, and the Reconfiguration of Eastern and Central European Apparel Production'. *Environment and Planning A* 35: 2191–2207.

Berndt, Christian and Marc Boeckler. 2007. 'Kulturelle Geographien der Ökonomie: Zur Performativität von Märkten'. In: *Kulturelle Geographien: Zur Beschäftigung mit Raum und Ort nach dem Cultural Turn*, edited by Christian Berndt and Robert Pütz, 213–58. Bielefeld: Transcript.

Callon, Michel. 1998. 'An Essay on Framing and Overflowing: Economic Externalities Revisited by Sociology'. In *The Laws of the Markets*, edited by Michel Callon, 244–69. Oxford: Blackwell.

Callon, Michel, Cécile Méadel and Vololona Rabeharisoa. 2002. 'The Economy of Qualities'. *Economy and Society* 31 (2): 194–217.

Creed, Gerald. 1998. *Domesticating Revolution: From Socialist Reform to Ambivalent Transition in a Bulgarian Village*. University Park: Pennsylvania State University Press.

Entwistle, Joanne. 2002. 'The Aesthetic Economy: The Production of Value in the Field of Fashion Modelling'. *Journal of Consumer Culture* 2 (3): 317–39.

Ermann, Ulrich. 2007. 'Magische Marken: Eine Fusion von Ökonomie und Kultur im globalen Konsumkapitalismus?' In *Kulturelle Geographien: Zur Beschäftigung mit Ort und Raum nach dem Cultural Turn*, edited by Christian Berndt and Robert Pütz, 317–47. Bielefeld: Transcript.

Featherstone, Mike. 2007 (1991). *Consumer Culture and Postmodernism*. Los Angeles: Sage.

Fehérváry, Krisztina. 2002. 'American Kitchens, Luxury Bathrooms, and the Search for a 'Normal' Life in Postsocialist Hungary'. *Ethnos* 67 (3): 369–400.

Gereffi, Gary. 1999. 'International Trade and Industrial Upgrading in the Apparel Commodity Chain'. *Journal of International Economics* 48: 37–70.

Gereffi, Gary, John Humphrey and Timothy Sturgeon. 2005. 'The Governance of Global Value Chains'. *Review of International Political Economy* 12: 78–104.

Goffman, Erwing. 1959. *The Presentation of Self in Everyday Life*. New York: Doubleday.

Holt, Douglas. 2004. *How Brands Become Icons: The Principles of Cultural Branding*. Cambridge, MA: Harvard University Press.

Humphrey, Caroline. 1995. 'Creating a Culture of Disillusionment: Consumption in Moscow, a Chronicle of Changing Times'. In *Worlds Apart: Modernity through the Prism of the Local*, edited by Daniel Miller, 43–68. London: Routledge.

Jackson, Peter. 2002. 'Commercial Cultures: Transcending the Cultural and the Economic'. *Progress in Human Geography* 26 (1): 3–18.

Kaneff, Deema. 2002. 'Buying into the American Dream: Reforming National Symbols in Bulgaria'. *Ethnologia Europaea* 32 (1): 35–48.

Klein, Naomi. 2000. *No Logo: Taking Aim at the Brand Bullies*. Toronto: Alfred Knopf.

Kotler, Philip, Gary Armstrong, Veronica Wong and John Saunders. 2008. *Principles of Marketing*, fifth edition. London: Prentice Hall.

Krăsteva-Blagoeva, Evgenija. 2001. 'The Bulgarians and McDonald's: Some Anthropological Aspects'. *Ethnologia Balkanica* 5: 207–17.

———. 2010. 'Food and Migration: The Case of Bulgarians in Munich'. In *Migration in, from, and to Southeastern Europe, Part 1: Historical and Cultural Aspects*, edited by Klaus Roth and Robert Hayden, 249–68. Münster: LIT Verlag.

Lash, Scott and John Urry. 1994. *Economies of Signs and Space*. London: Sage.

Lee, Roger. 2006. 'The Ordinary Economy: Tangled Up in Values and Geography'. *Transactions of the Institute of British Geographers*, n.s., 31: 413–32.

Lury, Celia. 2004. *Brands: The Logos of the Global Economy*. London: Routledge.

Miller, Daniel. 2000. 'Virtualism: The Culture of Political Economy'. In *Cultural Turns/ Geographical Turns: Perspectives on Cultural Geography*, edited by Ian Cook et al., 196–213. Harlow: Prentice Hall.

Moor, Elizabeth. 2003. 'Branded Spaces: The Scope of "New Marketing"'. *Journal of Consumer Culture* 3 (1): 39–60.

———. 2007. *The Rise of Brands*. Oxford: Berg.

Neckel, Sighard. 2006. 'Das Erfolgsprinzip der Selbstdarstellung: Marktgesellschaft und performative Ökonomie'. In *Wie wir uns aufführen: Performanz als Thema der Kulturwissenschaften*, edited by Lutz Musner and Heidemarie Uhl, 153–65. Vienna: Löcker.

Patico, Jennifer and Melissa Caldwell. 2002. 'Consumers Exiting Socialism: Ethnographic Perspectives on Daily Life in Post-communist Europe'. *Ethnos* 67 (3): 285–94.

Pickles, John. 2002. 'Gulag Europe? Mass Unemployment, New Firm Creation, and Tight Labour Markets in the Bulgarian Apparel Industry'. In *Work, Unemployment and Transition: Restructuring Livelihoods in Post-communism*, edited by Al Rainnie, Adrian Smith and Adam Swain, 246–72. London: Routledge.

———. 2010. 'The Spirit of Post-socialism: Common Spaces and the Production of Diversity'. *European Urban and Regional Studies* 17 (2): 127–40.

Pickles, John et al. 2006. 'Upgrading, Changing Competitive Pressures, and Diverse Practices in the East and Central European Apparel Industry'. *Environment and Planning A* 38: 2305–24.

Pine, Frances. 2001. 'From Production to Consumption in Post-socialism?' In *Poland Beyond Communism: 'Transition' in Critical Perspective*, edited by Michał Buchowski, Édouard Conte and Carole Nagengast, 209–24. *Studia Ethnographica Friburgensia* 25. Freiburg: Universitätsverlag Freiburg.

Rifkin, Jeremy. 2000. *The Age of Access: How the Shift from Ownership to Access is Transforming Capitalism*. London: Penguin.

Slater, Don. 1987. 'On the Wings of the Sign: Commodity Culture and Social Practice'. *Media, Culture and Society* 9: 457–80.

Smith, Adrian, John Pickles, Robert Begg, Poli Roukova and Milan Buček. 2005. 'Outward Processing, EU Enlargement and Regional Relocation in the European Textiles and Clothing Industry: Reflections on the European Commission's Communication on "The Future of the Textiles and Clothing Sector in the Enlarged European Union"'. *European Urban and Regional Studies* 12: 83–91.

Smith, Adrian and Alena Rochovská. 2007. 'Domesticating Neo-liberalism: Everyday Lives and the Geographies of Post-socialist Transformations'. *Geoforum* 38: 1163–78.

Stark, David. 1996. 'Recombinant Property in East European Capitalism'. *American Journal of Sociology* 101 (4): 993–1027

Stitziel, Judd. 2005. *Fashioning Socialism: Clothing, Politics, and Consumer Culture in East Germany*. Oxford: Berg.

Thrift, Nigel. 2006. 'Re-inventing Invention: New Tendencies in Capitalist Commodification'. *Economy and Society* 35 (2): 279–306.

Tokatli, Nebahat. 2007. 'Upgrading Among Contractors and Sub-contractors of Global Clothing Brands: The Example of a Hugo Boss Contractor'. *Journal of Economic Geography* 7 (1): 67–92.

Tokatli, Nebahat and Ömür Kızılgün. 2004. 'Upgrading in the Global Clothing Industry: Mavi Jeans and the Transformation of a Turkish Firm from Full-Package to Brand-Name Manufacturing and Retailing'. *Economic Geography* 80 (3): 221–40.

Tsing, Anna. 2005. *Friction: An Ethnography of Global Connection*. Princeton: Princeton University Press.

Žižek, Slavoj. 2002. *Revolution at the Gates*. London: Verso.

Chapter 11

GREEK (AD)VENTURES IN SOFIA: ECONOMIC ELITE MOBILITY AND NEW CULTURAL HIERARCHIES AT THE MARGINS OF EUROPE

Aliki Angelidou and Dimitra Kofti

Since the reopening of borders after the end of the Cold War, Europe has seen the revival of diverse forms of mobility and movement going in different directions, such as labour migration from or entrepreneurial mobility towards the former socialist countries. More specifically, the creation of new markets as well as the displacement and relocation of industries and services to postsocialist Europe have resulted in various kinds of business mobility to Eastern Europe.[1] In the case of Bulgaria, numerous foreign companies have established branches or moved their entire production there and as part of this process, entrepreneurs and managers followed this trajectory. A significant number of companies and investments as well as employees have come from neighbouring Greece.[2] In this chapter, we will focus on this elite migration and on the new relationships of power that have emerged between Greek employers and Bulgarian employees.[3]

Studies on migration and transnationalism in Eastern Europe have mostly focused either on the massive labour force movements coming from the former socialist countries towards Western and Southern European countries[4] or on the role of NGOs and other international organizations going eastwards.[5] Less attention has been given to the migratory movements of economic elites that have been constituted and/or reconstituted after the opening of borders and the emergence of new markets. Moreover, among the numerous anthropological studies on globalization that focus on elite mobility, postsocialist countries have been relatively neglected.[6] Our ethnographic example permits us to analyse some global phenomena after the collapse of socialism and the subsequent market expansion in this part of Europe in the neoliberal era. Our material suggests that these reconfigurations provide the means for new forms of mobility which reshape the relationships between two neighbouring countries and generate new cultural hierarchies at the margins of Europe.

As Kaneff points out (this volume), the neoliberal era is characterized by changing relationships between nation-states and markets. The previous political supremacy of the nation-state is gradually giving way to the neoliberal predominance of the market. However, this does not necessarily mean that the state is becoming a less significant actor (see Creed this volume; Duijzings this volume). The economic and judicial conditions and regulations that facilitate market processes such as business mobility are laid down and implemented by the state. For example, after the collapse of the socialist regimes in Eastern Europe, new tax conditions and labour law policies enabled new investments accompanied by new types of mobility.

Moreover, while nation-state border regimes permit the movement of people and economic transactions, national identities do not necessarily lose their importance. As Larry Wolff (1994) and Maria Todorova (1997) have argued, the reopening of borders after the end of socialism has led to renewed stereotyping, juxtaposing the East European or Balkan 'other' with the Western 'self'. This has also happened between Greece and Bulgaria, two countries which have a two centuries–long history of constructing images of national selves in mutual opposition and antagonism. Entrepreneurial mobility between them generates new representations of 'self' and 'other' and new claims of power in the context of the newly emerging free market economy. What is specific in our case is that the entrepreneurial mobility's routes are not between 'East' and 'West' but between two neighbouring countries that are both at the margins of Europe. Nevertheless representations of 'East' and 'West' play an important role in our subjects' self-identification and understanding of their position in Bulgaria, as we shall discuss.

As Steven Sampson (1996) has pointed out, mobility towards the former socialist countries includes flows not only of goods and people but also of ideas, models and representations. The economic activity across the Greco-Bulgarian national borders is a relatively new phenomenon for Greek businessmen, who form an economically privileged group in Bulgaria and, to a certain extent, in Greece as well.[7] They often use the English term 'expatriates' to describe their position. Because of their important role in the privatization process, they usually present themselves as pioneers of 'progress' and 'modernization' in the Bulgarian economy, claiming a more 'Western' and/or 'European' position compared to their former socialist neighbours. In this chapter we will analyse ways in which entrepreneurial mobility generates changes in the social and economic position and status of Greek managers. In addition, we will explore how new self-identifications and processes of 'othering' occur, linked to these transnational movements and new labour relationships. We will argue that Greek managers, through transnational economic activities and entrepreneurial discourses, claim a higher social and economic status and an unequal balance of economic and symbolic power between Bulgaria and Greece.[8] To substantiate this claim, we will first discuss how they employ their professional activities and daily practices. Secondly, we will analyse the ambivalences of Greek discourses on the 'expatriate self' vis-à-vis other categories such as 'Bulgarian employees', 'migrants' and 'other European or Western expatriates'.

Acquiring Power through Economic Mobility: New Positions, New Lifestyles

In setting the context of the Greek businessmen's new lives in Bulgaria, we will briefly distinguish between the different types of entrepreneurial and economic mobility. The great majority of Greek businessmen, who have been moving to Bulgaria since the 1990s, are men in their mid-thirties to mid-fifties.[9] Given their different employment types in Bulgaria and their diverse backgrounds, one may not describe them as a unified and homogenous group. In relation to their job positions, it is possible to identify four main (partly overlapping) employment categories which correspond to four different types of companies.[10] First, managers and key staff members (mainly engineers) of large Greek companies, such as telecommunication companies, banks, chain stores and mass production plants which have opened branches or transferred their entire production to Bulgaria. Second, the owners of small or medium-sized companies – mostly active in the clothing and food industries – which have ceased production in Greece and have transferred the entire manufacturing process to Bulgaria. Third, the managers of multinational companies, which have often entered the Bulgarian market through their Greek branches employing Greeks who have had previous experience of working in Bulgaria in a company of the above two types. Fourth, the former managers of major companies who use their recent experience working in the Bulgarian market to establish their own companies in Sofia, offering services such as consultancy and advertising.[11] In this chapter we focus on Greek entrepreneurs and managers working in Sofia, mainly managers of large companies and banks and to a lesser extent managers and owners of small and medium-sized companies.

The main reasons for Greek firms to establish themselves in Bulgaria are cheap labour, favourable tax conditions and geographical proximity to Greece. It is the latter especially that has facilitated the 'unavoidable expansion' of Greek firms, as emphasized by our discussants. As the owner of a construction company noted, 'Greece is a small market, and after its entry into the EU it has been gradually saturated. During the last decades – that is, after 1990 – we were forced to expand beyond Greece in order to survive.' In most cases, these companies prefer to employ Greeks in the higher echelons of managerial positions. Some of these managers were previously employed at the firm's parent company in Greece.

Due to the large demand for Greek staff in Greek enterprises moving abroad, the skills and qualifications required for managerial posts in Bulgaria are often less rigorous than those one may need for an equivalent post in the same company in Greece itself. Some of the managers indicated to us that they acquired a managerial position in Bulgaria with just an undergraduate university degree, instead of a postgraduate degree as is often needed in Greece. Previous experience from studies or work abroad is always considered a plus. Mastery of the English language is essential, but knowledge of Bulgarian is viewed as less important and it is usually not required, though it may be regarded as an advantage. For most managers, the decision to move abroad was the result of a request or proposition coming from their company rather than their own initiative.

Since the decision to work in Bulgaria is not always planned in advance, many Greek managers have ambivalent ideas about life outside Greece, which transpire when talking about their motives for accepting or rejecting a job position abroad. Moving to work in Bulgaria is often not viewed immediately as an attractive option by employees.[12] This is caused by the unwillingness to leave family and a familiar way of life behind in Greece. It is also reinforced by various negative stereotypes about Bulgaria, which they often represent as a 'backward' and 'dangerous' country.[13] As one informant said, 'When I first came here I had images of the Middle Ages in my mind. I knew it was a socialist country that had gone through changes and was not in a good condition.' Another said, 'I heard various negative things. There were all these rumours about robberies and that you cannot walk in the streets. But in the end it was not that bad.'

Family pressure is another reason that impacts negatively on the willingness to move to Bulgaria. Family members in Greece are often concerned that an unmarried (or married) man might establish emotional ties with women abroad, which is seen as one of the obvious risks when away from family and home. Few of those who are married move with their spouses and children to Bulgaria; the majority leave their family behind. Usually they stay in Sofia during weekdays and spend the weekends with their families in Greece: 'I cannot even imagine my wife's reaction if I were to not go back to Thessaloniki for the weekend. However, I am happy to go, I have nothing to do here except work', the 45-year-old manager of a major construction company told us. Some go back to Greece regularly, although not on a weekly basis. Only those who have a family or a relationship in Sofia visit Greece less often.

From the point of view of their social and professional trajectory, many businessmen experience an accelerated social mobility which is closely linked to their geographic mobility abroad. Bulgaria's proximity to Greece makes the decision to accept a job in Bulgaria easier for these businessmen, in spite of their initial reluctance. Economic disparities across the border generate and motivate movement as well.[14] Many of our informants often reiterated that proximity between the two countries allows easy and frequent commuting. As an IT manager commented, 'Athens–Sofia is almost like a domestic flight to me. It feels like working in another Greek town. The only difference is that I earn much more than I would if I would have worked in Larissa or Iraklio.' Apart from geographical proximity, businessmen often refer to a kind of 'cultural likeness' between the two countries, which is often presented as an advantage. As the owner of a small textile company told us, 'We understand Bulgarians better than, for example, Germans or Austrians who live in the country, so it is easier to work with them.' Moreover, they view the opening of the markets in former socialist countries as an attractive growth area for Greek businesses, as Greek companies have the opportunity to play a hegemonic role at a regional level. As the manager of an IT company told us, 'The Balkans provide a market that we can handle, they are in our courtyard.' Interestingly, Greek entrepreneurs often state that Greek investors are unlikely to play a role as important in markets other than the Balkans, admitting that their hegemonic ambition is geographically limited.

In addition, their new job positions and daily lives give them an opportunity to enjoy fast upward social mobility and act out their newly acquired position of power. As commonly admitted by our informants, high salaries and fast promotion are some of the most important motives to work abroad. Most of them immediately acquire managerial positions that would not be within easy reach in Greece, at their age or with the qualifications they have. They usually earn salaries double or more that which they would receive for the same position in Greece. On top of this, employment contracts often include privileges such as plane tickets for themselves and their families or expensive cars for daily use, sometimes with personal drivers who drive them around Sofia as well as to their homes in Greece. The companies often take care of accommodation, which is usually in posh areas of the city such as Boyana, Dragalevtsi and Lozenets or in large luxury apartments in the very heart of the city centre. The offer of these luxurious living conditions is also a strong motive to move to Bulgaria. A factory manager told us,

> When I first came here, the company had already rented a flat for me in an old building in the city centre. It was spacious but disgusting, one of those old flats from the communist period which have never been refurbished. I told them that I would go back to Greece. There was no point in me staying here if I would have to live in a house like that with old furniture. I did not come here for this kind of life. They finally found a house with a garden in Boyana and I decided to stay.

Finally, since the living costs in Bulgaria are much lower than in Greece and the managers' salaries are considerably higher, 'what counts is what is left in my pocket at the end of the month', the manager of a furniture company notes.

Managers get used to a way of life that many of them did not have in Greece. They hang out at expensive restaurants and hotel bars across town which most Bulgarians cannot afford, for both work and leisure. During winter weekends, when their families or friends pay them visits, skiing in the mountains around the capital or in luxury ski resorts such as Bansko or Pamporovo is a common activity. Other activities involve hunting, riding horses and flying sailplanes and aeroplanes. Shopping in the luxurious shops of the city centre or the newly constructed shopping malls of Sofia is another favourite pastime. For those who have school-age children living with them in Bulgaria, a private foreign language school, American or French for example, is the most common option. All these forms of conspicuous consumption allow them to demonstrate success and display a privileged and distinctive lifestyle both in Bulgaria and Greece. As we have noticed, many of our interlocutors did not have this luxury back in Greece. Interestingly, they often avoid speaking about their previous lives before moving to Bulgaria. Sometimes, during the more informal chats we had with them about Greece, many referred to the areas they had grown up in or the places where they would socialize, which showed that in Greece they had had a less prestigious lifestyle than the one they had acquired in Bulgaria, and that crossing the borders had significantly elevated their social status.

This new lifestyle includes socializing with colleagues and other expats after work. There are regular networking and business meetings for entrepreneurs and managers during weekdays in Sofia. For instance, such events are organized by the Hellenic Business Council in Bulgaria (HBCB) to allow people to get to know each other and to create tighter links between Greek companies, but also between Greek and Bulgarian companies. These meetings usually include company presentations and briefings by members of the HBCB and others about the economy and market developments. They take place in hotels in the centre of the capital, followed by cocktail parties or cultural events such as theatre and music performances dedicated to Greek culture or 'Greco-Bulgarian friendship'. In addition, some Greek managers participate actively in events organized by other organizations in Bulgaria, such as the American Chamber of Commerce. These events provide opportunities to establish contacts and meet new clients and potential business partners. Many managers regard these meetings as part of their job and they indicate that they feel obliged to participate for 'networking' purposes (for this they use the English term). Although some state that these are 'boring' and 'compulsory' events which they have to participate in, they also benefit from them as they meet 'important people' there. They sometimes boast about having 'friends' who have high positions in business or politics in Bulgaria and who may prove useful to further their career.

While prioritizing meetings and connections between Greeks, they also hang out with foreign or Bulgarian colleagues in higher managerial positions whom they meet during such events. Yet many of them have a strong sense of belonging to the Greek business community, which is strengthened through these social meetings. One can often hear them saying, 'We form a small village here, we know and help each other and meet regularly at places across the city.' These social events strengthen the ties between Greek managers in Sofia and make them part of an international community of people working in business, finance and politics.

Bulgarian journalists often report on these events and the economic activities of Greek companies, but the Greek media are also interested in this process of economic expansion in Southeastern Europe. They regularly write about Greek-owned companies in neighbouring countries and carry out interviews with investors and managers discussing their experiences abroad. It is the term 'expatriates' that is most commonly used in such publications to describe the position of these Greek businessmen, which adds to the prestigious social status of those working in Bulgaria. While store managers in Greece are hardly ever in the news, Greek store managers in Bulgaria are often in the media. When one of us had a meeting with a young computer store manager, the interviewer was left waiting for 40 minutes, after which the manager phoned and apologized for not coming. He asked to be reminded which newspaper would publish the interview, and it was postponed for some days later. He indicated that he had given many interviews both to the Greek and Bulgarian press in the course of the four years that he had been in the country. Initially he had felt honoured but later it became routine.

Their position of power is also symbolized and acted out through talk about numerous sexual relationships with Bulgarian women. Whether there is any truth in this or not, Greek businessmen often proudly discuss the 'ease' with which they can establish sexual relationships in Sofia compared to Greece. While talking to women like us, they usually refer to it as a possibility rather than an actual practice. The examples they give almost always concern 'other Greek men', who have several girlfriends at the same time or spend time with beautiful women at expensive restaurants and dance clubs to 'show off' their manliness. These discursive practices highlighting masculine competence can be seen as a performance and one more level of the display of Greek power in Sofia.

Another performance of power is their refusal to use the Bulgarian language. Although many Greek businessmen spend quite a few years in Bulgaria, the vast majority does not speak Bulgarian or even make an effort to learn it. Most of them are multilingual only to a limited extent in that they have a moderate command of English.[15] Some of them admit that things would have been better both in their daily lives and in business if they could understand Bulgarian. Yet they rely on Bulgarians knowing English or Greek. When recruiting local staff, Greek companies require knowledge of English and sometimes Greek as the language skills mentioned in the job description. Not being able to speak Bulgarian is commonly justified by saying that 'in business you have to be clear when you speak, and not put yourself into a vulnerable position'. A bank manager who had lived in Bulgaria for five years told us, 'I know the basics when I go to a restaurant or shop; however, this language is very difficult and I am not going to learn it. I never use it at work because I do not want to make mistakes or misunderstand what people tell me. I have to protect my position. It is their problem if they do not speak English.' Another reason given for not learning Bulgarian is the lack of spare time. A bank manager, who was married to a Bulgarian woman and at the time of our interview had lived in Bulgaria for nine years, said: 'I work twelve to fourteen hours per day; there is simply no time for language learning.' The lack of interest for the local language is also caused by a sense of temporary residence in the country. As a manager in a telecommunications company told us, 'I do not know whether I will stay here for a couple of years or only for some months, so why bother to learn the language?' Secretaries and drivers often help out with everyday communication and transactions, and Greek businessmen seem unmotivated to learn the language. Years pass with them living in the country without acquiring local language skills. This general refusal to learn the local language shows unwillingness to integrate into local society, while it also constitutes a performance in terms of displaying superiority and cultural hegemony.[16]

Many informants had previous experience of living abroad. Some of them had studied in the US or in Western Europe, while others had worked for Greek companies in one or more postsocialist countries. More interestingly, some of them had been involved in forms of economic migration in the past. For example, two had lived in Germany: the first migrated in his twenties, along with his wife, during the emigration wave from Greece in the 1960s; the other moved there as a child with his family in the 1970s. When discussing their migrant experiences, they avoided the term 'migrant' (or any related term); simply saying that they had familiarity with living abroad, which helped them in Bulgaria. Yet both freely used the English term 'expatriate' to describe their position in Bulgaria, a term we will further explore in our analysis.

Narratives about 'Bulgarian Employees'

Until now, the discussion has focused on how international mobility transforms the social status of Greek managers and businessmen, resulting in changing positions of power, status and lifestyle, and patterns of consumption. In this section, we will look at how they compare themselves with Bulgarians through stereotypical images that seem to be very popular among Greeks in Sofia. Since contact with local people frequently occurs inside the work place, they regularly comment on how Bulgarians work compared to Greeks. One of us once visited a small factory in Sofia to interview the owner, to whom we had been introduced by a Bulgarian friend employed at his company. At the start of the conversation, he would open the drawers of his desk and check his email and mobile phone while grudgingly responding to questions, avoiding eye contact and expressing surprise that the interviewer spoke Greek so well. It was only when the latter answered that she was born in Greece that he started to pay proper attention to the discussion, offering her a coffee and talking much more keenly, reiterating how much he suffers from the Bulgarians' unwillingness to understand 'his fight for progress' and their refusal 'to cooperate and work'.

Greek managers constantly reiterate that Bulgarians are not motivated to work and that they are 'not flexible enough' to handle complicated situations, while being at the same time 'obedient'. Characteristics that might otherwise be considered positive by employers, like 'obedience', become less so when comparing Bulgarians to the Greeks. As the Greek director of a large-scale factory commented, 'Bulgarians are obedient because they are not very bright – they are not like the Greeks, who are much more clever and cause problems all the time by going on strike.' Something that is often considered negative by employers in Greece (that is, going on strike) becomes a positive characteristic that distinguishes Greek employees from Bulgarians. As we have noticed, these strong stereotypes are reproduced by Greeks (as well as other foreigners) who seldom come in direct contact with Bulgarians: Greek managers rarely visit the work floor, managing the company from the safe distance of an office and using highly qualified local managerial staff as intermediaries. In some cases, when we asked them to give specific examples to illustrate their point that Bulgarians are not 'flexible and motivated', they had to admit that they had no clear example because they had no time to deal with Bulgarian employees. They just 'knew' that this information was correct, having heard it from other managers.

The above characterizations are often reinforced by comments on and comparisons between the two countries. Managers often present Bulgaria as 'backward', imposing a hierarchy according to which Greece is 'more advanced' in terms of business, the market and European integration. As a consequence, Bulgarians are seen to be in need of profound training to become more 'market and business oriented'. A country manager of a big chain store said, 'They [Bulgarian employees] do not have a career plan in mind. This is obvious in their CVs as well. They work in our sales department for 400 leva and leave our company to do something totally different if somebody offers them 450 leva per month. Hence they jeopardize their career for just 50 leva – they do not have any business logic in their head. It is a really difficult task for us to change this and train them.'

Many of our interlocutors emphasized the importance of organizing training for their Bulgarian employees. The director of a computer chain store explained, 'Extensive training is very important in this country; we need to do much more training than in our country for the same things. What is needed here is deep training.' Greek managers often see themselves as helping 'the expansion of the market', as 'changing the work mentality' in Bulgaria through the introduction of training programmes, and thus they regard themselves as contributing to 'progress' both for Bulgaria and the EU. As a bank manager indicated, 'I consider myself part of this society. I fight for it and for its economy to expand and advance, and I do more than any Bulgarian citizen, since we [expatriates] build the economy here, we financially help businesses and individuals and we give jobs to people. We try to change the mentality. We earn more money and pay more taxes.' The narrative that is constantly repeated by Greek managers is that the local economy and Bulgarian society benefit from Greek companies and businessmen. Sometimes they do indeed admit that they gain large profits as well, but that comes at the cost of huge frustration; they present themselves as victims of a Bulgarian disinclination to contribute to progress. They perform a kind of missionary role, distancing themselves from the 'unwilling Bulgarians' and creating a sense of proximity with fellow European expatriates as well as with an idealized European economy. Through this process of distancing, Greek employees articulate and enact their own Europeanness and impose a sense of superiority over their Bulgarian workers and colleagues, who are still in the process of 'becoming Europeans'.

The Construction of the 'Expatriate' Self

This kind of missionary role, in combination with local resistance, profit making and the adoption of a luxurious lifestyle, form the basic ingredients of the Greek business experience in Bulgaria. As indicated above, most of the managers do not label themselves as 'migrants', preferring to call themselves 'expatriates'. Yet they sometimes use with a degree of hesitation and irony the phrase 'entrepreneurial migration' in order to describe their situation. An 'expat' is, in the eyes of our informants, someone whose work contributes to the 'elevation' of local society through the introduction of new ideas and practices. At the same time an 'expat' is also seen as someone whose work engenders profit both for him personally and the economy of his country of origin. The image of the 'expat' combines the elements of temporariness in Bulgaria and permanence in Greece. As an executive manager of a large IT company explained, 'I am paid by the parent company in Athens; my base is there. If I was a migrant I would receive my salary here, from a local firm. I never know for how long I am going to stay here; I have a short-term contract which is renewed regularly, but at any time I can be called back by the company in Greece or asked to go to another country.' In many cases, Greece is perceived as the place of eventual return, although temporary migration to another country is always a potential option: 'If my company proposes me an equivalent or better job in another country, I am ready to go. I have done that before', a bank manager explained to us. Nevertheless, few people are looking for a job in places other than their neighbouring countries, for example in Western Europe or in another continent.

Interestingly, the term 'expatriate' is a self-definition less commonly used by Greek businessmen who live permanently in Bulgaria and are married to Bulgarian women. Most of them feel more integrated into Bulgaria and frequently designate themselves as 'migrants' or as the 'Greek diaspora'. They are critical of colleagues who use the term 'expat': 'You are not an expatriate when you live just four or five days a week abroad, but many people use this term because it helps them to make a career', a manager of a large computer company commented. Nevertheless, other permanent residents readily adopt the designation 'expatriate' for themselves, through which they demonstrate social distinction and the quest for a higher social status compared to the local population.

The term 'expatriate' is often used with pride, having connotations of power and wealth, whereas the word 'migrant' is avoided, signifying lower social status and economic hardship. The term 'expatriate' also implies inclusion of Greek expats into the highly desirable category of Western (that is, European and American) managers. Even if so, many of our informants talk about what they are doing as a 'sacrifice' for the benefit of their companies and careers, and so another dominant discourse is one of victimization. They often complain of having been pressurized into accepting their job by their companies in order to advance professionally, but without enjoying the same work and living conditions and privileges as 'real expatriates', such as their French, British or American counterparts. One of the main complaints is that neither the Greek state nor the company takes care of Greek education for their children. In addition, many of them complain that they are in an unstable position that does not permit them to do any long-term planning either professionally or privately, comparing their situation to that of 'real expatriates' of other nationalities who enjoy more stability. Many point out that their transient existence means they have difficulty maintaining long-distance relationships with Greek partners, yet having Bulgarian partners is frowned upon by their relatives and friends in Greece. Finally, some of them feel indeed trapped into continuing their career outside of Greece, as they see no opportunities to obtain a better position on return. As a consequence, they plan to use their expat experience to work for another multinational company in Bulgaria or another former socialist country. 'After all', as the general manager of a large company told us in confidence after sharing a bottle of wine once the interview was over, 'I am a migrant with luxuries, forced to stay away from home, family and friends, I would not have the same conditions were I to decide to move back to Greece.'

The term 'expatriate' is thus used situationally to express various meanings, revealing ambivalent positions and self-identifications. On the one hand, it signifies elite mobility, disassociating itself from the lower 'migrant' status. The 'expat' claims symbolic power through conspicuous consumption, geographic mobility and the acting out of cultural dominance at work, justifying his role as having a higher mission that is beneficial for the local economy and that is not to be confused with that of 'migrants' who struggle economically. On the other hand, Greeks who employ this term often lack confidence in its appropriateness. As a consequence, they do not see themselves as the 'real expats' – those coming from Western countries. During these moments of doubt and ambivalence the designation 'expatriate' is no longer convincing, and its condition starts to resemble that of the 'migrant'. It seems that one may better understand the term 'expatriate' in this context through its relation to the terms 'migrant' and 'real expatriate'. These ambivalences reveal that

Greek businessmen are sometimes insecure about their newly acquired position of power and seem to be engaged in ongoing cultural performances in order to attain this status.

Conclusion

As our ethnographic material shows, business mobility both shapes the cultural construction and performance of Greek identity as well as contributes to the production of new power relations. At a personal level, business expansion in Bulgaria has provided Greek entrepreneurs and managers with the opportunity to significantly renegotiate and transform their status and lifestyle. They enjoy higher prestige as a result of material rewards and related privileges. Their position is also defined through the use of the term 'expatriates', which suggests closeness to the European or Western business elites and distance from 'obedient' but 'incompetent' Bulgarian employees. Nevertheless the 'expatriate self' is an ambivalent construct, which positions itself between the less prestigious forms of economic migrant mobility and the more prestigious forms of global elite mobility enjoyed by the 'real' Western expatriates.

Moreover, cross-border entrepreneurial activity has produced new hierarchical cultural discourses and national antagonisms inside the newly emerging regional economic networks. Greek businessmen have adopted a powerful role, claiming a leading hegemonic and asymmetrical position in neighbouring Bulgaria. By employing managerial discourses of 'economic performance' and 'progress and backwardness', they claim a position of symbolic supremacy, enhanced by their own self-definition as 'expatriates', by their linguistic and positional power, and by the sense that their work represents a pioneering mission to establish market economies in the former socialist countries. As a consequence, transnational entrepreneurial mobility has not necessarily contributed to the elimination of cultural boundaries; on the contrary, new capitalist forms of entrepreneurial activities play a key role in creating new boundaries, stereotypes and antagonisms at the margins of Europe.

Notes

1 On this topic, see Dematteo's study on Italian entrepreneurs in Romania (2009) and Redini's work on Italian relocations to Romania (2007, 2008).

2 According to a report on Foreign Direct Investment (FDI) published by the Central Bank of Bulgaria in 2009, Greece is the third-largest investor after Austria and the Netherlands. Investments have taken place mainly in the banking sector, the clothing industries, financial consultancy, import and export, construction, real estate, and communications.

3 Our material is based on fieldwork conducted individually by both authors over different periods in Sofia. By comparing our diverse fieldwork experiences we have been able to develop our thinking and enrich our (common) writing. We are grateful to the French National Research Agency (ANR) (BALKABAS project ANR-08-JCJC-0091-01) and the French School of Athens (EFA), which funded, respectively, Aliki Angelidou's and Dimitra Kofti's research.

4 See for example Angelidou (2008), Kaneff and Pine (2011), King and Black (1997), King et al. (2005), Passerini et al. (2007).

5 See for example Brown (2006), Mendelson and Glenn (2002), Pandolfi (2002), Sampson (1996), Vetta (2009).

6 See among others the work of Abélès (2002, 2008), Appadurai (1996), Eriksen (2007) and Friedman (1997, 1999). Furthermore, Vered Amit's volume (2007) on middle-class elite travellers has no references to such movements in Eastern Europe.

7 Yet it should be pointed out that entrepreneurial and labour mobility is not exclusively a postsocialist phenomenon. It has a much longer history in the Balkan region. During the late Ottoman period, Christian entrepreneurs and merchants were operating throughout the empire and beyond. But the situation was nevertheless different from today's conditions because the Ottoman territories were lacking national borders. On Southeastern European merchant activity in the Ottoman Empire, see the classical contribution by Stoianovich: 'The Conquering Balkan Orthodox Merchant' (1960). Greek merchant mobility and the role of the Greek diaspora since the formation of the Greek state has also been the object of numerous studies, such as the works of Hadziiossif (1980), Mandilara (1998), Pepelasis-Minoglou (1998), Harlaftis (2007) and Sifneos (2009). After World War I this mobility gradually diminished as a result of the creation of national borders between the Balkan states, and almost vanished after World War II, in the context of the Cold War which followed. Between the end of the nineteenth century and the 1980s, labour mobility to Western Europe, Australia and the US became the dominant form of mobility from Greece. This was considered as 'emigration' by people in Greece and in the academic literature.

8 Since we conducted fieldwork in Sofia between 2008 and 2010, our analysis does not touch upon changes in position, practices and viewpoints that occurred after the Greek economic crisis and the effects it has undoubtedly had on Greek entrepreneurial activity abroad.

9 Some women work as managers in the banking sector or in managerial positions in small or medium-sized companies. Very few women have established their own company in Sofia.

10 The above categorizations reflect our informants' viewpoints: they do not perceive Greeks working in Bulgaria as a unified group but distinguish a wide range of employment types with significant differences among them. For example, working for a large company which provides managers with a variety of services in their daily lives differs quite fundamentally in their eyes from being an owner of a small company, requiring different levels of involvement with the Bulgarian economy and society both at work and beyond. While employees of large companies enjoy benefits such as accommodation, cleaning services, medical insurance, drivers, etc., owners of small-scale companies have to organize such things themselves. Additionally, it makes a difference in terms of involvement with life in Bulgaria whether somebody stays permanently in the country or commutes. Finally, Greek businessmen draw differences between companies based in the country's capital and those located in the Bulgarian–Greek border area. Still, these categories are very fluid

and permeable. Here we use the term 'businessmen' to describe both entrepreneurs/ owners and managers. We use the terms 'entrepreneurs' and 'owners' to refer to the companies' owners, while we use the term 'managers' to refer to people employed at higher managerial positions who are not the company's owners.

11 Two other smaller groups, which are not the focus of this chapter, have extensively lived in Bulgaria since socialism. These are people who studied at Bulgarian universities during the late socialist years or second-generation refugees from the Greek Civil War who moved to Bulgaria or were born there from the late 1940s onwards. Due to their knowledge of the language and their participation in local social networks they have found themselves in a privileged position, from which they have benefitted when establishing or managing companies since the 1990s.

12 This has gradually shifted, especially since the global financial crisis, which has hit Greece hard, to the extent that these opinions have almost completely reversed: a managerial position in a Southeastern European country is now considered by many to be a very good employment option.

13 On the use of these stereotypes by Greek day tourists who cross the border to buy cheap goods in Bulgaria, see Kofti (2009).

14 This case shows similarities with the US–Mexican border, as described by Michael Kearney (2004): values are created as a consequence of the disparities that exist between the two sides of the border.

15 Greek managers with excellent knowledge of English are much rarer – they are mainly those at high managerial levels who previously studied, worked or lived in the UK or the US and have had an international career ever since.

16 Things work out differently for the owners or managers of small and medium-sized companies who feel obliged to learn the language. As a director of a small transportation company said, 'We are obliged to multitask compared to the managers of large companies, we do not just stay in the office; and we are unable to work if we do not know to speak Bulgarian.'

References

Abélès, Marc. 2002. *Les nouveaux riches: Une ethnologie de la Silicon Valley*. Paris: Odile Jacob.
_____. 2008. *Anthropologie de la globalisation*. Paris: Payot.
Amit, Vered. 2007. *Going First Class? New Approaches to Privileged Travel and Movement*. London: Berghahn.
Angelidou, Aliki. 2008. 'Migrations in the "Neighborhood": Negotiations of Identities and Representations about "Greece" and "Europe" among Bulgarian migrants in Athens'. *Balkanologie* XI (1.2). Online: http://balkanologie.revues.org/index1152.html (accessed 28 June 2013).
Appadurai, Arjun. 1996. *Modernity at Large: Cultural Dimensions of Globalization*. Minneapolis: University of Minnesota.
Brown, Keith, ed. 2006. *Transacting Transition: The Micropolitics of Democracy Assistance in the Former Yugoslavia*. Bloomfield: Kumarian Press.
Central National Bulgarian Bank. 2009. *Report on Foreign Direct Investment (FDI)*. Online: http://www.bnb.bg/Statistics/StExternalSector/StDirectInvestments/StDIAbroad/index.htm (accessed 4 October 2012).
Dematteo, Linda. 2009. *La ruée des entrepreneurs italiens en Roumanie: Circulations, asymétries et narrations*. Paris: Notre Europe.

Eriksen, Thomas Hylland. 2007. *Globalization: The Key Concepts*. Oxford: Berg.

Friedman, Jonathan. 1997. 'Global Crises, the Struggle for Cultural Identity and Intellectual Porkbarrelling: Cosmopolitans versus Locals, Ethnics and Nationals in an Era of De-hegemonisation'. In *Debating Cultural Hybridity: Multi-cultural Identities and the Politics of Anti-racism*, edited by Pnina Werbner and Tariq Modood, 70–89. London: Zed Press.

———. 1999. 'Class Formation, Hybridity and Ethnification in Declining Global Hegemonies'. In *Globalisation in the Asia Pacific: Contested Territories*, edited by Kris Olds et al., 219–37. London: Routledge.

Hadziiossif, Christos. 1980. 'La colonie grecque en Egypte, 1833–1856'. PhD thesis, Université Paris-Sorbonne (Paris IV), École Pratique des Hautes Études, Section IV, Paris.

Harlaftis, Gelina. 2007. 'From Diaspora Merchants to Shipping Tycoons: The Vagliano Bros'. *Business History Review* 81: 237–68.

Kaneff, Deema and Frances Pine, eds. 2011. *Global Connections and Emerging Inequalities in Europe: Perspectives on Poverty and Transnational Migration*. London: Anthem Press.

Kearney, Michael. 2004. 'The Classifying and Value-Filtering Missions of Borders'. *Anthropological Theory* 4 (2): 131–56.

King, Russell and Richard Black, eds. 1997. *Southern Europe and the New Immigrations*. Brighton: Sussex Academic Press.

King, Russell, Nicola Mai and Stephanie Schwandner-Sievers, eds. 2005. *The New Albanian Migration*. Brighton: Sussex Academic Press.

Kofti, Dimitra. 2009. 'Acquiring Power across the Borders: Greek Tourists in Bulgaria'. In *Greece in the Balkans: Memories, Conflict and Exchange*, edited by Othon Anastassakis, Dimitar Bechev and Nicholas Vrousalis, 219–36. Newcastle: Cambridge Scholars Press.

Mandilara, Anna. 1998. 'The Greek Business Community in Marseille, 1816–1900'. PhD thesis, European University Institute, Florence.

Mendelson, Sarah and John Glenn, eds. 2002. *The Power and Limits of NGOs: A Critical Look at Building Democracy in Eastern Europe and Eurasia*. New York: Columbia University Press.

Pandolfi, Mariella. 2002. 'Moral entrepreneurs, souverainetés mouvantes et barbelés: La bio-politique dans les Balkans postcommunistes'. *Anthropologie et Sociétés* 26 (1): 29–51.

Passerini, Luisa, Enrica Capussotti, Dawn Lyon and Ioanna Laliotou, eds. 2007. *Women Migrants from East to West: Gender, Mobility, and Belonging in Contemporary Europe*. New York: Berghahn.

Pepelasis-Minoglou, Ioanna. 1998. 'The Greek Merchant House of the Russian Black Sea: A Nineteenth-Century Example of a Trader's Coalition'. *International Journal of Maritime History* 10 (1): 61–104.

Redini, Veronica. 2007. 'Del dare e togliere corpo al lavoro: Luoghi, merci e persone nel processo di delocalizzazione delle aziende italiane in Romania'. In *Arcipelago produttivo: Migranti e imprenditori tra Italia e Romania*, edited by Ferruccio Gambino and Devi Sacchetto, 171–206. Rome: Carocci.

———. 2008. *Frontiere del 'Made in Italy': Delocalizzazione productive e identità delle merci*. Verona: Ombre Corte.

Sampson, Steven. 1996. 'The Social Life of Projects: Importing Civil Society in Albania'. In *Civil Society: Challenging Western Models*, edited by Chris Hann and Elizabeth Dunn, 121–42. London: Routledge.

Sifneos, Evridyki. 2009. *Ellines eboroi stin azofikh: I dynami kai ta oria ths oikogeneiakhs epixeirhshs*. Athens: EIE (National Research Centre).

Stoianovich, Traian. 1960. 'The Conquering Balkan Orthodox Merchant'. *Journal of Economic History* 20 (2): 234–313.

Todorova, Maria. 1997. *Imagining the Balkans*. New York/Oxford: Oxford University Press.

Vetta, Theodora. 2009. '"Democracy Building" in Serbia: The NGO Effect'. *Southeastern Europe* 33: 26–47.

Wolff, Larry. 1994. *Inventing Eastern Europe: The Map of Civilization on the Mind of the Enlightenment*. Stanford: Stanford University Press.

LIST OF CONTRIBUTORS

Aliki Angelidou is lecturer in social anthropology at the Department of Social Anthropology, Panteion University, Athens. She obtained her PhD from the École des Hautes Études en Sciences Sociales, Paris, exploring socioeconomic transformations in postsocialist rural Bulgaria. She currently conducts research on migration, borders and transnationalism with a special focus on economic elite mobility in the Balkans and migration from former socialist countries to Greece. She is also interested in the comparative analysis of the institutional and conceptual history of anthropology in Southeastern Europe.

Gerald Creed is professor of anthropology at Hunter College and the Graduate Center of the City University of New York. He has been conducting research in rural Bulgaria since 1987 on a variety of topics including political economy, foreign aid, consumption, ritual, gender and nationalism. His books include *Domesticating Revolution: From Socialist Reform to Ambivalent Transition in a Bulgarian Village* (1998), which won the John D. Bell Memorial Book Prize from the Bulgarian Studies Association, and *Masquerade and Postsocialism: Ritual and Cultural Dispossession in Bulgaria* (2011), which also won the John D. Bell Prize as well as the William E. Douglass Prize from the Society for the Anthropology of Europe.

Ger Duijzings is reader in the anthropology of Eastern Europe at the School of Slavonic and East European Studies, University College London. He has published widely on identity, religion, ethnic conflict and nationalist violence in the former Yugoslavia, and is currently carrying out research on urban transformations, social inequality and new elites in Romania, conducting fieldwork in Bucharest. His books include *Religion and the Politics of Identity in Kosovo* (2000) and *History and Memory in Eastern Bosnia: Backgrounds to the Fall of Srebrenica* (2002). He is also co-editor of *The New Bosnian Mosaic: Identities, Memories and Moral Claims in a Post-war Society* (2007).

Ulrich Ermann is professor of human geography at Graz University, Austria. His research interests lie at the intersection of economic and cultural geography, exploring geographies of consumption and production, and commodities and brands, particularly in the postsocialist economies and societies of Europe. He has published on regional economic circuits and local food labels in Germany, and on fashion markets in Bulgaria. He obtained his PhD from the University of Erlangen-Nuremberg, after which he was postdoctoral research associate and research coordinator at the Leibniz Institute for Regional Geography in Leipzig. He was also visiting lecturer at the University of Sofia and interim professor for economic geography at the Catholic University of Eichstätt-Ingolstadt, Germany.

Christian Giordano is full professor of social anthropology at the University of Fribourg, Switzerland. He has done extensive research in Mediterranean societies and Southeastern Europe, as well as Malaysia, mainly in the fields of political and economic anthropology. He has published numerous articles, book chapters and edited volumes. His most important and relevant publications are *Die Betrogenen der Geschichte: Überlagerungsmentalität und Überlagerungsrationalität in mediterranen Gesellschaften* (1992) and (as co-editor) *Bulgaria: Social and Cultural Landscapes* (2000). He received an honorary doctorate from the University of Timişoara, Romania and is permanent guest professor at the universities of Bucharest (Romania), Murcia (Spain) and Bydgoszcz (Poland).

Petko Hristov is associate professor at the Institute of Ethnology and Folklore Studies with Ethnographic Museum at the Bulgarian Academy of Sciences. He obtained a PhD in ethnology from the Ethnographic Institute and Museum in Sofia. His research interests include labour migration, transborder migrant networks, family and kinship, cultural identities, traditional religiosity and political anthropology. He is the editor of *Migration and Identity: Historical, Cultural and Linguistic Dimensions of Mobility in the Balkans* (2012), and co-editor of *Kurban in the Balkans* (2007) and *Labour Migrations in the Balkans* (2012). He has published numerous book chapters and articles in edited volumes and refereed journals.

Deema Kaneff is a reader in social anthropology at the Centre for Russian and East European Studies, University of Birmingham. She has carried out extensive fieldwork in Bulgaria and Ukraine, in both rural and urban areas, and during socialist and postsocialist times. Her work focuses on a number of topics relating to postsocialist reforms including politics and the past, property relations, poverty and inequalities, and global–local processes (especially with respect to migration). She has published widely in refereed journals, is the author of the monograph *Who Owns the Past? The Politics of Time in a 'Model' Bulgarian Village* (2004) and (co-)edited several other volumes, including *Global Connections and Emerging Inequalities in Europe: Perspectives on Poverty and Transnational Migration* (2011).

Dimitra Kofti recently obtained her PhD in anthropology from University College London, focusing on the changing everyday politics of labour in postsocialist Bulgaria. Her research is in the fields of economic and political anthropology, with a particular focus on relationships of work and labour in the context of privatization and flexible capitalism. She has conducted fieldwork research in Bulgaria and Greece, and is currently a postdoctoral fellow at the Max Planck Institute for Social Anthropology in Halle, Germany.

Daniela Koleva is associate professor at the Department for History and Theory of Culture, University of Sofia. Her research interests are in the fields of oral history and anthropology of socialism and postsocialism, biographical and cultural memory, biographical methods, and social constructivism. She has published a monograph on the 'normal life course' in socialist Bulgaria and a number of book chapters and articles in peer-reviewed international journals. She is the co-editor of *Negotiating Normality: Everyday Lives in Socialist Institutions* (2012) and *20 Years after the Collapse of Communism: Expectations, Achievements and Disillusions of 1989* (2011). She is a member of the editorial advisory boards of the journals *Oral History* and *L'Homme: Zeitschrift für feministische Geschichtswissenschaft*.

Dobrinka Kostova is a professor at the Institute for the Study of Societies and Knowledge at the Bulgarian Academy of Sciences. Her main research interests are in the fields of political, economic and historical sociology. She has published numerous articles, and is author of *The Economic Elite in the 1990s: Continuity and Change* (2003) and co-author of several books on postsocialist transition, multiculturalism and trust.

Liz Mellish is completing her PhD at the School of Slavonic and East European Studies, University College London. Her research focuses on the lives and movements of urban dancers in Timişoara (Romania). She has conducted fieldwork on dance and music practices in Romania and Bulgaria, having a wider interest in Southeastern Europe. Both a dance researcher and practitioner, she has published articles in journals including *Narodna umjetnost* (Croatia) and *New Sounds* (Serbia) and is co-editor of several books on the region. She is currently secretary for the International Council of Traditional Music (ICTM) study group for music and dance in Southeastern Europe.

Lenka Nahodilova holds a PhD in social anthropology from Charles University in Prague. She was a Marie Curie Fellow in the Department of History, University College London, and had a temporary teaching position at the School of Slavonic and East European Studies, University College London, where she is an honorary research associate. Trained in social and medical anthropology, she has conducted fieldwork in Bulgaria, Russia and the former Yugoslavia, and is a specialist on Muslim minorities and European Islam. She currently works as an advisor to a major medical charity, while completing the book *Islam, Communism and Modernity: Muslim Minorities in Central and Eastern Europe* (forthcoming). She has published her work in journals such as *Contemporary European History* and *Anthropology and Medicine.*

Galia Valtchinova is professor in anthropology at the University of Toulouse II – Le Mirail. Before this she was senior researcher at the Bulgarian Academy of Sciences, Sofia. She obtained a PhD in history and a DSc in ethnology from the University of Sofia and the Bulgarian Academy of Sciences. She has conducted fieldwork in Bulgaria, Macedonia and Bosnia-Herzegovina, at locations close to political borders and cultural boundaries. Her work deals with religion, politics and identity, ethnicity and the notion of minority, boundaries and transborder exchange. She has published widely in the fields of the anthropology of religion and historical anthropology. Her publications include a book on twentieth-century Balkan female visionaries (2006). She was also guest editor of a special issue of *History and Anthropology* entitled 'Ethnographies of "Divine Interventions" in Europe' (2009) and editor of the volume *Religion and Boundaries: Studies from the Balkans, Eastern Europe and Turkey* (2010).

www.ingramcontent.com/pod-product-compliance
Lightning Source LLC
Chambersburg PA
CBHW022356280326
41935CB00007B/208